'Heart stopping. A bullet-by-bullet account of one man's journey from Ireland to Libya's International Brigade'
Sam Kiley, Middle-East correspondent for
Sky News and author of *Desperate Glory*

Housam 'Sam' Najjair was born and grew up in the suburbs of Dublin. His father came to Ireland from Tripoli as a student in the 1970s, where he met and married Sam's mother, Joanna Golden, daughter of Geoffrey Golden and Maire O'Donnell, two famous Abbey Theatre actors.

From the age of nine, Sam lived with his family in Libya for three years before returning to Ireland. By sixteen, he had moved out of home, having been expelled from school. He worked in restaurants and in the Liberty Market and, at nineteen, took over a small restaurant in Dublin city before returning to Tripoli for two years. There, he worked for a diamond jeweller and in a travel agency that specialised in desert and mountain trips. He returned to Dublin at the age of twenty-one and worked in construction for several years before his fateful decision to fight against Gaddafi and help in the liberation of Libya.

Soldier for a Summer

One man's journey from Dublin to
the frontline of the Libyan Uprising

SAM NAJJAIR

HACHETTE
BOOKS
IRELAND

First published in Ireland in 2013 by
HACHETTE BOOKS IRELAND

Cataloguing in Publication Data is available from the British Library.

ISBN 978 1444 743 83 8

Typeset in AGaramond and Rockwell by Bookends Publishing Services.
Printed and bound in Great Britain by CPI Group (UK) Ltd, Croydon, CR0 4YY.

Hachette Books Ireland policy is to use papers that are natural, renewable
and recyclable products and made from wood grown in sustainable forests.
The logging and manufacturing processes are expected to conform to the
environmental regulations of the country of origin.

Hachette Books Ireland
8 Castlecourt Centre
Castleknock
Dublin 15, Ireland

A division of Hachette UK Ltd
338 Euston Road, London NW1 3BH

www.hachette.ie

Two things in my life have transformed me above all else –
becoming a father and surviving a war.

I dedicate this book of survival to my beautiful daughter, Layla.

They shall be spoken of among their people,
The generations shall remember them,
And call them blessed;
But I will speak their names to my own heart
In the long nights …

from 'The Mother' by Pádraig Pearse

'It is little I would care,' said Cuchulain, 'if my life were
to last one day and one night only, so long as my name and
the story of what I had done would live after me.'

from *Cuchulain of Muirthemne* by Lady Augusta Gregory

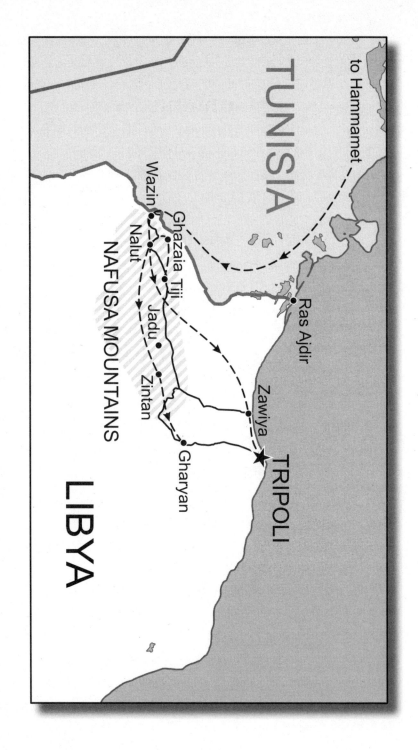

Contents

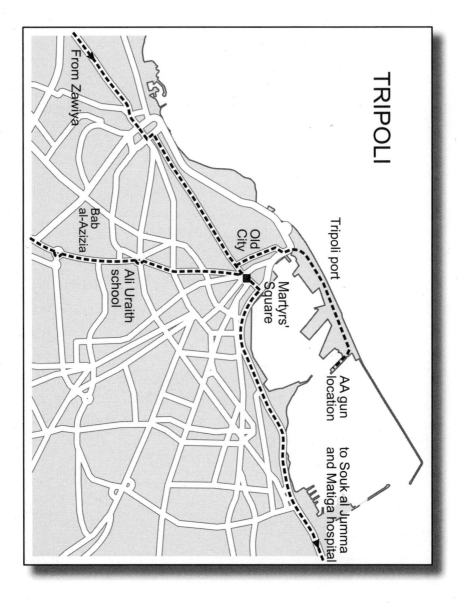

TRIPOLI

From Zawiya

Tripoli port

Old City

Bab al-Azizia

Ali Uraith school

Martyrs' Square

AA gun location

to Souk al Jumma and Matiga hospital

'When tyranny becomes law,
rebellion becomes a duty'

Inspirational motto

Preface

October 2011, Portobello, Dublin

My mind's all over the place, jumping from scene to scene, cutting back and forth across the many different things that have happened to me in the past four months – the amazing people I've met, the intense training I've been through, the life-threatening battles I've survived and the heartbreaking suffering I've witnessed. There have been emotional lows that I've struggled through alone and highs of excitement that I've shared with others. All of it totally unimaginable even six months ago when I sat in this very apartment, watching the news bulletins about the escalating trouble in Libya. All of it rushing through my mind now, in a storm of memories, flashbacks and stories.

Part I

Trouble on the Horizon

February–June 2011

The decision to go

The Chatterbox café, just beside where I live on Portobello Road, was run by a Libyan friend of mine, Mustafa Al-Ahimar, and because I didn't have an internet connection in my apartment, I'd drop in regularly, both to surf the web and to meet up with friends. We'd sit in a line at the computers, shoulder to shoulder, updating our Facebook pages, chatting in Arabic, drinking strong coffee and stepping outside regularly for a smoke. It was a typical gathering spot, but with a particularly Libyan feel to it.

The atmosphere was always light-hearted and easy-going – at least it was until February 2011. When the Arab Spring erupted in Libya and some local demonstrations flared up in the east of the country, all that changed … 'changed utterly', as Yeats put it.

I heard other customers asking Mustafa, who everyone knew was anti-Gaddafi, how 'events' in Libya were unfolding. The odd comment about the possibility of this being the end for Gaddafi crept into conversations. Sceptically, I started looking into what was going on in more detail, and, before I knew it, me and my friends had stopped talking about our night lives in Dublin and were suddenly only thinking about life in Libya. What was going to happen in our country? How would Gaddafi react to calls for him to step down after forty-two years? Every day, we trawled through social media sites for updates about what was happening on the ground, we sent each other links to YouTube clips and talked non-stop about what the latest news reports were saying.

At the time, my main concern was the unity of the country. I worried about Libya becoming like Iraq, descending into a nightmare playground for international warmongers keen for better access to oil. I prayed that the protests wouldn't escalate into some kind of horror of violence and destruction.

❖

Colonel Gaddafi had ruled Libya since 1969, when he orchestrated a military coup against King Idris. Although I was aware of the corruption in his regime, I was relatively tolerant of his rule because the Libyan side of my family wasn't directly affected by it. When I was young, I took the attitude that maybe Gaddafi's regime was a necessary evil, something that Libya had to suffer in order to remain united and to help it prosper.

Libya was a rich country and enough people did well from its resources to pull Gaddafi through for a long time. For the rest, the less fortunate people, Gaddafi was able to put on a display of trying to do what was right for Libya. For many people, his supposedly humble origins combined with his confidence created a convincing picture of a leader. His early success in getting a better price for Libyan oil, and thereby improving the infrastructure and healthcare in the country for a time, made him very popular. His apparent pride in Libya and in Africa – even though he expressed this in strange way – was also appealing to many people. In name at least, he gave the impression of supporting democratic principles of government, and his anti-imperialist and socialist talk gave him credibility with a lot of ordinary people.

But there were other ordinary people like my sister's husband Mahdi al-Harati, who had a very different view of him, who knew very early on that all his fine words were just talk and, in fact, a big cover-up for something fundamentally rotten. When you think how important education is to a democratic society and of how relatively little Gaddafi did to improve the education system of the country, you can start to see the telltale signs of the oppression that Gaddafi subtly but surely imposed on Libya for forty years.

Mahdi, whose father died when he was very young, was born into a religious family, and so was immediately branded a dissenter because of Gaddafi's anti-religious stance. Mahdi's uncle, Mohamed al-Harati, was imprisoned by the regime for ten years for his opposition to Gaddafi's ways. Fearing for Mahdi's life, his family sent him to his mother in Egypt at the age of sixteen, making him a teenage exile. It's no wonder that he developed an acute awareness of Gaddafi's regime from a very young age, and saw evil in it where many, including me, just turned a blind eye. Mahdi spent a few years moving around different places in Europe and only settled when he came to Ireland. He met and married my sister, he taught Arabic, became an Islamic preacher and started to become an activist for various causes, regularly protesting outside the Israeli embassy about the plight of Palestinians, and, in 2010, joining the Free Gaza Movement as a passenger on the Freedom Flotilla.

❖

No, after so many years of getting away with it, Gadaffi was in trouble. There were some small-scale demonstrations against him during January in areas around Benghazi in the east of Libya and Zintan in the west. By early February, calls for a 'Day of Anger' on 17 February began circulating on Facebook – they were even reported on Al Jazeera. Inspired by similar events in Tunisia and Egypt, our call was for people to go out and demonstrate their opposition to Gaddafi and demand something better. However, after Gaddafi's totally over-the-top reaction to these early demonstrations, particularly the shooting of protestors in the east on 15 February, the Day of Anger was bound to be confrontational. Everyone expected a violent response from Gaddafi.

I remember one of the first pieces of footage I saw on YouTube was taken outside a Gaddafi building in Tobruk in east Libya. It showed an enormous crowd gathered in a big square, chanting and whistling and milling about. Near a burned-out car, some had gathered around a statue of Gaddafi's 'Green Book', and were heaving and hauling at it. Eventually through the sheer physical force of the group working together, they managed to topple the hulk of concrete to the ground, to big cheers and waving arms from the onlookers. It was amazing to see this symbol of Gaddafi's hold on Libya being toppled by citizens of the country, and in full view of cameras. Brave, brazen or just crazed with excitement? I wasn't sure.

More serious violence erupted in Benghazi. From the safety of our internet café, we saw a steady stream of photographs and video clips of the terrible things that were happening on the city's streets. We saw pictures of civilians being fired at and murdered by their own security forces. It was horrifying to think that Libyans were killing Libyans in cold blood.

I was particularly impressed by a group of young men, who, despite the shooting around them and despite knowing that their lives were totally on the line, pushed out their chests towards the gunmen up on a military barracks, defiantly and bravely making clear targets of themselves.

Watching, we discussed how the demonstrators' Molotov cocktails and rocks were going to be no match for the live ammunition being fired at them.

We all felt that these protests would be stamped out. However, one man in particular did something to turn things around in favour of the protestors – and he wasn't some experienced leader with a military background. Having witnessed the brutality of the regime's backlash against the demonstrators, Mahdi Zeyo, an engineer at the state-owned oil company, had spent days helping to bury the young protesters shot by Gaddafi's security forces. Then, on 20 February, he said goodbye to his wife and daughters, filled his car with gas canisters and gunpowder and headed for the military base in Benghazi with a plan. He drove his car at full speed towards the gates of the base, knowing that he'd be shot at – and, of course, he was, and was killed in the resulting explosion. Such a selfless act! That explosion breached the base's defences, allowing the protestors to rush in. Even though those out front were being fired at and killed, other protesters continued to run towards the base and they eventually overwhelmed the loyalists and took over the barracks. Protesters who had been imprisoned were released and, finally, they had the arms and a stronghold from which they could begin the revolution.

I realised that Mahdi Zeyo – a man who by all accounts loved life – would be seen by some, especially in the West, as having some kind of death wish. But things had obviously got so bad around him that he felt that if he didn't do something extreme about the brutality he was witnessing, he was going to be killed anyway in the round-up of protestors that had begun. He did a very brave thing.

❖

It wasn't long before I heard that my brother-in-law Mahdi had gone to Benghazi himself. When the Arab Spring began in Tunisia and started spreading to Algeria and Egypt, Mahdi had reflected on what he would do if it reached Libya. He had a quiet life in Dublin as a family man and teacher, but he knew that he could not and would not stand idly by if a chance came to help end the regime he had opposed all his life.

Because of Gaddafi's influence, Mahdi was barred from Libya's neighbouring countries, so he had to fly to Sudan and make his way from there through the desert into eastern Libya and on to Benghazi. At that stage, all we knew was that he had joined other volunteers from Tripoli and that they were receiving training in Benghazi.

❖

In March, news came through that a young man by the name of Mohamed Nabbous had been killed. He was a young entrepreneur in Benghazi and, on 19 February, he'd started broadcasting coverage of the demonstrations online and had set up a TV station to provide independent news reports – something that was unheard of in Libya, where the state had controlled all forms of media since Gaddafi's coup. In a bitter irony, Nabbous captured the audio of his own death. He seems to have been shot by a loyalist unit while exposing the lie of the Gaddafi ceasefire in Benghazi.

Seeing all this brave personal sacrifice in response to the state's brutality, I started to think about going over myself, *If only I could get away from everything here more easily. I've just got too much holding me back.*

I knew there were other Libyan fellas my age in Dublin who didn't feel the same pull I did, maybe because they hadn't experienced Libyan culture and Islamic values first-hand, as I had. Very few had spent the same amount of time in the country that I had, learning Arabic and getting to know the people, and they didn't feel the same strong attachment as I did – and the more threatened Libya and her people were, the stronger that attachment became.

Some of the young Libyans in Dublin had the misguided idea that you had to be religious to join the fight or be old-fashioned to fit in with it. But looking at any of the footage of the protestors, I could see there were all kinds of people – young and old, bearded and clean-shaven, conservative and trendy, men and women. It truly was a revolution of the people that was unfolding before our eyes thousands of miles away.

❖

Another thing I started to notice was the changing make-up of the regime's forces. Even during the early demonstrations, Gaddafi brought in mercenaries from different countries to help in his campaign of terror. He did this because his ranks were being depleted because of all the soldiers leaving the army to join the revolution, and also because many Libyan soldiers found it impossible to fire on their own people.

The story of Ali Obeidi reached us. He was an officer who had left the Libyan army and joined the revolution in Misrata. When he had arrived in the city, he had spoken to the revolutionaries about his decision to defect, and a clip of what he said was posted on YouTube. He spoke in a very gravelly voice with great passion.

I am Air Marshall Brigadier Ali Attalah Obeidi. I asked myself, If I stay, how could I live with myself? How could I ever lift my head high in front of my people again? I escaped from Matiga Military Airport in Tripoli and joined our beloved revolution. I wanted to join my fellow Libyans. I wanted to pass on whatever experience I could, and I know that in all areas of Libya there are men just like me. Men who will do what it takes to defend their country, defend their dignity, defend justice.

I was one of those who couldn't be part of this massacre of our people. A man who would ship in mercenaries and let them loose on his own people, I mean, who would do this? Does he believe he owns this land? I can say this with all confidence, He will not win this war. We are headed for the capital. It will be you who will be in the rubbish heap of history, you the rat in front of us lions. We are not rats. We are men with history and glory. We are men who walk on the blades of sharp swords.

I was originally going to Zintan but something drew me to here, Misrata. It took me fifteen days to walk here. I slept under trees. This is what Misrata has done, Misrata has sacrificed everything. Misrata is a military miracle, pioneering the revolution. And I swear by Almighty God, I swear by Almighty God, I swear by Almighty God that I have never seen the like of what I have seen here in Misrata. It is history in the making. Misrata has given herself to the cause and we will not betray her. I advise anyone in the army to defect immediately if they have a conscience. Join the will of the people. Join the revolution with our sons.

I felt the power of Obeidi's words very directly. I was no longer worried about Libya in terms of unity or prosperity. All I cared about now were the people, the innocent people being betrayed by their state. I felt terrible all the time about what was happening to them, and wanted to do something to protect them from the brutality they were suffering.

Throughout March and April, I read more about the reason for and objectives of the revolution. I knew from experience that it was very important to have a complete knowledge of something before speaking out or taking action against it and I started to open my mind to the realities of Gaddafi's regime, seeing clearly for the first time how ruthless a tyrant had ruled Libya for forty-two years. I built up a profile of what I would be up against if I was going to go over and fight. I spent all my time reading about the recent history and current affairs of the country. I barely slept or ate in those weeks, I became so immersed in it. One of the most horrifying revelations I read about was the 1996 Abu Salim prison massacre in which, according to the prison cook, nearly 1,300 prisoners were shot systematically in a courtyard where they were protesting about the lack of judicial process.

❖

'I'm going over.' I said it out loud in the café, angry and frustrated after watching more horrific videos from Libya.

But every time I did think about going over, and even though I felt drawn to help my countrymen, I realised immediately how impossible it was for me to leave. My life had too many complications and I had no resources to enable me to get away. There were people going over from the community in Dublin, mostly transporting vehicles and supplies into Tunisia for the revolutionaries to use, rather than actually fighting. 'Maybe that's what I should do,' I said to myself.

Then one day my mother rang, elated with the news that my younger brother Yusef had joined Mahdi in Benghazi and was getting on great, training with good people and apparently showing himself to be a sharpshooter on the range. She was very proud. I was impressed.

'Are you going?' she asked. 'I would have thought you, being so practical and strong, would have been among the first to go.'

'I want to, Mam. I've been trying to organise it, but I can't just walk out of the flat and leave all my stuff.'

More news came in of mercenary fighters being brought in to build up the ranks of the regime's forces. I watched videos that had been leaked out, showing the convoys of mercenaries heading into the outskirts of Benghazi – I could hear them shouting about the terrible things they were going to do to the people. I heard that they were being given free rein to wreak any kind of havoc on the revolutionaries and on anyone associated with them. We even heard that they were being supplied with alcohol and drugs. This was bad enough, but when I heard about them going out in gangs, plied with Viagra, and raping Libyan women, it became just too much for me to bear. The thought that someone from my family could become the victim of these scumbags made me sick. I decided to do whatever it took to go. One of the guys in the café said to me, 'Make yourself ready, Allah will do the rest.'

Then, proving the truth of it, my mother rang in late June and asked me to be the *muhrim*, or chaperone, for a trip to Tunis that she was planning for herself and my sister to meet up with Mahdi. I realised, of course, that my mother had probably planned the whole holiday knowing that I just needed the means to enable me to take this step. She also knew that my life needed sorting out nearly as much as Libya did, and she might have felt that this was the only thing that would do it.

Before I tell you about my part in Libya's revolution, I should tell you a little about myself and about the way my life needed sorting out at that time.

The Goldens and the Najjairs

My mother's name is Joanna Golden. She is the daughter of the famous Abbey actors Geoffrey Golden and Mairé Ní Dhomhnaill. Geoffrey lived in Cork when I was young and I didn't have much contact with him, but my grandmother, Gra Wa, as I called her when I couldn't say Grandma, was like a second mother to me. I think I was drawn to her because of her sense of adventure and drama, as well as the love and attention that she always showed to me. When my grandmother was only twenty and had just started working for the Abbey Theatre, she was given the part of a possessed woman in a play entitled *The Righteous Are Bold*. She was so convincing in the role that the St John's ambulance brigade had to be present to attend to swooning audience members who fainted when she smashed the statue of the Virgin Mary nightly, whilst acting possessed. She used to tell me stories about Irish history, the fight against British rule in Ireland, and about her father, Bill O'Donnell, who had been a member of the Tipperary Brigade in the 1920s. His father, my great-great grandfather, was a quartermaster for Pearse Buchanan's brigade in the early days of the Irish Republican Army. Even though the area around Cashel where the family lived was loyalist, some of my family were well-known IRA activists. There was one story about Bill walking into a pub and shooting an English officer who had raped a girl he knew. (These stories came back to me very strongly when I encountered for myself similar brutality in the Gaddafi regime.) Gra Wa once featured in the 'Fiche Ceist' series in one of the national newspapers. She was asked, 'If you could change one thing about the world, what would it be?'

She answered, 'I'd want a united Ireland.'

That always impressed me.

Gra Wa lived with us on and off later in her life, at least when she wasn't drinking. Whenever she hit the bottle, my parents wouldn't have her in the house. My mother's attitude was understandable in light of her faith, and it may be that her conversion to Islam was partly a reaction to her own mother's lifestyle.

My mother was only seventeen when she first met my father in the 1970s, and even though she had been raised Catholic, she was interested and open minded about other religions. My father had come to Dublin from Tripoli as a student at a time when a lot of young Libyans received scholarships from the government to study abroad. She overheard him one day in a restaurant – Gig's Place on South Richmond Street in Dublin, just downstairs from where I am writing now, in fact – talking about Islam. He was handsome and she became curious.

She started questioning him about the way Muslim women were treated and, rather than argue with her, my father suggested she visit the Dublin mosque to talk to the women themselves. Later, she wrote an article explaining her feelings at the time:

> I felt women were treated dreadfully and put down, and I was foolish enough to think that I could free all these women from their enslavement. But when I visited the mosque, they were so nice to me that I couldn't say anything against them. So I thought I'd free them on my next visit.

She kept returning to the mosque and began to read the Quran. She was so impressed with its message that she converted to Islam shortly before her eighteenth birthday, taking the Muslim name, Rabia. Not long after that, she married my father. She was one of the first Irish women to wear the hijab, at a time when it would have been very unusual and brave to do so in Ireland. She didn't inherit the acting bug, but she was outspoken on many issues and went on radio and television many times to discuss Islam and the true status of women within it.

My father, Mohamed Najjair, is from a suburb of Tripoli called Souk al Jumma, which was a hot-spot in the early days of the 2011 Revolution – it was one of the locations where Gaddafi tried to suppress the people's protests with extreme violence. Historically, Gaddafi never had huge support in the area, so it was an area where the regime often came down hard. This treatment was a factor in my father's decision to stay in Ireland after his studies were finished. Even just being from Souk al Jumma was enough to mark you and make your life difficult in Libya. But my fatherr discovered that even in Ireland, he couldn't escape the paranoia of the regime – the Libyan authorities made it clear that they were keeping an eye on him, despite the fact that he wasn't involved in politics in any way and made sure not to attract attention to himself. There were Gaddafi spies, known to everyone as 'antennae', in every Libyan ex-pat community in the world, including Dublin, and everyone knew who they were. After Libya had been liberated, I saw one intelligence report written by prominent Muslims in Dublin that had labelled my father as an extremist. So if it wasn't for various strings he pulled back in Libya through family and contacts, he could well have ended up in prison himself.

When I was in my early twenties, there was always a steady stream of Libyan political asylum-seekers coming into the country. We would meet them at the mosque, especially on Fridays, when the community congregated for prayers. Most of the asylum-seekers were highly educated, down-to-earth, decent people, and my dad seemed to be friends with nearly all of them.

At the same time, he also had relatives who had connections with the Gaddafi regime back in Libya. In the early days of his career, Mukhtar Farrara, a lovely man who was the husband of my father's sister, was the chauffeur and personal friend of Ahmed 'Hamad' Ramadan, a top adviser to Gaddafi. However, the level of corruption in the regime eventually got to be too much for Mukhtar, and he took early retirement to get out of his situation.

In 1979, when I was born into this Dublin Islamic community, there were only about thirty people in it. My very first memories of Islam are as a young child of maybe four or five going to Friday prayer at the first ever mosque and Islamic centre in Dublin, on Harrington Street. It was a great multicultural environment for me to experience, bringing together Arabs of different nationalities, as well as Pakistanis, Malaysians and Indonesians. In 1983, the Donore Presbyterian church on the South Circular Road, which had been constructed in the 1860s in the style of a thirteenth-century English church, was bought by the the Islamic Foundation of Ireland and converted into a mosque. I think of this level-headed, tolerant approach in contrast to how, in 2012, some extreme Islamists in Libya completely levelled a perfectly good mosque just because it had had a shrine attached to it, and shrines are associated with certain Islamic sects of which they disapprove.

I remember that time as being a lovely Islam for me, a peaceful, kind Islam, especially our Quran classes, which were given by an English convert, and the Young Muslim Circle that was set up by a Malaysian doctor, Oteh. I was blessed to have these men as teachers because they weren't stuck up in any way. They didn't look down on us as some might have done, and we accepted them and what they were saying enthusiastically. These experiences formed the foundations of my faith, and I see now that they were laid down very well.

In our early teens, we'd have camps, a bit like the scouts, including sleepovers at the mosque, sermons from special sheikhs and trips to places like Quasar in Tallaght – we even did the Wicklow Way when we got a little older. I remember the list the leader gave us detailing all the things we needed to pack in our rucksacks – a torch, a penknife, a water bottle, and so on – there was even mention of the shared things, like pots and pans, that we had to leave room for. I loved all the preparations and was very excited by the whole experience.

In Quran class, we were told the great stories of Islam, like the story of the prophet Yusuf, peace be upon him, who went through so many trials and tribulations in his life but kept his faith in God through it all and who was eventually rewarded with peace and happiness. The story taught me how life can test you but that you have to accept these challenges and never give up.

The Quran says, 'And when he attained his full manhood, We gave him wisdom and knowledge, thus We reward the doers of good.' I remember these stories as being really beautiful and that we loved to listen to and talk about them. I actually cried at some, I found them so moving. The line 'The struggle of a nation burned in his eyes as he relived his wars on homelands' is from a song about Yusuf from a CD by Dawud Wharnsbey that my mother gave me. The song brings me right back to those innocent days and I am always close to tears when I sing it.

We had to learn long passages from the Quran, and we'd have competitions to see who could recite them the best. That's how the verses came to lodge in my mind, little pearls of wisdom and help that are on standby in my brain, ready to be called up when required.

Islam was all very unified in Dublin in the late 1980s, as I remember it – everyone was friendly and respectful, irrespective of background. Sadly, today there is, in my view, a good deal of judging of one another and fighting within the community and tempers occasionally flare, reflecting divisions that really shouldn't exist in Islam, which is a universal religion.

As I grew, I became conscious of the very different set of experiences my religion gave me compared to other children in my neighbourhood. I liked the fact that after school or after hanging out with friends in Rathfarnham, I escaped off into this parallel life. I knew that none of the other kids I was growing up with had ever met or become friends with, for example, Kurdish kids whose families had escaped from Saddam Hussein's genocidal attacks. I could see the blessing it was for me to have this extra dimension to my life, learning about the experiences of people from so many different backgrounds.

In the late 1980s to early 1990s, my mother learned Arabic and consciously educated herself about the position of women in Islam. I remember her being very knowledgeable and I was impressed with her ability to discuss things authoritatively. She got on very well with everyone in the Islamic community. The beauty of Islam is that when everyone's head is bowed to the ground in a prayer room, everyone is equal in the eyes of God, irrespective of background, social class, race or nationality – so her Irish background was never an issue. Of course, with four kids under eight to take care of, she was very busy just being a mother, and she was a very nurturing and caring mother at all times. In contrast, my father was the classic disciplinarian, strict and a little distant from us kids. Between 1986 and 1988, his work took him to Cork a lot and, eventually, the family moved down there for a while.

Gaddafi's milky soft hands

In 1989, when I was nine and still very impressionable, we filled two forty-foot containers with most of our belongings and moved to Tripoli for a fresh start. My dad wanted a change, even though he had been making good money in the thriving Irish–Libyan cattle trade synonymous with Charlie Haughey in the 1980s. (Haughey visited Tripoli in 1983 to meet Gaddafi and help promote the sale of Irish cattle in Libya.)

We lived with our Farrara cousins for a few months, then Mukhtar helped us to get an apartment of our own. Meanwhile, I went to school. At first I was just an onlooker, as I didn't have any Arabic. My cousin, Mukhtar's daughter, was my Arabic teacher, and as I had a mind like a sponge at that age, it only took me a few months to get my Arabic up to speed so that I could become a full participant in class when the new school year started. Learning Arabic was a defining experience for me, and I became fluent, Tripoli accent and all. It has stood to me in so many different ways since then, and I am forever grateful that I had the chance to learn it at such a young age.

Interestingly, I actually met and shook hands with Gaddafi at around that time. He was in the neighbourhood, the Old City, to officially rename the historic structure called Bab Bahar, or 'doorway to the sea'. It was now to be called Bab Muammar.

A relative of ours through marriage, Farhat Doma, who I would later work for, was a very important businessman in the area. But he was also a marked man, partly because he was independently wealthy but also because when he was a teenager, he had been arrested for praying at the graves of men who had been hanged for their anti-Gaddafi activities. Doma had made his fortune in the gold trade, importing gold and making and selling traditional jewellery pieces. Even as a young fella, I would sometimes go over to the workshop to watch the ingots being flattened in the machine until they had the long strip from which a piece would be cut out and shaped. It was a trade that attracted a lot of attention and required some shady dealings with the regime, including pay-offs. Doma was penalised for not playing by their rules, and both his business and health suffered.

Nonetheless, Doma took full part in this local ceremony, and that meant that me and my cousins were dressed up for the procession in fancy traditional clothes: white cotton trousers, a long shirt, a waistcoat and a little black hat. As Gaddafi walked by, we stood in a line and threw flowers in the air. For some reason, maybe because I looked different, Gaddafi walked up to me, smiled at me and shook my hands. I don't remember much about it, but one thing remains clear in my mind – the milky softness of his hands. Softer than my mother's, they were.

I'm glad to say, meeting him was never something I was proud of or bragged about to people. Although he wasn't my enemy until I was grown, at least I can say that he was of no interest to me even when I was young and impressionable. I was not impressed by his type of success and what he represented.

I remember this time in Libya as being very enjoyable, even though there were difficulties at home, including a lot of tension between my parents, especially after the second year. My mother's strong belief in the teachings of Islam came into conflict with some of the more relaxed Libyan traditions that were followed in the area of Tripoli where we lived, and this was also a cause of distress for her. Eventually, she came home to Ireland to have my younger brother, Yusef. Her decision was partly because of the lack of decent hospital facilities in Tripoli and partly just to get away from the tensions. It was lucky that she did too, because Yusef was born with a condition that needed immediate medical attention, and with the way Gaddafi's healthcare system was, that treatment wouldn't have been available in Libya.

Mam did not want to return to Libya afterwards, and, in hindsight, I couldn't blame her. Libya was suffering at the time from an embargo by the US, which aimed at punishing Gaddafi for 'biting the hand that fed him' in a sense, but which also impacted on the people of Libya. I remember one of my older cousins trying to be extra nice to us, giving us cornflakes for breakfast one morning. It didn't matter to me, I was happy to have the usual eggs or tuna, but he insisted. I remember that the box of cornflakes had cost something like 20 dinar, when an average wage was, say, 300 dinar a month. Gaddafi liked saying things to the people like, 'Why would you want chocolate when we have dates, which, remember, the Prophet loved? Eat them instead!' He only ever used religion when it suited him, and usually in the most ridiculous ways.

'Sam' Najjair

Soon after Yusef was born, the whole family moved back to Ireland. Mam was delighted. We moved into my grandmother's place for about three months, until we got a house in Whitechurch in Rathfarnham. That was where, through secondary school and puberty, I went from being a well-behaved thirteen-year-old Muslim boy to a tough, streetwise sixteen-year-old Dubliner. I remember the roll call on the first day.

'John McDermott?'

'*Anseo*.'

'Niall Smith?'

'*Anseo*.'

'Rachel Farrelly?'

'*Anseo*.'

'Des Brennan?'

'*Anseo*.'

'Housam Najjair?'

'Huh?'

Everyone turned to look. I became Sam.

I made lots of good friends and enjoyed Whitechurch, but both in and out of school I discovered that I had a choice to make: either put up with being picked on about my religion or push my religion aside and be accepted as one of the lads. Because I was sociable by nature, I naturally drifted towards becoming one of the lads. It was just part of my personality that made me want to fit in and be respected, and because it was a mixed-sex school there was suddenly a whole new group of people to try and impress.

❖

Since the age of seven, I have been taking part in the daytime fast of Ramadan, which lasts about a month. One year, when I was about thirteen, I was walking back home from the games arcade eating a packet of crisps. I knew it was wrong and I did feel guilty, but I did it anyway. I didn't want to resist the temptation because that would have made me different. I'll never forget having the packet in my hand, walking down the road munching away, and then suddenly spotting my father driving by. He looked from me to the bag of crisps and gave me that look that said, *Wait till you get home*. I got a serious hiding.

Soon, being one of the gang meant that I had to get streetwise. I started hanging around with friends in different parts of the neighbourhood, sometimes even during school hours. Inevitably, the hanging around led to getting into trouble. But I was actually recognised in school as being bright, and when I was in the B class and got into trouble, instead of moving me down to C or D, I was moved up to the A class. With curfews and groundings, my parents also tried their best to haul me back into line.

But it was too late. The forces of energy, curiosity and puberty had combined to set me on a very different path. Escaping from the house, I started hanging out in the fields after school with friends, making bonfires and messing about, usually to impress girls.

Pretty soon, drink came into the equation, and I took to it like a duck to water. For a while, I was able to hide it from my parents, but they found out in the end – and my father hit more than the roof. It just wasn't acceptable to him and it must have depressed my mother to have alcohol back in her house again. By this time, there were seven children in our family: five girls and two boys. (Another brother, Yaseen, had died when he was six months old because of complications.) My parents' concern for me was overtaken by their worry about the influence I might have on my sisters. At the age of seventeen, I was eventually suspended from school for causing trouble and, after this, they didn't try to stop me from moving out of home as well. They were glad to be able to shield my sisters from the kind of life I was leading.

I started working in restaurants and as a trader at the Liberty Market on Meath Street at weekends. I made good money easily, but with a girlfriend and no parents to hold me back, I blew it just as easily. I began to lose my way and to live quite a wild life.

In a sense, I no longer knew who I was, so my only option was to fit in where I was, and that was Dublin. I went out a lot, and hung about a lot with my Irish friends. You could have taken me for being no different to them, and sometimes I almost thought I was no different – I was Sam. But there was always something that separated me. I could be out with them for the whole weekend, for example, having a great time, everyone's pal, but then when it came to the big soak-up full Irish breakfast on Sunday morning and I would refuse to eat a sausage, it was as if I was an alien again – I was Housam.

Islam was like a song I'd forgotten the words to, but the tune was still running through me. My faith couldn't keep me from wanting the buzz of going out at night with my friends – but I never rejected Islam, and I never denied who I was, even when fellas saw me drinking and asked me if I was a Muslim.

Then, at nineteen, not long after I'd taken over the running of a restaurant – Leptis Magna on Aungier Street – and just as I was becoming relatively settled (by starting a computer micro maintenance course and juggling my new duties to both aspects of my life), my cousin, Abdarouf Farrara, who was called Abdu for short, invited me over to Libya to attend his brother's wedding. I told the landlord, my girlfriend, and my family and friends that I'd be back in two weeks. I was gone for two years, or, as we would say in Libya, two Libyan weeks. It was not totally by choice – my father actually arranged for my passport to be quietly hidden from me so that when I did consider going back to Dublin, I could never find it. But I was also having such a good time that I rarely considered returning. Life was very different, of course, a culture shock – like going from Windows to a Mac – but I was young and excited by the new scene.

Of course, in contrast to Dublin, Islam was all around me in Tripoli, but I could not hear its calls to me. I never turned my back on it entirely and whenever I found myself with practising Muslims, I took part in prayers and other observances, but I didn't keep it up for any length of time. It's a very difficult religion to maintain on a daily basis, and I had other things to keep me occupied. I didn't want to be a hypocrite about Islam, or lie to myself or pretend to others that I was more religious, on a day-to-day level, than I actually was, so I let my adopted lifestyle take over.

I made a name for myself in the neighbourhood where I worked, the gold market in the Old City, and also in Souk al Jumma, my dad's locality. I suppose I stood out and I made the most of that fact, getting to know all kinds of people and socialising a lot. I worked in a diamond jewellers first, and then in a travel agency that specialised in desert and mountain trips for tourists to places like the Roman city of Leptis Magna, the northern extremes of the Sahara desert, and the Nafusa Mountains.

I met some really cool, like-minded Libyans, and we lived it up. This was at a time long before Facebook, so to have found a group of guys who listened to the same music and were into the same things as me was great, and I am still friends with many of them to this day. My friend Hussam Zugaar, for instance, was a very talented entrepreneur but was kept down by Gaddafi's regime because of his refusal to play the corruption game, a little like Doma. (After the liberation of Tripoli, it was important to me to find out how these guys were, and I was pleased to discover that Zugaar had been made an official of the Tripoli Council.)

I spent a lot of time with my cousin Abdu and from time to time, we got into a bit of trouble together. Once when we were going to another family wedding, we rented a car and got the loan of a really fancy movie camera, which happened to belong to the family of one of Gaddafi's top generals, Abdul Salam Jalloud. Beforehand, being all dressed up for going out but with time to kill, we decided to go to the college and have some fun pretending to be a film crew conducting interviews on the campus – as you do! While we were there joking around, I noticed the police pulling across the barrier at the entrance and suddenly turning in our direction. We jumped into the car, thinking there must be something dodgy going on in the buildings behind us. As we sped off it became clear that they were actually after us. We were caught and arrested. As it turned out, not only was it illegal to film in colleges, but this college was a special one. First, Gaddafi used it as a venue for some of his speeches, and, second, and this only became known after the revolution, it had an underground prison where enemies of the regime were held illegally. Throw into the mix the fact that they knew my father had been living abroad for years, and the fact that the camera was owned by one of Gaddafi's generals, and the fact that the car was a rental, and you can see how an already paranoid bunch might see a major conspiracy.

Luckily, for some reason unknown to me, the police left me out of the picture and my cousin took the rap, overnighting in prison, missing the wedding and receiving a beating for his troubles. Eventually everything was explained to the cops' satisfaction, but the way things operated in Libya, we both might have ended up in prison for a very long time.

❖

When I eventually came back to Ireland in 2000, I experienced a kind of reverse culture shock. I'd forgotten how to do things the Irish way. I tried though. I was now twenty and Libya had given me more confidence in my identity. Ireland, too, was a little more multicultural and tolerant in some ways. I didn't have to hide my Libyan side. I still went out a good bit and enjoyed the company of my Irish friends, but everything was more toned down and blended with my renewed level of faith in Islam.

My girlfriend was a constant through this time and when I returned to Dublin, we sorted out our relationship and got serious. We decided to start a new life, so we got a house in

Northern Ireland – my parents had already moved up there – and had a child together, our lovely Layla. From the natural birth in Craigavon hospital to the first few months of new-found purpose in life, Layla seemed to be all we needed to keep us on the straight and narrow. Being a father was a huge change for me. I began to obsess about Layla's future, and all the things I needed to do for her and be for her. My mentality changed dramatically. My partner's too. Together, we began to take our responsibilities as Islamic parents seriously.

As well as my parents, my sister Eftaima and her husband Mahdi al-Harati had also moved to Craigavon and lived near us. With Mahdi as my teacher, I began to explore more deeply the religion that I had been born into but had drifted away from. Because of his character, and the fact that I trusted him entirely, Mahdi was the perfect teacher for me. I even began to act as his translator at the mosque. My moral compass was back in working order.

Not for long, though.

Sadly, things didn't work out between me and my partner, and eventually she moved back south with Layla. Losing both of them in one go was too much for me. My life turned upside down again, and all the bad stuff I'd managed to bury for so long came right back on top, all the old wounds opened again.

I started an extended period of being unsettled, hanging out in the wrong places and getting into trouble. I just felt I had nothing more to lose, so it didn't matter how I behaved. Much to my parents' disappointment, I lost my way again. I moved away from my religion, even though I knew, deep down in my heart, that my faith was still there. My mother used to ring me from time to time and try to talk sense into me. 'Take one step to God, son, and He will take ten towards you,' she used to quote. But it was no use. My behaviour, which could no longer be put down to teenage rebellion, was heartbreaking for her, but not even that mattered to me.

Eventually, I moved back to Dublin, via Manchester, and tried to start again. I got work in the booming construction sector in 2005 and started to make good money. My partner and I got back together, for a while, and I was so happy to be with Layla again, I actually thought it might all work out. But sadly, even after ten years together, we broke up again. When we split finally, there was a lot of bad feeling between us. Despite many attempts to secure what I believed to be fair access to Layla, who was four by that time, I was well and truly defeated by the court system. Not being able to see and connect with my daughter really tore me up and, with a nothing-left-to-lose attitude, I gave in to my demons again.

The twin I never had

Another element in all this was my lifelong friend, Adil Essalhi, who was like a brother to me. My dad and his dad, Frag, became friends when they first came to Ireland from Libya. As a child, Adil's dad had been orphaned, but was lucky to avoid the orphanages in Libya, which acted as recruiting grounds for Gaddafi. He was also fortunate that even though he is black, he was adopted by a wealthy Arab couple and had a very good childhood. While an arts student in university, he had the option of studying abroad and chose to come to Ireland. There he met Geraldine, they married, and soon Adil was born, a year or so after me.

For a few years, our families lived in neighbouring apartments in one of the Ballymun Towers before that area developed so many problems. My mam and Geraldine would sometimes take it in turns to mind Adil and me, and a bond formed between us that never broke fully. Even when Adil's family went to live in

Greenfort in Clondalkin and we went to Killinarden in Tallaght, our families often got together and Adil and I played. As we got older, we were sent out to the shop to buy sweets, and, on those first short trips out into the world, I became aware that Adil's skin colour was marking him out. I remember him being called names, and I remember him reacting angrily and me joining in with him.

Maybe because of such experiences, he started to learn taekwon-do, and he became very good at it. I used to go to see him in competitions and was very proud of him for always winning in his category. He went on to become an all-Ireland champion.

We both grew up under the watchful eyes of old-fashioned Muslim fathers, and both got the occasional hiding for stepping out of line. We recognised in each other the sting it left and, in our wordless way, we would comfort each other. In hindsight, I realise that the tough-love approach was like our fathers training us for the challenges that they knew lay ahead of us, but at the time, it was another reason to rebel.

Then came the first major step apart for us when, at the age of nine, I moved to Tripoli. While I got the chance to learn Arabic and soak up the culture of Libya, Adil stayed in Greenfort and had to soak up something very different – racism. I was twelve when we returned to Ireland and could meet up with him again. His body and face already bore the marks of a difficult life. He told me all about the fights he got into and the fellas who would pick on him. With his taekwon-do and just the courage of him, he was usually well able to defend himself, but there were times when he was overwhelmed by the number attacking him. He was a good-looking fella and never had a problem attracting girls, but that just attracted even more trouble.

When I was with him, I would always jump in to help, without hesitation. If he was picked on, I took it personally and gave back as good as he got. Of course, then I'd get the same abuse, and the whole thing would escalate. When we were teenagers, we started hanging out at bonfires and drinking with whoever was around. I knew that, given how I looked, I could stay quiet and just have a good time if I really wanted to. But I never did. It wasn't in me to keep out of it if Adil or anyone else was being picked on for any reason – be it the colour of their skin, their religion or anything else. I knew all the comments were said out of ignorance, but that didn't mean I was going to let it go. And I knew Adil would do the same for me.

We always knew we could only really count on each other. While some guys would talk about being friends, about doing stuff together, me and Adil lived it. More often than not it was just me and him left standing, looking at each other, outsiders. And that's a moment when you recognise, even as a youngster, that you are bonded to each other.

A coded warning

We weren't all goodie-goodie with each other all the time, though. The opposite, in fact. We slagged each other to bits and fought a lot, like brothers. Because we knew we could get away with anything with each other, we used each other to work out all our frustrations.

We both went to extremes in our behaviour, but maybe because he'd had the harder time growing up, Adil seemed to take longer to find his way back. He was so troubled in himself at times that he would test the people who loved him, including me, seeking the limits of our love. Although he never found those limits with his family and true friends, there were times when I just had to get away from him for a while to find my footing.

One such time coincided with my need for a change of direction when myself and my partner went to Craigavon. I did well moneywise for a few years, but there was a lot of racism to deal with there, and there was always tension between us and some of the locals. It ended with a shotgun being fired in through the window of my parents' house. First Mahdi and my parents left, and then my relationship fell apart.

Around this time, I met Adil by chance while on a visit to Dublin. I could see he needed my help. I was on a downward spiral myself after the break-up and not being with my daughter, so I didn't mind the idea of us hanging out together again. He had no job at the time, so I persuaded him to move to the North with me, but our troubles only got worse, as did our rowing. Often our tempers, fuelled by alcohol, would flare up and we'd end up fighting.

I remember one night we were really laying into each other. He grabbed me by the throat with his claw of a grip. He used to use those spring-based hand exercisers and had huge popping muscles between his thumb and first finger. He was choking me so hard, I could feel the life draining from me. The only thing I could manage was to grab him by the groin and then I was able to get a grip on his shoulder, and I lifted him off the ground and banged him against the wall. We both fell back on the ground, the two of us gasping for air and totally exhausted. After a few minutes of silence I said to him, 'If anything ever happens to me, Adil, make sure you're always there for Layla.' He said the same to me about his son, Aleem. And we just lay there afterwards, eventually falling asleep.

The trouble with our carry-on was that we were both in such a bad way that we didn't care who knew about it. Whatever about the trouble we attracted in Ireland for being different, we multiplied it in the North by being different and loud. Finally, one day the cops came to my place, totally unannounced. They didn't seem to have any specific reason for visiting, but they stayed for a cup of coffee and a chat, asking me if everything was all right. I took this as some kind of coded warning, even though I didn't know what it was about or who it was from. Adil and I packed up our stuff right away, left everything we couldn't carry, including the contents of my fully furnished house, and just got out of there. (Looking back, it makes me think of the Libyan people who had to leave behind everything they owned to escape the Gaddafi regime.)

We went to Manchester, again following my family, but this time we stayed well clear of them. I wanted to keep my distance given the state I was in. Even though I was finding it hard to cope myself, I took care of Adil as best I could. I found him a place to stay, but we continued the pattern of fighting, making up and fighting again. With both of us being so low and on paths to self-destruction, I knew I just had to make a break and leave. That's when I came back to Dublin and tried to start over again.

The good die young

I didn't see Adil again for quite a few years – until December 2010 in fact. I bumped into his father one day out on Aungier Street and invited him in for a cup of tea. He told me that things weren't good for Adil and that he was now in Dublin hanging around with the wrong people, though he was trying to change his ways. He'd just had his jaw broken very badly in some incident and it was held together with plates and a couple of bolts. He asked me if I would speak to him and spend a bit of time with him. Inside, I was anxious about the idea of letting him too far into my life again because I had been burned so many times before – but I looked past this, as a brother would. I explained to him that I was off to Libya to attend a family wedding but that when I got back I would ring him and arrange to meet.

The following day, Adil was in the neighbourhood by chance. Someone told him I was in the internet café, so in he walked. For the first time in five years, we were face to face. Without hesitation, I jumped up and went over to him, smiling and greeting him warmly. I could see all the new marks on him of the troubled life he'd been living. There was no anger, no resentment between us. We hugged and we chatted for an hour or so. He told me about all his kids, including the daughter he'd had since I'd last seen him, who he'd called Layla. He told me he was trying to get his act together. I promised to meet up with him as soon as I got home. That was the last time I saw him.

I flew to Libya the next week. I heard afterwards that some days after I left, by an amazing coincidence or God's intervention, Adil had visited his mother and when they had been sitting down by the fire together, watching TV, he'd turned to her and said, 'Mam, with all that's happened to me in my life, all this damage to my body and these scars, do you think if I die God would have mercy on me for all the hardship I've been through?'

His mother had reassured him as best she could. Apparently, he'd also gathered up all his papers and documents that week and had given them to his dad to mind for him.

Meanwhile, I was best man at Abdu's wedding. On the last big day of the lengthy celebrations, I got a phone call from a mutual friend in Ireland. She asked me if I'd heard about Adil. 'He has been murdered,' she said.

At first, I just didn't believe it. How can something like that sink in? I escaped from the celebrations and fireworks for a few moments by sitting in a car and I rang another friend to confirm the news. Then I broke down crying. I must have been in the car for an hour before Abdu, on a search for his best man, spotted me from a distance and came up to check on me. I dried my eyes quickly, put on a brave face and got on with the end of the celebrations.

I spent the rest of the trip in a daze, as if part of me wasn't actually there.

When I got back to Ireland, I went straight out to visit Adil's parents. Geraldine was in bits, totally torn up, totally inconsolable over what had happened to her son. Through her tears and anger, she told me what they knew about what had happened, how he'd somehow found himself in the company of some very brutal people and been beaten and stabbed to death, and then how his killers had attempted to burn his body using bleach as a fuel, and ended up throwing him in a stream. Such awful things for a mother to have to contemplate happening to her son. She cursed the people who had done this to him.

I heard the name of the suspect for the first time, and was told that he had previously been convicted of manslaughter for killing an eighty-six-year-old man who was tending his wife's grave in Glasnevin cemetery, as well as being convicted of cruelty for hitting three of his girlfriend's children with a belt and electrical cable. How could such a criminal be free in our society? How could such violence go unpunished?

This terrible new low of violence in Ireland left us all in an awful state. We knew what had happened, or at least a lot of it, but we didn't know why. We all knew what Adil was like, that he might get into drunken fights with friends, but we also knew that he wouldn't be mixed up in anything that would explain this kind of brutality from hardened criminals. Of course, the journalists didn't know this and their speculation about Adil just added to our distress. We would have to wait months for the court case to find out the why, and to clear Adil's name.

Adil's funeral

Fortunately for me, because of the autopsy Adil's funeral didn't take place until after I had returned from the wedding, so at least I got a chance to pay my respects properly. On the day of his funeral, I drove up to the mosque and saw that all the Irish side of his family were already there. I took it upon myself to take care of them so that Geraldine wouldn't have to worry about it. I showed them where they needed to go, how the women were separated from the men, and explained to them how the service would proceed and I gave them sheets with the Islamic prayers in English.

After the funeral, we drove down the N7 to the Muslim burial ground in Newcastle – where my brother Yaseen is buried. I followed behind the three black funeral cars and instinctively found myself wanting to protect Adil on his final journey, as if he was in a convoy of VIPs. I pulled out slightly into the right-hand lane and made sure that no vehicles came too near them or tried to pass.

When the coffin was being brought out of the hearse, I took one of the corners and acted as a pallbearer. It was very gloomy, damp weather. I joined the chorus of prayer knowing that it was the only thing I could do for him now. 'Lord, have mercy on his soul. Lord, have mercy on his soul. Lord, have mercy on his soul.'

When we were lifting the coffin from our shoulders and starting to lower it, I remember looking across the top of the coffin and being able to see a crack of light showing through the gap under the lid. Suddenly, I got this very faint smell of earthy dampness and I realised it was the smell of the stream that Adil's body had lain in for a week. I laid my hand gently on the coffin before it was lowered into the ground.

I then took one of the two shovels and dropped a pile of earth into the grave. Two queues had formed for this, but being experienced with a shovel, I found myself quickly getting into the familiar motions and got almost frenzied about it. The anger and emotion mixed and I broke down. Somebody steadied me and took the shovel. I went over to Geraldine and gave her a hug.

I felt so thankful to have had that chance to say goodbye to Adil in the café. If I hadn't been there that day, Manchester would have been the last thing on our record together. I felt lucky to have been able to give him one last proper hug and erase in that short reunion all the shit that had come between us. It seemed to me to have been the hand of God that allowed that.

This was the first time I had been intimate with the rituals of a funeral, the first time that one meant something to me. I had been too young when my brother had died to have been able to take comfort from his funeral and since then I had always had a thing about funerals; I just couldn't deal with them. But Adil's meant a great deal to me. It made me confront death head on for the first time, and ultimately I think it took away a large part of my fear of dying. I came to terms with the fact that you can die at any time in any place for no reason. 'So,' I concluded, 'why not die for a reason?'

❖

Looking back over these events, you can see how bad things were by the time my mother told me about the trip to Tunisia. What I needed was something to take me out of myself, something to help me become someone new.

My life had been trapped between opposites. I was Sam, I was Housam; I was Irish and Libyan; Western, Muslim; father, childless; partnered, single; good, bad. I needed a showdown between all these opposing forces in my life to achieve some kind of new balance. And then along came the revolution – Libya's chance to sort out its problems, and my chance to do the same.

Part II

Owls in the Mountains

July 2011

Call of duty

It was all hours of the morning on 2 July 2011 when we landed at Enfidha-Hammamet, Tunisia's brand-new international airport. It was dark in the arrivals area, almost empty of people, and it gave me the creeps completely. Tunisia's revolution wasn't long over and the place was still far from safe. I was in protective mode, watching out for my mother and my sister and her children in a country where I knew anything could happen at any time.

At passport control, the guard looked like he was about to let me through quite casually, but suddenly spotted something he didn't like and his mood changed. Like some kind of symbol of my life up to that point, I had mistakenly left my Libyan passport inside my Irish one, and the guard decided he'd dig a bit deeper. He asked me the purpose of my visit, probably guessing himself what I was up to, and whether I had any electronic equipment in my luggage. I told him I didn't, but he wasn't convinced and started to search through all our luggage. I was annoyed and frustrated, but realised there was no point putting up any resistance.

❖

I was thankful for the familiar touristy atmosphere of the Sunway coach when we got on board and headed towards our hotel in Hammamet. At reception, I asked if my brother-in-law was about, only to be told, 'It might be best to wait and see.'

I guessed he had some sort of a surprise planned for my sister and the kids, as he hadn't seen them for about five months.

When I opened the door of the hotel room, there was Mahdi. He looked extremely tired and his beard had a lot more white hairs in it than I remembered, but he was very happy to see us all. His kids rushed past me to get to him, screaming with joy.

I introduced myself to the guys Mahdi had with him – a group of Tripoli Brigade volunteers. I left the family to their reunion and went off with the lads to hang out for a while. There were five of them, though two more were in Tunisia but not in the hotel.

Ahmed Falolo was from downtown Tripoli. He had been active in the revolution in Libya from the very start, so by the time I met him, he had already had plenty of battle experience in different parts of the country.

Mohammed Tayari, who I called Che because of his resemblance to that other famous revolutionary, was from Surmaan, near Tripoli. He was young, fit and very brave. He was actually famous in the brigade for having attacked a tank armed with only a knife – he had jumped up on the turret, gained access by the hatch and killed the operators.

Waleed Zumeet was from Tripoli but had lived in Norwich. Like me, he had a daughter from a relationship that had ended so we had a lot in common and often spoke about how much we missed our children. He was a big stocky guy and had been training with the brigade since it was formed in Benghazi. He turned out to be a great 14.5-mm AA gun operator.

Wa'el 'the Greek' was from Tripoli but had lived for quite a while in Greece. He was a peculiar character and reminded me of Private Pyle from the film *Full Metal Jacket*, as he seemed like he was ready to blow a fuse all the time. However, he had an extensive knowledge of mortars, RPGs and cannons from the time he'd spent serving in the Greek armed forces, and so he was a great guy to have along. Typical of him, one of the first things he said to me was, 'I can see you being a martyr.'

'Really? How?' I answered, feeling a little awkward.

'I can see you being hit by a 106-mm cannon shell and blown to pieces. But think of it – you will be a martyr, so you will welcome that shell with open arms.'

Of course, I laughed it off, but I remember thinking of it as a very unusual thing to say to someone you had just met and that if I was the sensitive type I might have grabbed the next flight out of there.

Mustafa al-Waar was a calm, collected guy, mature and wise. He was a real gentleman and very helpful, at one stage driving me to a local hospital when I became badly ill. Unfortunately, he had to leave the brigade later in our campaign to take care of his ailing mother.

This was the first time I had met these guys, but I immediately gelled with them, and soon felt I could trust them with my life. Wa'el was the only one that seemed unsure of me at first. I noticed him looking at me in a weird way, staring as if he was trying to suss me out.

I asked myself, 'Is he testing me to see am I up for this? Or to see what kind of a heart I have?'

It was nothing so deep, as it turned out – Wa'el was just a bit paranoid. The guys were always slagging him. He was an easy target, being so uptight, and constantly biting his nails and fidgeting.

I remember one night I had a bit of a row with him. We were in a hotel room and he was watching some film on the TV. I switched over to catch the latest news from Libya, and Wa'el got really pissed off and started remonstrating with me. I immediately stood right up to him, full on, and I think the surprise at how I reacted was enough to end the matter and he stormed off. The problem was when we were leaving the following morning, we couldn't find him anywhere. It turned out he'd spent the entire night outside on a lounger under a palm tree. I felt really bad, but apparently this was the kind of thing that Wa'el did and it was quickly forgotten.

But on that first night, we talked together about Libya and the revolution, and I heard all kinds of amazing stories about the things they had been through so far. They told me how Mahdi had gathered together a group of Tripoli men he trusted and had co-founded the Tripoli Revolutionary Brigade. I hadn't realised that he was the main man – but was, of course, very excited that he was and very proud. According to the guys, it was because of Mahdi's popularity and charisma that the brigade had quickly received approval among other brigades and attracted many volunteers.

They had gone to eastern Libya to get some training, but with the stalemate there, it was decided to shift operations over to the west. They travelled by boat to Tunisia, from where they made their way south and crossed the border into what I called the Western Mountains. I soon found out that Gaddafi had forced that name to become the official name and, in fact, the local people called them the Nafusa Mountains. It goes without saying that that's what I started calling them too.

The guys told me about a battle they had been in a few weeks before – the first on the western front. Forty men, thirty with assault rifles and ten armed with only daggers, had left the brigade's base in Nalut and driven down from the safety of the mountains towards the town below, called Takut, to take on a fully equipped force. Mahdi had tried to persuade some of them to stay back, knowing that he couldn't arm them properly, but they had insisted on joining in the assault. They weren't successful and one of the guys, Tabuni, who I hadn't met, was hit by a bullet in his elbow, for which he was receiving treatment in Tunisia. I was inspired to hear about their bravery.

During our time in Tunis, the guys were very respectful towards my mother – and my mother was very good to them. She even gave them a few quid at one stage, knowing that they had hardly anything for themselves while they were with the brigade. Mahdi didn't give them cash. Instead, he made sure they had good meals and comfortable hotel rooms (when they could get them). The portions of food they ate while in Tunisia were huge, but they all said to me, 'Wait till you see what we're were eating back at the base!'

One of them came up to me after we'd all shared a meal in the hotel, saying how nice my mother was and to make sure to thank her from them.

Even though we were in a hotel, with tourists and a holiday atmosphere all around us, I didn't go out much at all, just to the pool now and again to relax with the lads. I spent a lot of time thinking back over the many mistakes I had made in my life up to that point. In particular, I thought about what impression my daughter might have of me – being separated from her for so long troubled me a lot. I found myself thinking that if I died fighting for my country, it might make up for the wild things I had done in my youth and at least leave my daughter with some kind of positive idea of me. I also thought about Adil and how, if he had still been alive, he would have definitely been there with me.

On our second day there, my family was sitting by the hotel pool with no other people around when I announced to Mahdi that I had decided I was going to join the brigade and would leave Tunis with him when he was heading back to Libya. He was happy, but my mother was overjoyed. They had both known that this decision was inevitable, I think, but it was a relief for us all to have it finally announced and settled.

Even though the closest thing I'd ever come to a gunfight was playing *Call of Duty* on the Xbox, and even though the small civilian brigade I was joining was up against a massive professional army helped by drug-fuelled mercenaries and the best military equipment oil money could buy, and even though hundreds of people had already lost their lives in the fight against Gaddafi, and even though, let's face it, I was much more likely to come home in a body bag than as a hero, my mother was delighted.

I know a lot of people will find this attitude hard to understand, but maybe a good comparison is with that of the mothers of the Irish revolutionaries in 1916. Think of their hearts aching at the thought of what the British would do to their sons, but also their pride in what their sons had done for their country. My mother believed this fight against Gaddafi's tyranny was a just cause, so what she pictured as a worst-case scenario was not so much burying her son's body in a hole in the ground, but celebrating her son's spirit going off to heaven as a martyr.

She looked at me proudly and said, 'My son, you are about to discover what you are made of.'

Mahdi just smiled calmly in his usual quiet way. The fact that he was there with a small group of guys who had made the same life-risking decision months ago, and would soon be heading back to a camp full of hundreds more like them, showed that from his perspective, this was *the* call of duty.

'We're not here to have fun'

The next morning, my third day in Tunisia, my new life started. Even my Facebook updates changed suddenly, from being all about my favourite music to being all about Libya. 'Streets on Fire' is my update for 2 July 2011 – a YouTube medley of images about the February protests and Gaddafi's backlash. In the video, a protester outlines their demands:

> We want a little dignity. We want them to stop imprisoning people and killing them in prison. We want corruption to end, for education and health service to improve.

The final still shot of the video shows a woman holding a green flag with words handwritten in black ink on it:

> We will not surrender. We will win or we will die. This is not the end! You will fight us + you will fight the generations that follow us until LIBYA IS FREE!

I got up very early that morning and went off with Mahdi and the others to a meeting with the brigade's financers. One of the vehicles the guys drove was a right-hand-drive navy Mitsubishi Pajero. As all the lads were used to left-hand-drive cars, I was the obvious choice to be driver. 'Waleed drove it the other day, Tayari said, and nearly crashed it. And Falolo is not the best driver in the world. You have a go, Housam.'

I was pleased. Immediately I had something to offer, because I knew I was a damn good driver. It was just something I had taken to from a very young age – from the age of nine, in fact, when I first had a go in a big old Chevrolet in Tripoli and had impressed all the adults with how well I was able to handle it. So the Mitsubishi soon became part of my identity in the brigade, and unlike the other vehicles which were shared, I hardly let go of the keys from that day until the day the chassis finally cracked during a battle some weeks later.

Now that I had made the decision to join the brigade, I was anxious to head for Libya and start making a difference, but, of course, that's not how it was going to be. Mahdi had arranged quite a few meetings around Tunisia and I found the delay a little frustrating, but at least I was able to join him and the guys and go to these meetings.

From the very start, without making it too obvious or looking too much like a greenhorn, I began taking things seriously, adapting to my role as part of the security. While Mahdi was at the meetings, we would wait around outside keeping an eye on things. Of course, this being Tunisia none of us was carrying a weapon, but we looked the part – jeans, tank top, army shirt, sunglasses, stocky and serious.

I found it easy enough to stay alert, keeping my eyes peeled for anything out of the ordinary. For instance, there were a lot of Libyan-registered cars around, which was not unusual in itself given the relations between the two countries, but with so many people fleeing across the border, there were a lot more than usual. It might sound crazy, but I tried to take note of them all, even on longer journeys going so far as to try to remember the registrations in case I came across them again. My theory was that if Mahdi was an important figure in the revolution, he could well be a target, and any one of those cars could be carrying the assassin.

One day, we were attending a meeting at a luxury hotel in Carthage. I was struck by the number of very fancy Libyan-registered cars, including Porsche Cayennes, in the parking lot and assumed they must be owned by Gaddafi loyalists. I was concerned, but Mahdi explained that these were, in fact, owned by our allies – Libyan businessmen based in Tunisia to escape the fighting, and keen to finance revolutionary brigades as the fastest way to return the country to business-as-usual.

At one of the last meetings before we left Tunisia, some of the guys took the opportunity to head off on their own for a while, and when Mahdi came out and they still hadn't returned, he said to the rest of us, 'OK, let's go.'

'But the fellas are—' I started to say.

'It'll teach them,' he interrupted. 'They'll know not to do it next time. Remember, we're not here to have fun.'

'If I had twenty sons, I'd send them all'

It was an emotional goodbye on the morning we finally left Tunis. Even the Sunway tour rep, who I had got on well with, was crying. My mother hugged me and started crying too, but they were mostly tears of happiness. Her sending me off joyfully like that was something people around us couldn't understand – just as some viewers of the *Late Late Show* at a later date would have trouble understanding how she could say, 'If I had twenty sons, I'd send them all.' It makes perfect sense to people who have a faith like hers.

'You will discover who you are,' she said to me again. 'No matter what happens, don't forget how much I love you.'

When we'd said our goodbyes, we drove off in our convoy, heading south down the whole length of Tunisia towards the western border of Libya. We were all in high spirits in the Mitsubishi – myself, Tayari, Falolo, Wa'el and Zumeet. Mahdi and the others were in a second jeep. I was particularly happy to finally be on our way, ending the frustration I'd felt in Tunis. Even though I might have been driving to my death, I had this feeling that it was what I was meant to do, and I wanted to get on with it.

We drove pretty much all day, with me at the wheel, and we talked and listened to music, especially this one revolutionary song that was banned in Gaddafi-controlled areas, 'O Bless You, Revolutionaries' by Salah Ghaly. We sang it over and over again. If our mission was successful, we talked about how it would be heard openly and freely throughout Libya.

At Medinine, I followed the sign eastwards to Libya only to have the other jeep quickly overtake me and indicate to me to turn back. The route I had taken was the quickest to get us into Libya, but it would have led us straight to the Gadaffi-controlled town of Ras Ajdir. We needed to take the much longer route south to get to a safe crossing point.

The landscape gradually became more desert the farther south we drove. We were on the fringes of the Sahara, near where George Lucas shot the *Star Wars* scenes of Luke Skywalker's early life – we even drove through the town of Tataouine which inspired him so much. Lucas was inspired by the underground Berber dwellings of this area when he was imagining Luke's family home. Ironically, Gaddafi had tried to eliminate the Berber culture from Libya in a way similar to the British attempts to eliminate Irish culture from Ireland. Irish culture has survived and hopefully Berber culture will reassert itself in Libya.

During our journey, we picked up the other two volunteers

who had previously travelled with Mahdi. Housam Kafu was from Tripoli but lived in Dubai. He had been with the brigade from the beginning, often going into battle alongside Tayari, and had great stories about the early days of the revolution when they had little or nothing by way of weaponry.

Mohammed Tabuni, who had recovered from the treatment he'd needed for his shattered elbow in Tunis, was from Tripoli but had lived in LA and spoke with an American accent. He was a big, bald-headed crazy dude and had trained in an American SWAT team. I clicked with him right away. Both of us were into hip-hop and I was really impressed when he told me he was friends with some of my favourite underground rappers and DJs. I felt relieved in some ways that I had found a truly kindred spirit, a guy who had tasted the same side of life as me – and who had also left it all behind him.

By midnight, we reached the foothills of the mountains in the south and started to climb slowly upwards. Near the border, we visited a villa to meet up with Shukre Mashaiykh, a friend of Mahdi's who was supporting the revolution by protecting the route for rebels crossing the border. Mashaiykh helped us at various times during our campaign, and later became an important figure in the new administration.

Later, when we arrived at the border in complete darkness, there was no need for security checks or searches as the Tunisian guards knew what we were about. This was a very active crossing, both for refugees leaving Libya and for revolutionaries entering the country. Mahdi gathered all our passports, including my Irish one, and the Libyan guard, protecting our national borders even in this time of war, stamped them. On Mahdi's advice, I used my Irish passport so that my Libyan one would not show any signs of me having been at the revolutionary-controlled crossing. This would keep open the possibility of me being able to enter Tripoli as an infiltrator if needs be at a later stage.

We were met by the brigade's border official and welcomed to Libya. Wazin, the nearest town on the Libyan side of the border, had bounced back and forth between loyalist and revolutionary control, but was now held firmly by friendly forces, though it was still empty of normal life because of all the uncertainty. Keeping it liberated was vital to the revolution, as it enabled the crucial movement of people, arms and supplies, especially fuel, across the border.

We got to our destination, the city of Nalut, at about 4 a.m. It was like a ghost town, totally lifeless and eerie. When we arrived, it had been under revolutionary control for some months, but most of the local people had moved away because of the relentless firing of Grad rockets by the Gaddafi troops from the plains below.

Nalut had been liberated without much bloodshed early on in the war. There had been about 150 loyalist troops stationed in the city and when the revolution started, the elders approached them with a request to leave. They did so, under pressure. Ironically, they were then accused of disloyalty by the regime and some were even murdered.

Following their success in Nalut, the elders then went down the mountain to another town, Ghazaia, and invited its inhabitants to evacuate to the safety of Nalut. The locals' reply was a loyalist slogan, 'Only God, Gaddafi and Libya', so the elders gave up. When mobilised Gaddafi troops subsequently arrived in Ghazaia, the locals soon realised that, in reality, the troops didn't care about the loyalty of such towns. The people were treated appallingly and in ways previously unheard of in Libya. Many of the troops were mercenaries, plied by the regime with drink and drugs to make sure they instilled as much fear into the countryside as possible. How low would the regime have to sink before Gaddafi's supporters realised how much he had betrayed Libya?

When we got to our barracks most of the brigade were asleep, but even so, there was soon a line of guys wanting to welcome back Mahdi. The way people hugged him really brought home to me the huge affection they had for him. There was nothing formal about it. They were hugs of real friendship, and they were being given to everyone in the returning group too, even me. That sense of welcome was a great boost and made me feel part of everything immediately.

The fellas I'd travelled with introduced me to everyone, and it helped that there were quite a few who knew my brother, Yusef, from his brief time with the brigade in Benghazi. In fact, I was soon being asked all about my family and about Ireland. Libyans are like that. They want to hear what you have to say for yourself, your stories, your perspective on things, especially when you're not a local.

There was this one older man who was crying as he told me how proud he was to see Libyans leaving the comforts of other countries to come to Libya's aid. 'You mean more to me than my own sons,' he said. That had a powerful impact on me.

Number 329

The brigade had been in place in the mountains for about a month before my arrival. According to my identity card (and we were the first brigade to have properly produced dog-tag-type ID cards), I was number 329, which meant I was the 329th person to join the brigade. Better late than never.

Eventually that first night, I was shown to the room in the barracks, which had been converted from a school, where I would sleep. The makeshift quarters were in many different rooms off the main corridors, with every room sleeping between five and ten people. Each room had a different vibe about it because we came from so many different backgrounds. There were all sorts of guys; the educated and the illiterate, liberals and conservatives, the outgoing and the quiet, some very religious, some not so. Most were from Tripoli but some were from the countryside, and we tended to stick with people from similar backgrounds. But one of the things I came to appreciate most about our campaign was how it united us in spite of our differences. With a shared enemy and common purpose, people who otherwise would have had no reason to hang out together were suddenly co-operating as if they had known each other all their lives, and always as equals.

Because I had got on so well with the guys I had met in Tunisia and had a similar outlook to them, I was immediately accepted by the others at the base as one of that gang. In the room with me were Isa Burqeeq, Hisham Breki, Abd Wahab, Waleed Fezan, Sami Bin Musa, Tayari and Falolo.

Isa was a cool dude – a tall, bald-headed guy who had spent some time in the UK. He was wise but fun, and commanded a lot of respect from everyone. Hisham was great at those perfectly timed off-the-cuff remarks that left us all in stitches. He helped us get through many a journey with funny stories about how tough it had been to grow up in Gaddifi's Tripoli. Abd Wahab was from Nalut, although he had been living in Tripoli for years. He spoke Berber and during battles became the brigade's translator for all the Nalutian conversations we'd hear on the walkie-talkies. He and I often tuned in to the CB radios at night-time and he would tell me what was being said. Waleed was a big stocky guy from the Old City and was very streetwise, like me.

Our room and one other were known as the *joojmats'*

(mavericks') rooms. We were seen as being a little crazy, taking bigger risks, pushing ourselves to extremes, up for anything. We were never put into a particular platoon or rostered for training because, well, we were the lads. We had attitude. We had the gear. We had the chants. We beat on our jeeps when we arrived on the scene and everyone knew it was us.

Because of my association with Mahdi, some people were surprised that I hooked up with these guys, but it wasn't long before they saw why!

Our mattresses were only about two inches thick and so not what you'd call comfortable, while the pillows were as thick as normal mattresses but as hard as rocks. It wasn't the bedding, though, that kept me awake that first night – it was my mind, working overtime with everything new that was happening.

Unfortunately, my insomnia didn't come to an end even after the first few nights, and it actually caused me some health problems after a while. In the meantime, I learned to function on very little sleep. I took the opportunity to keep a diary about what happened each day. I'd get odd looks from people about it sometimes, but I managed to keep it up and record my own little bit of history. Each time I wrote in it, I was conscious that it could well be the last thing I'd write, and I also thought how maybe the diary would reach Layla someday. I certainly never thought it would become the basis for a book.

'We're not soldiers, we're revolutionaries'

On that first night, I hadn't been in bed long when we were called for *Fajr*, or dawn prayers. Each morning, our brigade commander, Marwan Jamhoor, would walk the corridors singing the traditional call, 'Prayer is better than sleep.' Sometimes this would be altered for fun to something like, 'Wake up you sleepy lot, there are dying men on the front.'

A mosque had been established in the main school hall upstairs and most of us gathered there soon after the call. I could see that for many fighters, their faith was an important element in the revolution. What the Quran says about pure motivations in war gave a lot of them the courage to risk their lives, knowing that they would be rewarded in the afterlife as long as their intention was to serve God. As the Quran says, 'Do not think that those who fall for the sake of God are dead, for they are alive with their Lord prospering.'

I witnessed the full power of this faith some days later when one of the men started crying during *Fajr*. We learned that while Gaddafi's thugs had been searching for him in Tripoli, they had murdered his mother. It was moving to see all the brigade members go to the man, and hug and comfort him. Later that same day in the canteen, I saw this man again and the slight smile on his face was proof to me that through our faith and through sharing in his grief, we could dilute his pain and sorrow among us. Even if we couldn't erase his suffering, we could help him to go on for the sake of others.

Dawn prayer was usually followed by a little more sleep before breakfast, but on that first morning, there was a physical training session to undertake. Even though I wasn't rostered to do it, I decided it would be a good start. I knew I wasn't physically fit and that this was something I needed to work on. However, what I lacked in fitness, I made up for it in my determination. Even that first morning, tired as I was and in temperatures my body wasn't used to, I made myself keep up with the guy leading the training so that everyone would know I meant business.

I had built myself up so much for this mentally during that week in Tunisia that I literally hit the ground running as soon as I got the chance. I was extremely fired up about all aspects of training and wanted to be involved in everything. I didn't just want to be involved with the brigade – I wanted to distinguish myself and be an important part of it. I wanted to put as much effort as I possibly could into the brigade, physically and mentally.

Later that day, after a short nap, I got my first good look around the sandy grounds of the buildings and I visited the security hut at the gates of the barracks. Falolo and another guy were on duty, and they had guns. We weren't well supplied at that stage, so it was a bit of a novelty, especially for me of course, and I immediately took it as a great chance to learn. It was the first time I had held a Kalashnikov or an FN FAL, both of which would become important weapons for us, and I was determined to get to know them there and then, inside and out. Falolo gave me a quick run-through and I learned as much as I possibly could. I pushed myself very hard like that from the outset. I took every opportunity to learn, not just how to take apart the guns, for instance, but how to do it fast. I even timed myself.

The atmosphere in the barracks was an odd mixture of things. In some ways, it was like a prison, a bit run-down and isolated from the real world, but an open one in that we could come and go, within limits – though, of course, there was nowhere to go. The town was mostly uninhabited and everything had shut down. The barracks had been a boarding school, and with between 300 and 500 of us living there, it certainly felt like an institution – with its twenty sinks and ten showers, and with dormitories, canteen and recreation room.

The food available to us was very simple. Lunch was based around things like milk, bread and dates, or eggs and a bit of cheese. Dinners were very bland, often just unflavoured pasta or something like that, as everything had to be made to suit a lot of different dietary requirements.

However, alongside the institutional feel, we had a lot of freedom and fun too. There was revolutionary graffiti on the walls, for example, and plenty of carry-on. A uniform was issued to us, but guys took a lot of liberty with it by cutting off the sleeves or wearing a tank top or a beret with it. Individuality in uniformity, I suppose you could say. This wasn't the army, after all.

The leaders had a tricky time finding the right balance between discipline and personal freedom. Sometimes, orders were met with the objection, 'We're not soldiers, we're revolutionaries and free men!' This was said a lot, for instance, when Mahdi tried to ban smoking inside the building. This attitude was sometimes a problem during training, with some guys not always willing to put in the effort. I'd say to them that it was for their own benefit and could make the difference between killing or being killed, but not even that approach worked. Some of them thought I was just lecturing them because Mahdi was my brother-in-law, but I was saying it out of genuine concern. 'Don't do it because you're being told to,' I'd say. 'Do it to stay alive.'

In those early days, our main focus was on training, which got more intensive as the days went by. Specialist trainers were brought in to work with us on different skills, making it like a crash course in soldiering. I took part in as many of the training sessions as I could, because I wanted to make myself the best soldier I could be in order to have the greatest possible impact. And I wasn't doing it for personal glory or any such thing. It was always for the cause and to put an end to an evil regime and to the oppression of my people.

Soon, however, I was put on duty as a special security officer to

Mahdi and so had to juggle training with those duties. Mahdi had already been the target of a number of attacks, so it was a case of when the next attack would happen, not if it would.

First mission

Early in the morning of 13 July, when I had been at the camp about a week, Tabuni woke me with a nudge in the pitch dark. He winked and said, 'Come on, Housam.'

'What is it?' I asked groggily.

'We have a mission', was all he said.

Myself, Tabuni and four other guys – Waleed Ghariany, Abdaroof Jojma, Anis Zawy and our commander, Marwan Jamhoor – made up the group. With just two FN FAL rifles, a bunch of cameras and a few scopes, we bundled into a powerful Dodge pick-up, and I left the relative safety of the barracks for the first time.

Still in darkness, we sped through the empty streets of Nalut, through two revolutionary checkpoints and were off into the open terrain of the Nafusa Mountains, known to locals as the Nalutian Ocean because the mountains seem to go on forever, filling the view in every direction. The most amazing bright moon lit up the road, the surrounding desert plateau and the rocky landscape around us. With Waleed reading from the Quran beside me, I could feel the adrenaline pumping through me, putting my senses into overdrive. The dust we were lifting flew off behind us, the sounds of the engine roared in my ears, the cool morning air was like water against my face, grit from the road stuck to my teeth and the cigarette smoke jagged roughly in my throat. It was surreal.

Suddenly, with a bang on the cabin, Abdaroof signalled to Marwan to stop. Marwan jammed on the brakes, no doubt thinking there might be trouble. Abdaroof jumped out, went around the back of the pick-up, and with two swift jabs, smashed in the rear lights with his rifle butt. 'What the hell?' We looked at each other, confused. But then we figured out what he was doing. He had realised that all the sudden braking needed to manoeuvre through this terrain meant the lights could give away our position and so needed to be taken out. After Abdaroof climbed back in, cool as a hero in a movie, we took off again.

We drove out to the edge of the mountain range, from where we could look down at the town of Ghazaia and the surrounding desert plains. The massive mountain range we were on runs across a portion of the northwestern corner of Libya, from the Tunisian border at Wazin to the town of Gharyan 250 kilometres to the east. The southern end of the range slopes down to become a desert plateau, while the northern edge – where we stood – falls steeply down in an escarpment to the Jafara Plain below, which then stretches off northwards in a dry desert landscape to the coast.

Two east–west roads run roughly parallel to the escarpment, one across the plain below and the other through the plateau up behind the mountain range. At intervals along the way, a north–south road climbs from the plain road up through steep valleys in the escarpment to meet up with the mountain road. A number of towns were joined up by the mountain road, from Nalut to Jadu to Zintan to Yefren to Kikla and on to Gharyan; many of these towns were in the hands of revolutionaries. Along the plain road were the Gaddafi-held towns of Ghazaia, Takut, Huamid, Tiji, Badr and Al Jawsh, until you got as far as the north–south road to Tripoli.

The outcrop we were on had been referred to as Elders' Point since the start of the revolution. Apparently, the elders of Nalut had banned young people from visiting the area because they had seen Gaddafi's troops in the town below raping women out in the open as a fear tactic. This brought home to me how rape was not at all just an incidental by-product of lawlessness, but a consciously employed weapon that was being used by Gaddafi to terrorise Libyan society.

Our mission was simple – scout for positions for the planned assault on Ghazaia. We calculated that the distance from a safe point at the bottom of the mountain to the gates of the town was about 8.5 kilometres. Because the terrain near the town was totally open, we knew they would see us coming from miles away, and that we would therefore have to plan for being bombarded all the way in. We discussed different strategies, even the idea of some groups paragliding in. At a later stage, a unit of the brigade consisting of thirty-three men did go along that route, but without success. It was led by a guy we called Uncle Naji, a really sound guy who had lived in the UK for a while and knew my dad. He was as fit as a fiddle, even though he was in his mid-fifties. He took his specialist unit on such extreme missions to toughen them up. He was as tough as nails himself, and it was said he was able to sleep standing up in his armour if required. He called the guys in his unit 'ya ghawaly', which means 'my lovelies'. 'What's wrong, my lovelies?' he'd say when his men complained about another day in the searing heat and a night of sleeping rough.

At sunrise, we performed the Islamic ablution called *Wudu* and prayed together on the side of the mountain. For me, it was such a rare thing to be able to pray to God in so beautiful a place, on that barren, sculpted mountainside with an expansive view of what felt like the whole world stretching out before me. That moment of praying as the first light of day comes is like a direct line to God, and keeps you in touch with your creator. I was beginning to see how prayer would play an important part in my revolution, like a compass pointing me in the right direction.

One of the local Nalutian elders very kindly invited us to join them for *Fajr* and brought us to a well that had been created from a stream they had filtered and protected with a cover. Very graciously, and against tradition, the elder insisted on being the one to lift the lid and pour the water for us. He poured the water for me, which I took into my hands and used to wash my face, then my arms and head and, symbolically, my feet. He chatted away as he did this, and I got to know him a little. I found the experience very special and moving. Maybe because my skin is more pale in colour, and similar to the Berbers, he seemed to be treating me almost as one of their own.

We spent the whole day in the area, observing vehicle movements below and trying to gauge the size of the force we'd be up against. It wasn't very exciting stuff, but it was my first experience of the peculiar nature of recon work, and I took it seriously.

First target practice

The next morning, I got up at dawn and after prayer did two hours of intensive training with our trainer, Bu Muslim. I grew to admire this guy enormously over the weeks that followed. He was a giant of a man physically and he had a huge heart to go with it, and both were matched by his intelligence. An unusual combination of pharmacist and judo black belt, he was a force to reckon with in the brigade.

His type of training was only possible at the crack of dawn because it was just too hot for it any later than that. It involved crazy stuff like carrying your partner on your back while doing the laps that you'd normally only just manage to jog. Then, when you could take no more, Bu Muslim would blow the whistle and you'd have to do a squat, with your partner still on your back, before carrying on. My legs were in agony for days afterwards. Another example involved holding someone who was 'playing dead' under the arms and dragging them around the pitch at full speed. Instead of weights, we lifted each other. It was far from the fancy gyms of Dublin that I'd been to, but just as effective, and much more in keeping with the nature of war, in which you rely on each other and make do with what you've got.

That afternoon, we had our first interaction with the media. Some film crews came to the barracks to report on our brigade, and we put on a bit of a display for them. We wanted to get the message out that we were going to be an important force in the revolution.

We organised some training exercises and drills for the cameras, and the troops were filmed singing revolutionary chants. One went: 'Libya has called, Libya has called, and we have answered that call. Our strength has doubled, our strength has doubled, we won't let our martyrs fall.' Another had the lines: 'Muammar we're coming for you. Muammar we're coming for you. Do you not know who we are when you say, Who are you?'

Being always mindful of security and my duties, I stayed with the commanders, sticking close to Mahdi, while the speeches were made. Most of us wore masks to protect our identities because we knew that the Gaddafi regime in Tripoli might identify us from the footage and target our families and relatives. Compared to a professional army, we were a bit of a raggle-taggle lot – some in uniform, some in military khakis, some in jeans – but we showed ourselves to be a lot more organised than other brigades. With our actions, discipline and pride, we showed the film crew how passionate we were about our cause, how well trained we were becoming and how determined we were to remove the Gaddafi regime, no matter what the risk to ourselves.

That evening, I also fired my first shots in front of the brigade with the FN FAL assault rifle. There was a queue of lads at target practice, all waiting for their turn to shoot at the dummy – a few sandbags with a helmet on top – about 150 metres away. Each person was only allowed to take two shots because we didn't have much ammunition to spare at that stage. I was just passing by and Bu Muslim said to me, 'Have you taken any shots yet, Housam? Come on.'

While I waited for my turn, my heart started to beat like mad. I would have preferred not to be taking my first shot while being watched by a platoon of lads. My connection with Mahdi meant that everything I did was scrutinised closely by everyone, as if they were waiting for me to show a weakness. So I was extra nervous, though still confident. I knew that when it came time to line up the FN FAL with the target, I'd focus and steady. And I was right. Boy was I relieved when I hit the helmet twice. Everyone gets scared and nervous on the battlefield sometimes – if someone says they don't, they're telling you a lie – but it's how good you are at controlling it that counts.

After spending some time chatting with the guys, I also saw Bu Muslim shoot the PKT machine gun, holding the beast of a thing himself in one arm and cocking with the other, even though it's usually mounted on a T-72 tank and fired via remote control. We all got a big charge of pride seeing one of our own being able to manage this massive gun single-handedly and firing it so confidently.

❖

The next morning, 15 July, I woke up feeling the effects of my new world – waking up at dawn every morning for *Fajr,* the intense training, the broken sleep and the barracks food. Because I was not getting enough sleep, I was a bit stressed, and I was starting to think that I might need the sleeping tablets that I'd brought with me. It wasn't easy changing from my nightclub lifestyle to this tough regime, and the difference was starting to take its toll on my body and my mood. That morning, I found myself thinking up an excuse that I could give Bu Muslim to get out of training. But I managed to overcome that urge and decided it was best to just do it. But what a thrill it was to hear him declare after prayer, 'Back to the bunks, lads, it's Friday. Take the day off!' I made a beeline back to the room, the thin mattress looking like a plush pillow for my aching body.

I got about three more hours of sleep before being woken for breakfast. Afterwards, everyone started gathering in the square because there was a lot of talk about preparing for an advance. Some guys were becoming frustrated with all the waiting around, and were talking among themselves about all the action going on elsewhere in the country and complaining that things were going too slowly here. We found out that a section of the brigade was to go to Zintan, to another of our barracks, and maybe from there to the frontline. The commanders – Bu Muslim and Marwan Jamhoor – spent some time picking out who was to go, choosing vehicles and weapons and so on. I could have gone if I'd wanted to – and I was tempted by the idea of immediate action – but Mahdi's security was the main thing for me at that stage, and I knew I had to stay put.

Waleed Gharyani was one of the guys who was leaving. Though we didn't know each other back then, he did remember me from my time in Tripoli when I was a kid. It was my pale skin and unusual looks that had caught his attention, and I'd made him think of his own Berber people. He was the barracks photographer while he was with us. I gave him a hug, wished him good luck and said that I'd see him on the front.

Later that day, we went out into the mountain terrain for some arms training. I got to fire the 14.5mm anti-aircraft gun, the same one Gaddafi was using on unarmed civilians all over Libya. It's a big, seated, beast of a gun, and I could see how it would frighten the hell out of protesting civilians. I could also see the horrors it would cause when it was fired at people in enclosed spaces at close range, how bodies would be torn to pieces by its huge bullets – again, something we knew Gaddafi was guilty of ordering. It's really a terrifying machine. We learned how to load up the belts and feed them into the gun, then how to cock and fire it. I also fired the PKT, another belt-fed automatic rifle, and learned how to open the bullet cans and load the links.

All this technical detail suited me. I was used to working with my hands and with tools and equipment. I was also – there's no denying it – like a lot of lads and excited by guns and military gear. Some people can't understand this and are a little horrified at the idea, but it's hard to deny that boys have an attraction to guns – when you see a young fella get his first toy gun, he'll start running about the place pretending to shoot everyone and everything around him. I'm of the view that some boys are just into tools and weapons and we imagine having to use them … often to save the universe from its fiercest enemies.

After shooting practice, we made our way back to the barracks, singing songs and feeling pleased with ourselves. I could see that morale was high among these guys and it felt good. After a bit of food, we sat up late as usual, chatting and meeting guys we hadn't talked to yet or to new volunteers. There were guys organising classes in things like prayer and English language, but us crazy dudes were too wrecked every night to exert ourselves any further.

The cleaning revolution

The next morning, I slept in and woke up quite shocked that I'd slept so heavily. I was disappointed that I'd missed *Fajr* prayer and training. I sneaked off and went to the mosque next door to wash and pray. This was a little cheeky of me, as we weren't meant to leave the barracks casually like that, but the water wasn't working in the barracks at the time and I really needed the wash. It also gave me the chance to pray.

When I got back to the barracks, the mess in the place suddenly got to me and I decided to do something about it. I grabbed a sweeping brush and, starting in one corner of the large entrance hall, began working my way around, clearing out the dust and debris that had built up. It was amazing how quickly it made a difference to the look of the room, and it wasn't just me that noticed. Others started helping out, and soon guys saw what was going on and joined in the cleaning revolution, not just in the common areas but also in their rooms and everywhere through the barracks. I could see it had its own momentum after a while, so I went outside with another plan. I got a shovel and a barrow and started on the exterior of the building. From my background in construction, I knew what a big difference clean and defined edges of buildings, steps and kerbs make, so I started skimming away the sand that had gathered up against the concrete. Not only was this a great workout in the blistering heat, but it was also good for the soul. I felt much better about myself and about the place itself afterwards, and I think it helped lift everyone's spirits. 'Cleanliness is next to godliness' is also true in Islam.

After all our hard work, it was nice to find out that, by pure chance, the dinner was the best we'd had yet: a bowl of white rice with a kind of salsa made from strips of liver, sultanas, tomatoes and a few nuts. It was tasty and made a big change from the bland slop we often got.

Speaking of cleaning, at a much later date, during our advance north, when I was really down in the dumps in the midst of Ramadan and feeling the effects of the fasting and of not smoking, I calmed myself one morning by taking about three hours to hand wash all my gear. I had become used to getting in late and just throwing whatever I was wearing in the corner, and at that stage my clothes were really sticking with the sweat and filthy with the sand and grime. This was during a build-up to another battle, and I also took the opportunity of that downtime during Ramadan to service my car myself: fresh tyres, checking the fluids, cleaning out the interior, getting her battle ready. While others expected the fellas in the transport department to do all that, I took the initiative and responsibility to make sure my jeep was the way I wanted it to be.

Training, experience and confidence

I took a short nap after dinner that day after all the cleaning, before a mortar and cannon training session given by my pal Wa'el 'the Greek', which I had decided to go to even though I wasn't scheduled to. I was filling every free hour with anything that would prepare me better for fighting. From his training in the Greek armed forces, Wa'el was like a textbook in what he knew and the way he taught us about the mortars and cannons – he didn't just use markers and a white board, but different colours for different elements. I respected him a lot for that and learned a lot from him. For example, when firing a normal rifle when the wind is coming strongly from one side, you fire slightly into the wind to allow for it. With an RPG, though, you do the opposite because it is the tails on the rear of the grenade that catch the wind most and throw it off course into wind.

Another training session involved SWAT manoeuvres. I was chosen as squad leader for one team while the other squad was armed with sand-filled plastic bottles as grenades and positioned around the course ready to throw them at us. We had to make our way around the course without being spotted. I did a good job getting our team to work together as a unit and keep out of sight, but there was one guy, who I didn't know, and he caused me a lot of grief. He just wouldn't obey commands and kept breaking rank and doing his own thing. He gave away our location a few times and I got furious with him.

'Thank God I have my own pack to go into battle with and don't have to rely on the likes of you to watch my back,' I said to him before storming off in a fury and missing the last hour of the training.

I got my own back on the guy, though. At the debriefing afterwards, Bu Muslim told us that according to Islamic teachings, if a soldier doesn't listen to his commander in battle, the commander has the right to injure and abandon the soldier.

I turned to the guy and said as sharply as I could, 'Did you hear that?'

❖

One morning we did some stamina training and judo. Although he was a huge guy, Bu Muslim was as nimble as a child. He felt the judo would be especially useful for us in learning how to run and dive with a gun – a very tricky and risky thing to do.

The stamina session, when we set up another assault course, was so intense that I puked and had to rest. I asked if this was something to worry about but was told it was because of my smoking – my healthy side trying to defeat my unhealthy side! 'I have to give up,' I said to myself, knowing I wouldn't.

After a short sleep, I woke up with a ferocious pain in my upper abdomen. Like a wounded animal unwilling to attract the concern of the pack, I didn't want to say anything in case anyone thought I was weak, but it got worse through the course of the day, and when I heard some other guys had to go to hospital with pains, I knew there must be something up. So even though I really didn't want to miss sniper training, I got Mustafa al-Waar to drop me to the hospital.

It was the local Nalut hospital, yet I was treated by a Korean doctor. From one glance at me, he knew what was up and that I hadn't slept properly for a week. I was given tablets, and, feeling like something scraped off a shoe, I went back to the barracks planning to go straight back to bed. However, just as I arrived back, I was instructed to take three American NATO officials on a tour of the barracks. I could tell by the look of them that they were extremely professional soldiers. They were being hosted by the local Nalutian brigades in a safe house in the town, but had decided to make contact with the Zintani (with whom they had most of their dealings in the region) and then also with us. Having communication with NATO was very important to our plans, so we were happy to show them around.

I realised just how on the ball they were in the arms depot, where like heat-seeking missiles themselves, they immediately spotted the SAM7 missile launchers. They asked if I knew what they were and explained that it was the one weapon we had that was a problem, in that it could do serious damage to the international reputation of the brigade and of the revolution as a whole if we used them. If they fell into the wrong hands and were smuggled into terrorist countries or used against civilian aircraft, it would be a disaster for the revolutionaries.

On their way out, they retrieved their weapons – advanced M16 rifles with grenade capability and Desert Eagle pistols – from our security checkpoint and left.

I then had to go to another meeting, at which commanders from another Tripoli Brigade were trying to persuade Mahdi that he had no choice but to allow his brigade to be subsumed into theirs. I felt they were like vultures, testing Mahdi to see if he was weak enough for them to move in on for the kill.

I knew one of them, an elder who considered himself a sheikh (leader), from Dublin, and knew that he was nothing more than a trouble-maker. His tactic at the meeting was to insinuate that our motivations were too secular for our fight to be considered jihad, and so our revolutionaries were never going to become martyrs and be protected by Allah. This infuriated me, thinking of all the great guys who had given up so much for this fight, some of whom, like Aymen Krema, a good friend of Falolo's, Tayari's and Kafu's, had already lost their lives.

When he was on his way out, I took him aside and, ignoring his status as an elder, said to him as sharply as I could, 'Keep it up and I know a bunch of guys who would do you damage for what you are saying.' He looked shaken and had no answer.

I was pleased with myself for having spoken up for the people he was offending. As my mother had predicted, I was really starting to discover what I was made of.

❖

I went back to the dormitory, collapsed in agony onto the mattress, popped a sleeping tablet and was out for the count.

The next morning, I don't know how I managed it but I woke up for prayer. I didn't feel like I'd slept at all, so I went straight back to bed afterwards. The next thing I knew Tabuni was kicking me in the leg saying, 'Come on, Housam. Where were you? We've been looking for you, man. We have to do escort duty for a bunch of Tripoli VIPs.'

We left the barracks in three pick-ups and my jeep, and headed for the border town of Wazin to collect the VIPs – leaders of the yet-to-be-formed Tripoli Council. We waited there all day and I guessed that Mahdi had planned it this way so that no one would know exactly what time the leaders would arrive.

We spent a lot of time chatting and getting to know guys we hadn't had much of a chance to talk to before. I had a look around Wazin. The prefab building of the checkpoint was still scarred by the signs of battle, with bullet holes in the galvanised roof, through which rays of light hit your face. On display in the middle of the road was some kind of spontaneous monument, a massive pile of spent shells and bullet casings of all different kinds, as if to show everyone who drove by how much the town had been through.

Once the VIPs had arrived, among them Abdur Raheem al-Keeb, a professor and businessman who would become interim prime minister, and Abdul Razzak Buhajir, who would go on to become head of the Tripoli Local Council, I took control of setting up the convoy in proper formation. I followed the protocols I had learned in training, forcing cars to park until we had passed, keeping front and rear diagonals covered as much as possible, and so on. I was delighted to see Isa on the back of the pick-up swinging the 12.7-mm Browning machine gun from side to side, alert to anything in the landscape that could act as cover for an ambush.

The sense that Gaddafi's soldiers could strike us at any time kept the likes of Isa and myself on our toes. We expected it, even anticipated it at times. And yet, it never happened that way. This surprised some of us: where were the signs of Gaddafi's powerful military machine? Where were the spies? The crack units? Yes, the international forces had been implementing the UN Security Council Resolution against Libya since March, and, yes, NATO was enforcing the arms embargo and a no-fly zone, but wasn't there more to the regime than that, we wondered?

When we arrived back at base, there was a big reception for the VIPs and a display of force. This would have been the first time Keeb had seen such a professional brigade preparing to enter Tripoli. There were tears in his eyes as he looked on. Aware that many of us would not survive the campaign, maybe he felt how sad it was that this was the level of personal sacrifice Libya needed.

I got to have a little chat with him in English afterwards as we passed each other in the corridor. I took to him straight away, judging him to be a kind man with a good heart. He told me he had absolutely no political ambitions himself, but was willing to assist in the transition if required. Like me, he was answering the call of the people. Someone came to try to take him off to the meeting but he just said, 'Let them wait another minute, I'm just enjoying this chat with this young man.'

The next day was not eventful but I took an opportunity to go online on one of the computers we had got hooked up in the office and post a message on Facebook:

Just to let you all know I'm alive and well … Things are hot here and I don't just mean the weather, although that's hot too … Pray for us. We're doing our best to get rid of this war criminal … If you could see what I am seeing or hear what I have heard, you'd be sick … He has done unimaginable things to his people … But we are lions and our motto is … We'll never back down … we'll be victorious or die trying …

I also chatted via Facebook with a female friend of mine who I felt bad about, as we had fallen out. She came to mind because she was from the nearby town of Gharyan, and I just decided to contact her. It made me feel much better to have cleared the air. I was trying to make amends, I suppose, in preparation for what might lie ahead.

At a later stage I also rang Adil's parents, something I'd never usually do, but because of how I was feeling about things, I rang just to say hello and see how they were.

❖

Some nights later, I was woken up suddenly well before dawn by the sounds of people shouting and getting ready for battle. 'The time for battle has come,' I heard someone shouting.

I wasn't sure what was going on, but I grabbed my uniform, bag and equipment. From what I could gather at first, Gaddafi brigades had assembled a 2,000-strong force nearby in Takut and they were making their way up the mountain on a major advance against us. Our biggest fear was happening right there and then, because we were nowhere near trained or armed enough to take on such a force. I psyched myself up for battle and whatever else God had in store for me.

However, by the time I got to the common area, I found out that it wasn't battle stations at all. Somehow, maybe from some movement someone observed, a worry that it might be happening had grown into a rumour that it could be happening, and next thing everyone was acting as if it was happening.

As things were calming down, Abdaroof called to me to join the scouting mission to see if there were actually any signs of an attack. I was totally up for it, especially since I had all the adrenaline of someone prepared for battle flowing through me. I knew Mahdi wouldn't want me to go, so I avoided him, got my gun and headed for the pick-up. Of course, just my luck, that's exactly when he spotted me: sitting in the back. He was surprised and looked a little worried, but I gave him a please-don't-say-anything look, and he let it go … though not before telling me to make sure to follow orders. So while others were experiencing a major anticlimax and returning to their beds, I was still heading off for action.

It wasn't that action-packed, though. We drove to the edge of the mountains and looked down towards Takut, trying to spot signs of movement. We stayed there for about an hour and then went to another viewing point for a few more hours. We did see some movement in the town, but nothing to get too concerned about.

The Americans

A few days later, a contingent from the brigade met with the Americans again, this time in their safe house in the town. They had been set up there by Nalutians and Zintani, and had been mostly dealing with those local groups up to that point. However, since our brigade was getting bigger and Tripoli was now becoming a focus, they wanted to liaise with us more. Having two fluent English speakers – myself and our strategist, Bashir Rueben, who had co-founded the brigade with Mahdi – made communications with us easier too.

We chatted for a while, but you could just tell these guys were in work mode at all times. They made it clear that they didn't want media attention.

Bashir discussed our Tripoli strategies with them. And then we discussed their concerns about the SAM7s. I translated for Mahdi and he explained that he had decided to have the SAM7s destroyed altogether. I could see the relief on the Americans' faces about this and the respect for how this brigade was being run. They said that it might help them leverage more assistance for us.

We asked them what they could give us. 'Could you give us weapons?'

'No, can't do that.'

'Ammunition?'

'No can do, I'm afraid.'

It was a little disappointing how limited they were in what they could do for us, but they did give us a CB radio with a much better range than anything we had, two satellite GPS trackers and a couple of boxes of food rations for the field.

The field rations came in two parts and were very interesting. There were a series of small packs of things like raisins, Manhattan nuts, Kellogg's Frosties, sesame seeds, nut bars and snacks like that. Then there was a variety of different meat and vegetable meals in tinfoil containers, which came with a chemical sleeve. On closer inspection, I was happy to find they bore the Halal trademark and there was no pork – it was good to see that the Americans took note of our culture. You put these tinfoil meals into the chemical sleeve, added a drop of water and left it for a few minutes until they were piping hot from the heat of whatever chemical reaction took place. This is essential for producing a hot meal on a clear, dark night when a fire would give away your location. Funnily enough, there were guys who wouldn't touch these once they knew they were American. They had been totally sucked in from a young age to reject everything American. I never looked at it like that – and most of us were happy to take what we could get.

❖

Another American I met around this time was a new recruit in the brigade – 'American Adam', I called him, a big, strong and healthy guy. I remember seeing him going around one night in the barracks gathering up bits and pieces of food to make something.

'Can you cook?' I asked him.

'Look at me,' he said. 'Do I look like I have trouble cooking?'

❖

About this time, Mahdi wanted me and Nadir to bring two Libyans out to the Americans and translate for them. When I got there, I realised the guys were smugglers who were helping out with the revolution. Although smuggling would usually be frowned upon, in times of war even smugglers were able to help the cause. They had been into Tripoli, bringing guns to revolutionary cells within the city, and so they had unique insight into what was happening on the ground there. I was with them to make sure they were able to give the Yanks as much information as possible about the coordinates of the latest loyalist military installations and to give ideas about where Gaddafi might be hiding mercenaries. With NATO having bombed a lot of military buildings over the previous few months, Gaddafi had started relocating his forces into residential areas. The smugglers said they would supply the Americans with the coordinates of these new targets before leaving Nalut. There was also a worrying report of an eyewitness account of Gaddafi forces unloading boxes while wearing biohazard suits and masks. On the good side, they had reports of upwards of 6,000 armed revolutionaries in Tripoli ready to fight.

One of the strategies discussed was the idea of creating a 'green zone' from within, as had been done during the Iraq War. Part of our brigade would go in to Tripoli inconspicuously and link up with the revolutionaries in the city, specifically in the suburb of Souk al Jumma, where resistance was thought to be strongest. The plan was to destroy all the access routes to the area in order to secure it. We would then begin working our way out in ever-widening circles, securing more territory as we went.

It all sounded good to me, especially since Gaddafi's artillery had been placed in defensive positions facing out. With Ramadan only ten days away, I said to myself the sooner, the better. I was excited about the prospect that we could all be taken in by helicopter and lowered on zip lines.

When I was leaving the villa, I realised that I hadn't got my cap and went back to find it. One of the Americans immediately informed me that when I arrived I hadn't been wearing a cap. 'You guys don't miss a thing, do you?' I said as I turned around again to leave, seeing for myself how alert to everything these guys were at all times.

I was asleep the next morning when I got a call on the two-way radio from the Yanks to bring over the coordinates the smugglers had promised. When I asked one of the commanders where the smugglers were, I was told they had left for the border about twenty minutes earlier. 'Shit, they've forgotten to leave the documentation.'

I had to jump in the jeep and start a mad chase for them through the mountains – we had no phone contact. Needless to say, I went hell for leather. I remember the jeep going sideways, and the fella with me practically shitting himself. He really respected me as a driver after that, though. Incredibly, I made it to the smugglers just as they were about to cross the border. They were actually in the queue headed for the security gate on the Libyan side, just about to cross over, by the time I caught up with them. A few minutes later, and I wouldn't have been able to go after them as I didn't have my passport with me and it would have been too risky anyhow.

Love at first sight

On the night of 19 July, I walked into Mahdi's room and saw, among a few other fancy guns stored in the corner, a PSL sniper rifle. I was immediately drawn to this rifle and felt a connection to it – the first real sniper rifle I'd come across in Libya. I went into a trance of sorts, ignoring the other people in the room and walking straight over to it. I picked it up and felt it in my hands, admiring the skeleton design features, the smooth, beautifully machined and contoured wooden stock, the curves of the comb above the butt. I held it against my shoulder and felt like a piece of a jigsaw had fallen into place. It was like falling in love.

I noticed it had been made in 1978, which made it a year older than me. I knew I just had to have it and that I wasn't going to be able to take no for an answer. There was some talking going on behind me about something or other, but I wasn't paying attention and eventually casually slipped in a question: 'Is this ours?'

Mahdi explained that he had just bought it for 11,000 dinar (about €6,000), a crazy amount compared to the average AK price of 5,000 dinar.

I'm not usually forward when it comes to asking people for things, especially people like Mahdi, but I had to be brazen in this situation. When we were alone in the office, I said to him straight up, 'She's just got to be mine, is that OK?' I gave him that look that begged him not to refuse.

Mahdi knew how keen I was on the sniper idea. I'd told him back in Tunis that if I had the chance to learn how to be a sniper, that would be my first choice of duty. I think I'd even said to him years previously, in relation to nothing in particular, that if ever I was in the army I'd want to be a sniper. He was also conscious that my brother, Yusef, had been very good in target practice in Benghazi, so he knew this was a good match.

'OK,' he said, 'for now.'

Reluctantly, I left the rifle there that night, but I couldn't stop thinking about it. Ever since I was a kid, I'd always gone for the rifle in computer games. I'd jump into some corner or other in the game and try to pick off the enemy, one at a time. Any time I'd got to play Quasar in Dublin, I'd imagined I was a sniper. I'd be up on the cages, down on my hunkers, firing at the others as they moved around the battle zone. In the results, you'd find guys who had taken 600 or 700 shots, and I'd have taken something like forty, but my head count would be way higher.

I loved the sense of people thinking they were in the clear and then saying, 'What the hell', as they suddenly realised they'd been hit but couldn't tell who was shooting at them, or from where. verything about it – the concealment, approaching targets carefully and methodically, the one shot that made the difference, how personal it was, how each bullet seemed to have a destiny – appealed to me in some deep psychological way.

I was mad keen to get my rifle out on the range. The first chance I got was the next evening, after training. I went straight to the armoury and asked for the bullets, and then took the rifle off under my arm. At the other end of the training area, I stuck a shovel in the ground and hung a helmet on it. Then, I got up onto a landing in a derelict building overlooking the field, about 300 metres away. It was dusk at this stage, but I was using blue-tip tracer rounds – the ones that leave a light trail after them so you can follow the trajectory.

I put my eye up to the scope and studied what I could see. It showed the magnified target against the crosshairs. The horizontal axis of the crosshairs has a number of hash marks, ten to the left and ten to the right. These are to allow you to factor in wind drift. The vertical axis has four ^ symbols, each a bull's-eye for a different range. The farther the range, the lower the ^ you use to target with. Then there's a diagonal line marked from two at the top down to ten at the bottom indicating the height of an average man (or vehicle), depending on how far away he is. You line up your target to be standing on the horizontal line and if his head touches the two mark, then you know it is 200 metres away, though the calculation may be a bit rough compared to laser technology. When you get it right, it's good for up to 1,000 metres as long as you factor in wind, heat and, of course, gravity ('bullet drop'). So the final thing you need to be able to compensate for when you aim is the trajectory of the bullet, so there's a lot of personal ability in it.

I lined everything up as best I could, steadied myself, breathed as naturally as possible, and gently squeezed on the trigger.

Bang!

The very first shot I took with a real gun had been when I was only nine years of age. I was out with my Farrara cousins on a little hunting trip outside Tripoli. The idea was that whatever we shot, we would barbecue and eat together for dinner. The rest of the group was standing behind me for my first go, and I had the rifle in position against my shoulder. One of the adults was supporting me a bit to protect me from the recoil. Suddenly I saw something up in the sky. I shifted the barrel instinctively to line up with the bird and pulled the trigger. *Bang!* I must have closed my eyes with the sound because I wasn't sure what had happened.

Next, I heard everyone cheer and I realised I'd hit it, whatever it was. I remember being so thrilled with myself. We walked over to find it, everyone praising my aim as we walked. It turned out that it was an owl. I had never looked closely at an owl before and was immediately struck by how beautiful it was. While I felt a little remorse about killing such a beautiful bird, I was so proud of my kill that I insisted on bringing it home to have it stuffed.

And with the PSL? Even though I hadn't zeroed in the sights, two of my first three shots were on target. In fact, when the tracer round hit the helmet, it became lodged in it and the unspent tracer chemical flared up in the helmet, giving me a dramatic sense of just how vicious this gun could be. 'Now, if that's not chemistry!' I said to myself. I knew this was the gun for me. And I knew I was the right sniper for it.

The Lion Pack

One evening, I met with the brigade's head of public relations, Abdul Hakeem Meshry, and a core group of Breki, Isa, Anis, Tayari and Falolo to discuss setting up a special forces team within the brigade. We nominated some other fighters to make up the numbers required: Majedy Alagy, Atif Keblo, Ali Arara, Maryamy and Tabuni (who wasn't there at the time, as he had gone back to Tunisia to undergo more treatment).

This was effectively the mavericks in a different guise. Crazy, yes, and yet here we were getting very serious about the need to prepare ourselves for more extreme wartime situations. We were all like-minded, who recognised in each other a bond and a trust that went beyond the norm. We were creating a special group that would take responsibility for the brigade, protect its ideology and values in the event that commanders were lost. From then on, instead of the usual 'infantry' or 'gunner', our dog-tags stated that we were 'Special Forces'.

Some people knew us as the 'Lion Pack' and when the battles started, we tended to travel together and consult each other on strategy. But the momentum of the campaign was such that we didn't end up operating as a group so much as individuals who received a different level and type of training from the others.

Meshry was intriguing in how he was both very informative and yet totally secretive at the same time. To me, it felt like he had first-hand experience of the extreme events he was passing on to us, but that he wasn't telling us anything about how he had acquired the knowledge. I felt it would have been a contradiction to ask him how he knew all this stuff. It was as if he could have been an ex-Gaddafi operator, an insider, yet it was clear that he definitely wasn't – he was well known for having made a very powerful speech on Al Jazeera at the very early stages of the revolution, screaming the words, 'Tripoli is crying out.'

We started our training there and then had an extended theory session. This involved a series of presentations and discussions on different techniques for everything from evading capture and handling prisoners, to protecting VIPs and reading body language during interrogations.

No one else was allowed to enter the room, no matter who they were or how high ranking. Yet again, it was all hours of the morning before we got to bed.

Out on the roads

On one of our few free days during our training, I went with Hisham in the jeep to visit Housam Kafu in Naji's platoon – still posted out at the edge of the mountain for security.

They told us how, in the clear night-time air, they could hear Gaddafi's men down in Takut, with ammunition to burn, firing off rounds non-stop through the night. Looking down, you could see the glare of lights from the rounds in the distance. They were shooting at ground level to the bottom of the mountain so that anyone who even attempted to approach would face this barrage of fire. They shot in bursts and sometimes, they'd make a rhythm with their firing – they were that good. *Doo-doo-doo – duuf – duuf. Doo-doo-doo – duuf – duuf.* Looking down from above, you could see the sparks of the bullets as they hit the base of the cliffs.

To kill some time, one of the pranks Kafu's guys got up to once was strapping a torch to a dog and sending it down the side of the mountain. The Gaddafi troops saw the light moving around the place and started firing like crazy, except, of course, in the dark the dog moved too fast for them and got away no problem. I laughed to myself, thinking about how I'd need a disclaimer when retelling this story: 'No animals were injured in the making of this revolution.'

We brought the platoon some of the American food rations and they were delighted. They'd had nothing proper to eat since the previous night. It was a small thing, but I was glad to do it, to help keep up their morale and to boost the comradeship of the brigade. I unloaded the boxes of food and proceeded to show them how you poured a bit of water in the sleeve to cause the chemical reaction that heated up the food. Some of them were looking on at this, saying, 'Wow, that's got to be black magic. It's has to be the work of the devil.' They appreciated the food, though, American or not.

Afterwards, myself, Uncle Naji, Hisham Breki and another guy went down the mountainside to a place called Ain Ghazaia, the oasis of Ghazaia. This meant we were leaving the safety of the plateau and getting closer to enemy territory. Uncle Naji was so fit, he moved over the rocks like a mountain goat. I was able to keep up with him but Hisham and the other guy struggled and kept falling behind.

The landscape was beautiful except for one thing – every tree around us had been burned by Gaddafi's troops. I made a video on my phone and narrated my thoughts as I recorded the destruction:

> In Islam, it is specifically stated that we must not burn a tree, or destroy a well, and yet look at these monsters doing exactly what we are told not to as a basic rule of engagement in Islam.

I just couldn't understand what would possess a soldier to do such a thing. It made me realise even more that something was rotten in the state of Libya.

We found the spring of the oasis gushing out of a crack in the rock and we drank our fill. It was a real thrill to be away from training and duties for the first time since I had arrived, and to be able to just hang out, enjoy the cool water, the beautiful views and the peace. We washed and prayed.

Then we went out to a dirt road where there was an old, broken-down tank lying across the track as a barrier. I put a bottle down a good distance away and we did a bit of target practice. Eventually, we climbed back up to the rest of the platoon and chilled out with them for a while longer before heading back to the barracks.

❖

I woke up for early prayer one morning, only to hear the terrible news that three guys from the brigade, who I had just seen the day before preparing to go to Zintan, had been in a bad car crash on their way there, and two of them had died. The other car was from a Tripoli Brigade and had been heading back to the city. I rushed to Mahdi with the news and he gave me the keys to one of the ambulances. Abdaroof got an AK, and we joined another ambulance and two cars and rushed off to the scene, near Jadu, about sixty kilometres away.

When we arrived at the crash site, we were all saying, 'Oh my God, who could survive that!' It was seriously nasty – as you'd expect from a head-on collision at something like 140 kilometres per hour. We later heard that when the crash happened, the other car had been full of petrol and ammunition and had caught fire immediately. The rescuers had just about managed to pull the survivor from the flames. We left the scene after gathering whatever we could of their belongings, and went on to the hospital about forty kilometres away.

The guy from our brigade was being operated on when we arrived. On my way out of the hospital, I heard someone calling me. I looked over through a small group of people gathered around a trolley of one of the other survivors. 'Oh my God, Mohammed!'

I couldn't believe it. It was a neighbour of my aunty's who I knew from when I'd last lived in Tripoli ten years earlier. He was the person pulled from the flames. Imagine meeting an old friend in the middle of the mountains under these circumstances! He was seriously injured but stable, and, despite his state, he had spotted me and managed to call out. We hugged and chatted for a while, and once I knew he was being looked after, I left him to see to our dead comrades.

❖

After I woke from a sleep that evening, we went to meet the Americans to detail our plans for the advance and our military targets. Just as we were about to start the meeting, two commanders from a Nalutian Brigade rushed in with the news that there was a lot of movement both down the mountain and coming in from farther south. This made us all worry about a pincer attack, so we put off the meeting and left immediately.

Back at the barracks, everyone got suited up for battle, convinced that this was the real thing. We were told it was a very large convoy of up to 200 vehicles. Of course in the dark, no one could see whether they were tanks or jeeps or what. It ended up being just a tormenting wait, because though we were all ready for battle, and ready to die, nothing happened. The Nalutians fired off some mortar rounds at the convoy to warn them, and that caused them to turn back.

We heard later that the loyalist troops below had sent up a convoy of civilians with a small military element hidden within it. The Yanks told us they had seen lights on in the convoy – something that wouldn't usually be done by military at night. Apparently, there were buses filled with civilians. My suspicion was that it was an attempt by the regime to attract a NATO strike and then try to mislead the world into believing that revolutionary forces were bombing civilian convoys.

❖

I was on bodyguard duty once with Waleed Zumeet protecting Mahdi at a conference of commanders in Jadu. We were late leaving, so we had to speed all the way there. Then, when we arrived at the checkpoint into the town, we were told by a revolutionary from another brigade that we would have to hand over our weapons. We looked at each other and I said to the security guy, 'Sorry, we can't do that.'

He told me that that was the rule and I replied, 'Look, can you guarantee that there is not even the slightest chance of someone trying to harm us? You can call in to the conference and explain that if they want us to be there we will have to be permitted to carry our weapons.'

While the call was being made, we waited around outside, and watched on as more and more revolutionaries gathered. There were a lot of weapons around, but not a lot of discipline. I didn't like it. A row flared up between a few of the revolutionaries. Mahdi and I exchanged looks and I was glad when I saw that he clearly agreed that we should head for the jeep. As I was about to drive off, one the security guys ran over and tried to take a hold of my door. I immediately opened it with a snap and he fell back while I slammed it shut again. If it wasn't for Mahdi telling me to hold on, I would have sped off there and then. The security guy was actually coming back to let us in with our weapons. He pleaded with us, in fact, knowing that he'd made a mistake and not wanting to get into more trouble by having delegates drive off. So we attended the meeting after all, with me just a little more on edge than usual the whole time.

On the way back, we drove through a small town in the mountains named Tandamirah, where we were pleasantly surprised to see a diner-type place that was actually open for business: a sudden reminder of the normal lives we had left behind. We couldn't believe it and got all excited about it. We stopped so that we could get something.

Unfortunately, all geared up as we were, we attracted a lot of attention and got into another spot of bother with the locals outside. The owner of the café was going on about how they didn't want guns in their town, and his friends hanging around outside were giving us hassle. While Mahdi was doing his normal thing of being friendly and humble, I was seething in the background that people like this still didn't seem to get what we revolutionaries were doing for Libya. In the end, Mahdi's approach worked and they went from being hostile to being completely the opposite – all friendly and even wanting to pay for our coffee.

We went on to another meeting in the nearby town of Rejban. Mahdi was trying to persuade the local brigade of Tripoli revolutionaries to unite with us, offering to enlarge the administration so that the commanders wouldn't be giving up power. He wasn't having much success with this strategy, as a lot of the guys he was dealing with were only in it for the power and the ego trip, but you had to admire his efforts.

Knowing Mahdi, he probably knew full well it wasn't going to work, but he had a second agenda, which was to just make contact, open some channel of communication and thereby help to create a greater sense of unity. The lads in the local brigade, who numbered about a hundred and who had only just taken delivery of uniforms, were impressed with how well equipped and professional we were. Some of them were very curious about our brigade, even asking on the quiet how they could join.

❖

Back at the barracks that night, a group of us studied a particular video clip over and over on a laptop that was a real eye-opener. Watched casually, it could have been seen as nothing more than a terrible accident caused by incompetence, but careful viewing showed an act of horrifying sabotage. It was footage taken at our Zintan barracks and showed one volunteer and another guy I didn't recognise figuring out how to use a M72 LAW (nicknamed SPG in Libya), a one-off rocket launcher, like a disposable RPG. Nothing unusual about that.

The video showed them sitting on steps leading into the

barracks itself, with another guy recording what they are doing. They were working their way step-by-step through the operating instructions, which were shown in simple diagrams on stickers on the barrel. The guy I didn't recognise had the SPG on his lap.

You could hear them talking through the instructions: 'Step 3, extend barrel' ... so they extended the barrel.

'Step 4, take out safety pin' ... and then you could hear the guy doing the filming saying in a lower voice, 'OK, that's it – fire', and the other fella pressed the trigger.

There was a blast and the rocket entered the barracks. You could hear it whizzing off, and then there was an explosion.

The guy standing behind the SPG had half of his upper body incinerated and died instantly. The missile itself killed two or three guys in the barracks.

It made me very concerned and even more vigilant about the security of our own barracks and the safety of the commanders, especially Mahdi, of course. Even though we had a decent level of security at all times on the corridor that led down to where the commanders were based, I pictured someone walking past the guards and just throwing a grenade down the length of the corridor, without anyone being able to warn the people down there.

We sent orders to the Zintan barracks to apprehend anyone suspected of being at the scene, but it turned out the suspects had fled immediately. One guy who had been there and who didn't flee was then sent to our brigade. I was very put out by this, thinking that he could have been involved and should be treated as a suspect, but I was reassured that he had been questioned thoroughly and was found to have been an innocent onlooker.

❖

One night, a GRAD missile landed quite near the barracks. Nalut was being hit with them regularly, but this one was closer to us than usual. It didn't really bother me, in that we were well used to hearing them at this stage.

I considered them to be a ridiculous weapon in a way, maybe useful for 'softening up' a big sprawling city before a major assault, but not very efficient when it came to actually causing your enemy problems. They involved so much work just to get them ready, loading them into a truck, and moving them into place – and then, after all that, you couldn't even aim them accurately. My view was that if I got hit by a GRAD missile, I'd welcome it with open arms because to have found me, it most definitely would have to have been destined.

Mahdi's security was top of my agenda the next day, but it turned out to be a very busy day preparing for our long-awaited, much-anticipated attack on Takut and Ghazaia. We had a meeting about the strategy and then we got a call to collect thirty FN FAL rifles to add to our artillery.

Meanwhile, Mahdi got everyone together and gave a speech, explaining that we were now code yellow, meaning that at any time in the next forty-eight hours, we could receive the orders to go into battle. We had to be ready. There was a push by the Nalutians to put an end to the random GRAD attacks and end the constant threat of attack from the towns below. They were frustrated at having control of their town but not being able to have life there return to normal because of the loyalist troops below. Despite the threat, some refugees were returning to the town from Tunisia and that made it all the more urgent to liberate Ghazaia.

❖

Early the next morning, Wednesday, 27 July, Mahdi instructed me to get myself and four others from the Special Forces unit ready to take a trip to buy more weapons. We got armed up, collected the money and headed for Zintan. This was the one place in the mountains that I hadn't liked since I had arrived – even the thought of it made me uneasy. They did a lot of good in the war, but undid it all by various underhanded and self-serving actions, including robbing and looting in the cities they had liberated (or helped to liberate).

I was on high alert, looking out for signs of anything that was not quite right – paranoid, maybe, but I couldn't help thinking the worst, and felt we didn't know what the Zintani were capable of. We were meeting arms dealers who were selling the spoils of war and weapons donated by other countries. My view was that if they were true revolutionaries, they would have given us the weapons for free with their blessings, but, no, this crowd were just in it for the money. We did a deal and got our PKT machine guns, ten AK47s, ammunition and a big-ass American M60 that I thought looked like it was off the set of *Rambo*. Unfortunately, it didn't even work – we had paid €7,500 for it just in the hope that we could fix it.

We left the shady Zintani at all hours of the morning, and travelled along the road through the mountains. These late-night drives after so many long days on top of late nights were a surreal affair. I'd be so tired, I'd have one eye closed, and I'd be looking for anything to keep me awake, a chat or jokes or music. I laughed to myself when I saw the billboard on the roadside advising drivers who felt tired to pull over.

On this trip, Mahdi, who didn't have much time for jokes or our music, sang Libyan rebel songs to us over the walkie-talkies, including 'Nasheeds'. Another song was 'Ghoraba, Ghoraba':

'We are strangers, we are strangers. We are strangers,' Mahdi sang quietly, 'and we won't bow our heads but for Allah. Strangers and we accepted this, our fate. We don't care about dictators. We are the soldiers of Allah. Our path is the hero's path.'

Judging by our silence and our reaction, these words meant a lot to all of us. Even though the original reference would have been to Libyan soldiers fighting abroad, we felt like strangers too – and we were strangers of another kind in these mountains. I thought it was really lovely – Mahdi's strong, sweet voice, his gentle and genuine way of singing, everyone in the four cars listening to his voice over the walkie-talkies as we moved through the night desert. 'That was lovely, Sheik,' one of the lads said after a few moments of silence at the end of the song. Everyone agreed.

We arrived back at the barracks at about 5 a.m. only to find out, after a day without contact, that we were going into battle that same day. We would be assisting the Nalutians in an assault on Takut.

Without any time for sleep, we started getting everything ready for battle and headed for the gathering point. Despite the lack of sleep, adrenaline kept me focused and alert to the point of having a spring in my step.

Part III

Lions in the Desert

August 2011

First battles

We were about 600 strong by the end of July. Many of the men with us had left Tripoli quiet recently, and rather than running off to Tunisia to safety they had come into the mountains to join the revolution. They were appalled by what they had seen and, like the rest of us, were willing to risk their lives to put an end to it.

Those who were battle-ready gathered at a mosque near the top of the road that led us off the safety of the mountains to the plains below. The start of the road was like something you'd see in Monaco, winding and bending back on itself sharply as it snaked steeply down through the rocky terrain.

Tanks that the Nalutians had captured a few months earlier from the local Gaddafi barracks thundered about us like roaring steel monsters. They were old T-62 and T-72 Russian beasts, first used by the Libyan army in the 1970s but still very powerful. They packed a far-reaching punch, up to five kilometres, with great accuracy. The Nalutians had learned that Gaddafi's men had removed the firing pins, thereby turning them from game-changing killing machines into colossal people carriers, but when interrogated, one of the PoWs had mentioned that the pins had been thrown down some well or other, but the information wasn't followed up initially. It wasn't until later, when he was being interrogated properly, that the PoW had brought the Nalutians to the hiding place and the pins had been found, carefully greased and wrapped up. Now, with the tanks back in action and drivers and crew trained up, we were delighted to see some serious firepower being rolled out onto the battlefield.

About 300 sand-coloured turbans were handed out to us and we discovered that they were the perfect protection against the searing heat of the sun. A good trick was to wet it on your head and then even a slight breeze catching it would cool you down very effectively.

I was on a high, pumped up in anticipation of what might lie ahead in my first battle. Because of the early start, I had missed the main *Fajr* prayer and so went into a small mosque nearby to pray – maybe for the last time, *that's* how I felt.

Before I knew it, I was encouraged forward, something Muslims traditionally do when new people join a prayer-time midway through. I then found myself being expected to lead the prayer, which I did, reciting some beautiful verses from the Quran. I was surprised when I had finished and turned around to see that lots of my friends had come in after me and were smiling that their 'crazy' Housam was leading prayers. The atmosphere of anticipation had everyone buzzing, and we all shook hands and hugged before leaving the mosque.

Outside, our media man, Meshrey, suddenly approached me from out of nowhere, with the camera trained on me, and asked what I thought about the battle ahead. I said something off the cuff: 'I believe we will be victorious over the evil Gaddafi mercenaries.'

He asked me where I got such confidence from and, without thinking, I just raised my voice aloud and said, 'From the faith that I have in my heart.'

Everyone around responded loudly, shouting out, 'Allah Akbar, Allah Akbar, God is great.'

I was surprised and delighted by the confidence in my own voice and by the strength of the reaction I got. It gave me a huge lift. Muslims are very vocal in their encouragement of each other, using phrases and chants all the time to call up courage in themselves and to instil it in others, and once you get into it, it becomes a powerful thing.

We lined up all the vehicles and troops and got everything ready for battle. There was one truck from where you could pick up ration bags, supplied by the good people of Nalut. These included things like a small piece of cake or a bag of nuts and, most importantly, dates – central to the diet of Libyan freedom fighters. While in battle, during Ramadan, I would often break my fast on nothing but a bag of dates, and yet it would feel like a feast.

When we were in our vehicles – Mahdi was with me in the jeep – we started driving in convoy down the mountainside. As we were driving, an American recruit named Malek flew over the handlebars of his quad and nearly killed himself – it was obvious that the spot would become known as 'Malek's Bend' from then on. Mahdi had acquired a bunch of quad bikes, and even though they were painted in bright, summery colours which used to make us laugh, they turned out to be brilliant on the battlefield for getting messages and small supplies around. Communication was always a big issue because the walkie-talkies would go dead in the space of a few hours, so the quad bikes helped us keep everything together.

Mahdi spoke to me about the previous advance along this route, when forty guys from the brigade, including the ten armed with only daggers and determination, had joined in the fight. He pointed out to me the gigantic concrete reservoir from where the Gaddafi troops had pounded them with heavy mortar, long-range sniper and AA fire for hours. I could see for myself just how impossible a task it would have been to take the position with only light weapons and small numbers. This time was different though, as having already removed the position with our own heavy artillery, the Nalutians were able to sail right past it, to within a few kilometres of Takut.

Meanwhile, our brigade took off into the countryside along a similar route to the one we had taken on my first scouting mission. For this advance, we were playing a supporting role to the local brigades. Our task was mainly to cut off retreat lines and possible reinforcement routes from the south, so we were to take up a strategic position above the town of Takut, a few kilometres away. We had to cross very punishing ground to get there, and I was proud of my jeep for being able to handle it. I was even able to help some of the other vehicles that didn't cope so well and got stuck.

Just as we got to the place where we had planned to stop, one of the tyres on my jeep got a major tear on the razor-sharp rocks. Mahdi jumped out and carried on towards the edge of the mountain with a couple of the other guys. I stayed back to change the tyre. This was the first in a string of problems I had with the wheels on various jeeps during the revolution.

As the battle got underway and we waited for the tanks to work their magic, the noise levels became incredible. This was the first time I had heard tanks in full flow and just how powerful and noisy they were really took me by surprise. The sound was overwhelming, filling up my ears and attacking all my senses. I could hear these almighty lightning cracks coming from somewhere off in the distance and echoing all around. Then I'd see explosion after explosion in and around Takut.

The first cracks sounded like explosions to me, and I couldn't figure out where they were coming from. It was all so intense, I thought for a minute that our position was sure to get hit. I actually took a video of myself with my phone, leaving a final message for my mother and family. It was only when I turned around that I understood that the tanks were actually many kilometres behind us on the mountain firing safely over us at Takut, and it was the echo of the shell travelling overhead that was causing my disorientation. It turned out that the Jadu guys, another brigade from the mountains, were positioned well back and had their tanks working from long range.

With the tyre fixed and my ears adjusted to the sounds of tank fire, I walked over to the very edge of the cliff and looked out across the few kilometres of desert that separated us from Takut. I could see sunlight reflecting off the glass of different vehicles that were moving along the road to Takut. I realised that even with the range of my sniper rifle, I wasn't going to be able to target anything meaningfully.

Suddenly, I sensed bullets hitting the ground near me and realised I was being fired at. Strangely, it took a moment for the fact to sink in. It was, after all, my first time ever to take fire. I hit the dirt, as they say, pulling back away from the edge and staying low to the ground. They were obviously AA gunners tasked with defending that side of Takut and they had spotted me. To them, two kilometres was nothing, so they just opened fire at the edge of the escarpment. Sand and dust sprayed up all around me from the huge bullets, any one of which would have ripped me open if it had found its target.

I shouted back to the others to stay down and gathered myself together. I was calm and knew from my reaction that I was up for this. I was pleased with myself for that. Considering the intensity of the tank battle and what had just happened to me, I might just as well have wanted to run and get the hell out of there. But my first thought was actually how to get into a position from where I could return fire. Like my mother had said, I was finding out what I was made of, and it seemed I had what it took to be a soldier.

Instinctively, sizing up the ground under me, I rolled down my sleeves, thinking that my bare elbows on the rocks would be no good as a base for the rifle. I got my turban together and crawled forward towards the edge, ready to take my first shots of the revolution.

I had nothing but a little plant for cover, but it was enough to enable me to look around without being seen. I took my time and tried my damnedest to figure out where the gunfire was coming from. The guys who had joined me pointed to a road on the right where a few vehicles were on the move. We speculated that they could be carrying reinforcements, or were possibly transporting heavy artillery, but whatever their purpose, they were now heading away from us at speed. We figured that they had probably been the source of the firing, but it was too late for me to return fire now.

On my way over to where Mahdi was positioned, I noticed a few Nalutian troops who had come with us jumping into their pick-ups and starting off in the direction of Takut, as if they might have heard something we hadn't. I wondered if it was time for us to advance. I knew we were there to do a job, but I reckoned that if the battle was already won, there was nothing stopping us from heading into Takut. We needed to be part of the clean-up so that our brigade could get some share in the arms and equipment the Gaddafi troops were bound to have left behind.

We had a Nalutian guy with us, a friend of Hajj Masoud, the

leader of the Nalut Military Council, who Mahdi trusted. Mahdi was listening to the Nalutians on the walkie-talkies and this guy was translating the Berber for him. We could hear orders being shouted and updates being given on the progress of the battle, but we couldn't be sure we were getting the full picture.

Eventually, Mahdi gave the order to advance and, in great excitement, we spilled over the edge and down the steep slopes towards Takut, shouting, chanting and roaring all the way. We came under some fire from the scattering Gaddafi troops but nothing major, and we made it through into Takut without injury. With the loyalists on the run, there was a massive sense of relief and joy running through the brigades. Some of our younger guys climbed up on a water tank, while others were firing rounds into the air constantly. Myself and a few other guys yelled at them to conserve their ammo, pointing out that the fighting was far from over.

Post-battle Takut was a mess. It could never have been described as a well-kept modern town to begin with – this was a very poor, desert community after all – but now it was devastated. Buildings had been battered and bruised and the ground was ripped up, there were mortar craters in the road, bullet casings strewn everywhere and abandoned and burned-out vehicles all over the place.

When things calmed down, we regrouped and relaxed for a while, drinking water to help us cool down and eating our rations. Everyone was in good spirits, delighted and a little surprised that it was so early in the day and yet we had already taken the town that had blocked us for months. We knew the plan was to push on to Ghazaia, farther to the west, but we had to wait for more details. We hung out in a vacated villa on the far side of Takut. Inside, you could see it had been ransacked and looted by Gaddafi's troops. What little there had been was thrown about the place, broken or torn.

A simple meal of rice in little tinfoil trays was produced from somewhere, and although it wasn't much, we were very thankful for it. Exhausted, I found myself a mattress in a quiet corner and got about half an hour's sleep. Being able to catch some sleep while in battle mode was seen as brave in its own way. 'When you can fall asleep in the middle of action, it means you don't fear war any longer,' I heard people say, and only the more experienced fighters would usually be so lucky.

I was woken by a nudge and was told we were heading out. I got up just in time to catch sight of the convoy being led off by the roar of the tanks and AA guns. After they had moved on a bit, the rest of us got back into our vehicles and followed.

Not far down the road, we came across a team of Nalutians securing the route and, just as we reached them, shots came towards us from a small shack across a field. We were on a two-lane road through a landscape of dusty fields and a few farms. Our guys were quick to jump down behind the vehicles to get cover – though we were still new to this business of being fired at. We all turned our guns in the direction the gunfire had come from, and plastered it with everything we had. It was totally over the top, but I thought to myself, *At least we're seeing some action.* Whoever was firing stopped and we just got out of there, leaving the Nalutians to follow up.

We passed the turn-off for Um al-Far, where a separate small battle was taking place, and headed straight on for Ghazaia. Even though we weren't out front, with Mahdi in the jeep with me, I was at the centre of the action as far as our brigade was concerned – spearheading, moving ahead, giving orders. On the few occasions that we had to park up and hold back, I always jumped out and set up to take some long-range shots. I could sometimes see loyalist troops in the distance, but mostly they were moving away too quickly to bother with. When this happened, I would take some shots, but it was more for the sake of getting practice at setting up under pressure and for the experience of using the gun in battle situations.

Again, by the time we reached Ghazaia, Gaddafi's men were already retreating. We took a few shots but there wasn't much of a force remaining. 'They're heading for the border. Quick, let's catch them before they get away!', was the kind of thing we heard shouted from time to time, through the cracking of bullet fire. There were times when Mahdi would listen to such opinions, and sometimes he would actually go out of his way to consult with others in the brigade about what to do next, but this situation, when he was responsible for hundreds of lives, wasn't one of those times. He wasn't going to take unnecessary risks, and so we let them go.

Moving around the outskirts of the town while others took in the sight of a freshly liberated Ghazaia, I came across an armoured personnel carrier, or 'battle taxi', a Russian cocoon-shaped, tank-like vehicle with giant wheels and blast doors at the back. It was parked behind a shed, maybe having been hidden away from NATO. Even though the bonnet was up and it looked like it had been tampered with, Anis and I scrambled over crates and boxes to get at it and see if it was still working. Unfortunately it wasn't, but it didn't dampen my spirits. I knew that all such efforts would add up to something in the long run.

We did a bit of a sweep around some commercial buildings and a few houses. I was very wary of booby traps. There were guys going headlong into rooms and lifting up stuff carelessly, but I was telling them not to open or even touch anything that wasn't already open. I told them that this was exactly the kind of tactic Gaddafi was known for. I'd heard his troops were trained to put AKs on the ground, with a bit of fishing cable on the pins of a grenade. 'You go and pick it up and … Bam!' I warned them. The thought of being killed that way, during a routine search, made me shiver.

We eventually made our way into the centre of Ghazaia. It was a great feeling looking around at another liberated town – to think that we were starting the process of becoming a free nation again, town by town.

There was a mixture of other revolutionary forces, mainly Nalutians, all around us, but they were keeping to themselves because they wanted to keep the spoils to themselves. It was frustrating because nearly all the loyalists' arms had already been lifted before we got there. We could see the mountain guys driving off with truckloads of stuff – guns, artillery, armour – their pick-ups were filled to the brim. And we were left with very little.

It was very much that way with the brigades, each wanting to be the top dog. Mahdi stopped and talked to one or two of the leaders to offer his congratulations, but it wasn't a friendly relationship. There was a lot of politics involved, something I was starting to understand. Of course, revolutionaries from all around Libya were starting to think about closing in on Tripoli. Everyone's goal was to travel all the way to Tripoli and, after liberating the city, to take as much of the glory and spoils of war in the capital as possible. Obviously our plan was to be in there first because it was our city. We needed and wanted them to help, but we didn't want them to come in saying it was in some sense their patch now.

In terms of spoils, we weren't, of course, taking people's belongings. There wasn't much in that way, anyhow. It was really eye-opening to see how neglected these people were and how basic their living standards were, judging by their dusty and bare homes. It was like stepping back in time for me. I walked into one old hut and I found a little Quran that looked like it had been there for years. It had yellowed, dusty pages. I decided to take it as my spoil and said to myself that I would come back some day and return it to the person who owned it.

The order was given to return to base – a wise decision, considering how things always got more dangerous the more tired the troops became. In fact, the next morning we discovered that one of our pick-ups with two or three of my friends in it had driven over a mine. Ali Arara was very badly injured and another lad, Muneer Na'agi, who was only eighteen years old, lost his foot. I visited him in hospital with Madhi and a few others the next day. (After a battle like that, we'd always go to the hospital to visit the wounded. Mahdi was always very moved on the visits, affectionate and full of praise for the guys.) I told Muneer that I'd never imagined someone who had been through such a traumatic accident would be able to smile and be so at peace and accepting of his misfortune. 'It's easy, considering the success we had,' he said. (He has since returned to Tripoli a hero.)

We drove back to Nalut that night, thrilled with our victory. The guys back in the barracks were expecting us and when we arrived at around sunset, they were already whooping it up with all sorts of banging and clapping and singing revolutionary songs.

Mahdi would always make a point of paying respect to those who stayed behind. 'Let it be said,' he called out, silencing the crowd immediately, 'that as we could never leave our house unattended, we thank these brave men who looked after it while we were gone.'

Our first taste of victory felt good. We felt more like a fighting force ourselves, and as a result of our participation the other brigades started to include us more in their communications and planning.

A taste of victory and freedom

That night in Nalut town, there were celebrations and an immediate return to some level of normality. You could see more cars out on the streets. There were horns beeping all over the place, and there were people out and about for the first since we'd arrived. The Nalutian revolutionaries themselves were in the back of their pick-ups shooting into the sky. Even a few shops opened up suddenly, selling the scant few things they could get together. We were really pleased to see this.

In theory, Nalut had been liberated months before, but it was now liberated in practice too. We were also delighted to be around some kind of normal life ourselves and started to buy a few treats from time to time. I managed to get my hands on some sachets of flavoured corn flour, and because we had a fridge where I could let it set, I became known for it around the barracks. Suddenly, our room became very popular with characters of all kinds from other rooms looking for corn flour puddings like they were the best thing they had ever tasted.

It was such a satisfying thing to see Nalut come back to life, and to have played a small part in its revival. The place was becoming an important part of my life. I was in the town a couple of days later buying a few bits and pieces, and when I parked up I noticed a bunch of older men, the wise-looking elders of the locality. I always got a strange look from the older generation, as if they couldn't hide the fact that they couldn't quite figure me out. These guys made an effort to talk to me, standing up and shaking my hand. They thanked me for everything we Tripoli lads were doing to help them liberate their homelands. I found this very humbling.

Another time in one of the local shops, the shopkeeper wouldn't take any money from me for the few things I was buying. It was encouraging to get this acknowledgement.

Later on during Ramadan, some of us headed out of the barracks at night and would go to a local café in Nalut. It was another small taste of normality for us. Tents had been set up in the middle of the town and volunteers were providing food to people who couldn't feed themselves. People from Nalut itself, refugees and even some people from the brigades – anyone who couldn't afford to buy food or didn't have anything to cook with – was able to queue up to get a little bite to eat and somewhere to sit down. They had also set up a large screen in the car park showing the news.

There were always interesting people to meet about the place: some Western journalists were there to document life in a liberated town, people from other brigades, a Danish guy who was in charge of the UN landmine action mission in Libya. I got a new sense of how big and unstoppable our campaign was becoming.

❖

The next day, after a meeting with the local Nalutian Military Council to discuss our co-operation with them, we went on to a regional military meeting at the high council in Jadu. When we arrived at the building, I noticed in myself a new sense of purpose and confidence. I was now trained and finally had some battle experience under my belt after our victory. I felt charged up and ready for more action.

I started off in security mode, checking out the building,

noting cars and so on, extremely alert to everything, right down to the smallest detail. I knew I had to compensate for the slackness of the security set up by the organisers. While other lads took it easy and hung around chatting and smoking, I stood in front of the building, re-enacting the movements of the Terminator standing on guard, scanning everything around me, assessing all the information available to me, mentally taking note of anywhere that could hide an RPG or give cover to a crack squad. Everyone coming in for the meeting was trying to figure out who I was, standing out like that, looking so intense.

When I was happy with our own security set-up, I adopted a new role. I went into the meeting and, with his approval, sat beside Mahdi. He was at a large round table surrounded by the leaders of all the local town councils from Jadu, Nalut and so on, each with a microphone in front of him and all the necessary attendants. This was a first for me, to be at the level of the decision-makers, rubbing shoulders with the future leaders of the country. When Mahdi stood and introduced himself as the leader of the Tripoli Brigade, everyone paid attention.

'Tripoli is here,' he said, 'standing side by side with our brothers in the mountains.'

They thanked us for our help in the previous battles and our allegiance to the cause.

The maps of Tiji, Badr and Al Jawsh – the next towns to the east on our route to Tripoli – were spread out on the table. Plans were being discussed about how to keep the momentum going, and for pushing on to Tiji. There was also a discussion about how we would come up against stronger resistance there, because the whole city was loyalist. The sense was that this next battle would be messy because it wouldn't just be a battle against an army, but against the people: the Se'aan.

I played my part too. I made a few quiet comments to Mahdi about various aspects of what was being planned. I was particularly keen to have the issue of communications between the brigades discussed. The mountain brigades were talking a lot in Berber, as well as in code and a local slang to prevent Gaddafi troops from being able to understand them – the problem was that we weren't able to understand them either.

I was impressed by how wise the Nalutians were being about the Tiji plans. They were determined that as many groups from the mountains as possible would be involved in the assault, so that it could never be seen in the future as an act of tribal aggression by Nalutians against the people of the tribe of Se'aan. They explained that the people of Tiji had been approached with a proposal for a peaceful solution – that they stay neutral in our fight with the Gaddafi troops for the military base. This had been refused and so an all-out assault was necessary. Being essentially planters from Tunisia, the Se'aan people remained doggedly loyal to Gaddafi to the end. They did his bidding no matter what because he had given them everything they had, even though, as I saw for myself later, that didn't amount to very much.

The wisdom of the collective approach taken by the councils in this situation impressed me a great deal. Not only were we planning how to win local battles as efficiently as possible, we were also co-ordinating with other areas to win the overall war. Furthermore, we were thinking ahead to when victory would be ours, and to how peace would be restored as quickly as possible. There were aspects of the revolution that were far from seat-of-the-pants stuff and that were done totally independent of NATO.

❖

About this time, we grew suspicious of a guy who had joined the brigade out of nowhere, claiming to have abandoned his government post in internal security to join us. It had been discovered that he had since travelled across to Tunisia via a Gaddafi-controlled checkpoint at Ras Ajdir. He was also found to be in possession of a number of SIM cards. I was tasked with interrogating him to find out as much as possible about where he had come from and what he was aiming to achieve by joining us. I questioned him gently at first, and, as per my training, read his reactions carefully, in both what he said and his body language. Then I started to build up more and more pressure on him, leading up to asking about the SIM cards. I wasn't happy with his explanations at all, and in the end we handed him over to the Nalutian Military Council to have him put in their local prison.

Having to deal with him so closely was difficult for me when everything he represented made me so sick – his loyalty to Gaddafi and his involvement in that regime of terror, the fact that he had infiltrated our brigade and was trying to undermine our good work, and the fact that he was now desperately trying to get off the hook with lies. It took great effort to control the anger I felt, and I was glad to see the back of him. It was the first of many such encounters I had with regime loyalists and criminals.

With surprise being such a key element in our chances of success, the fact that we had had an infiltrator and may have had others worried me a lot. To take away the element of surprise from any of our strikes could have led to disaster and death for us all.

First assault on Tiji

The Battle of Tiji, which started on 30 July, was a turning point for our brigade. In the intensity of the firepower we were up against, other brigades pulled back much sooner than we did and took the soft option. We stood our ground. It proved to the mountain lads the real potential of the Tripoli Brigade. They were sturdy people themselves, of course, and called us 'the city boys', slagging us about waxes and creams and fancy clothes, but Tiji ended all that.

We had prepared very well beforehand, getting our munitions ready, cleaning and oiling everything, loading the belts, checking and double-checking the guns. There was great excitement among the troops and lots of talk of victory and of the end of Gaddafi.

Before dawn, we gathered outside the barracks and listened to the commanders outline the strategy. One of our men, Muftah Salak, was blessed with powerful vocal cords and he rallied everyone on. Such criers are very important and greatly respected. You hear them at all kinds of gatherings. Salak was injured later that day in an accident with a C5 rocket. The C5 is usually mounted in a launcher on the side of a helicopter, whereas revolutionaries often launched them from a very basic set-up, nicknamed Zenga-Zenga. Salak accidentally set one off in the sand beneath him as he was running. The flames gave him second-degree burns all over his face and chest. Later, a YouTube video showing him singing revolutionary songs to calm himself while the doctors treated his burned and bloodied skin became a huge inspiration for us.

He urged on everyone in the convoy, like something out of *Braveheart*:

We are the warriors of good. Do not fear. Make your hearts strong. This is our time and we are coming. Oh yes! Rest assured that we are coming.

Early that morning, we left the barracks to gather in Nalut. We got the convoy ready to descend the mountain by the same route as before, only this time advancing beyond the turn for Ghazaia and Takut to go deeper into Gaddafi territory, where we would join up with the other brigades. With all the new troops and vehicles that had arrived in the previous few weeks, the convoy had become so big that I felt myself swell with pride for it.

I was with Mahdi and a few others in the navy Pajero, which was still going strong. When we got going, there was lots of chatter on the walkie-talkies – 'Let's do this, guys. Today is the day Gaddafi will crawl back into whatever hole he came out of' – as well as the odd joke.

Mahdi and I were out front, heading down the mountain at quite a speed to catch up with the other brigades as quickly as possible. A few miles along the plain road, some movement made me glance over to the right and I thought I could make out a bunch of cars behind some trees and someone beckoning.

I said to Mahdi, 'Are you sure we haven't gone too far?'

'Yes,' he said, 'there've been no roadblocks.'

I wasn't going to risk distracting him needlessly from his preparations so I didn't push it, but then all of a sudden, a Nalutian jeep sped up and got us to stop. It turned out they hadn't got the usual sandbanks set up on the road to mark the frontline. We had been heading straight for the loyalist barracks in Tiji without any kind of cover. A few moments more and our entire brigade could have been decimated. We got everyone turned around and down the side road to join the rest.

Unfortunately some time later, two of our guys – Salem Beesa and a new recruit, who were delivering maps and other documentation to Mahdi – drove down to follow us without realising we'd taken that turn, and they drove straight into the path of three AA guns. As they told us later, when they realised what was happening they jammed on the brakes and started reversing, but the AAs opened fire and started spraying them. Very quickly, Salem realised they had no choice but to bail out and abandon the Passat at the side of the road. But, having bailed, Salem said to himself, 'I'd rather die than lose those papers', so he crawled over to his now-sprayed-out car without being seen, grabbed the documents, and hiked all the way back with the greenhorn. When we were coming back later, we saw for ourselves that the vehicle was totally destroyed.

In the meantime, the brigades were gathering in the grounds of a very impressive villa in the desert countryside that had already been taken by revolutionaries. It was about four kilometres or so from our target, the Tiji military base – so the base was easily within view – but was surrounded by boundary trees and a thick orchard, which gave it good protection. We drove in very slowly so as not to stir up dust clouds, and parked up under the trees in the orchard. The Nalutians and some others were already there, waiting for the order to advance.

While we were waiting, I got to meet a few guys from other brigades, including this one Nalutian guy who had, like me, a PSL rifle, the only other one in the force that I encountered. He picked it up as spoils in Ghazaia. We went up onto a roof together and I spent some time teaching him how to use the scope before he did some target practice on a scarecrow in the distance.

The rest of the time was just hanging around and waiting. We were under strict orders to stay as quiet as possible and it was all quite surreal being among all these heavily armed men who knew that their survival depended on not being noticed.

Eventually, it was decided for strategic reasons that we would stay there overnight and advance the next day. Because the villa stood out as a target, we all moved to a farm about half a kilometre away. Even though we were told there was to be no smoking in case the glow gave us away, we did smoke into Pepsi cans during the night. Anyone who lit up a cigarette in the open would get a jibe from the others: 'Go on out of that, you must be one of Gaddafi's fifth column!'

I started the night in the jeep but was woken up at all hours of the morning by guys on patrol who thought they had seen some movement. The story we'd heard about the special African mercenary militia that Gaddafi had trained to fear nothing started to wreck my head. We'd heard they could operate in the dark, approaching their victims in their sleep and stabbing them before slipping back into the night. I became freaked out and started scanning the horizon restlessly. I ended up climbing a small water tower, about a storey high, to get myself fully out of harm's way, and sprawled out uncomfortably on the top of the concrete rim under the star-speckled sky. There I lay in the moonlight for the rest of the night, getting just a few short snatches of sleep. It was one of the most bizarre nights of my life, a mixture of extreme anxiety from the possibility of being attacked at any moment and peace from the extraordinary serenity all around me.

❖

The next morning, Omar Hariri, who had previously been a general in Gaddafi's army, arrived in full army gear and gave us a rallying speech. We all listened enthusiastically. Mahdi said to Hariri, 'I brought the whole brigade with me. All the men you see around today are your sons.'

Meshrey, our media guy, conducted a public interview.

'What do you know about the Tripoli Revolution Brigade?'

Hariri replied, 'I know that it was formed in Benghazi and

An image from a 1957 production entitled *Boyd's Shop* by St John G. Ervine, with my grandparents Geoffrey Golden, as Andrew Boyd, and Máire Ní Dhomhnaill, as Agnes Boyd.

Almost in Confidence

MAIRE O'DONNELL

This week answers questions set by J.J.F.

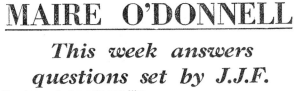

What is your favourite role?
Pet Clancy in "The White-headed Boy."

Favourite dramatist?
Sean O'Casey.

Favourite novelist?
Graham Greene.

Favourite composer?
Debussy.

Favourite painter?
J. B. Yeats.

Favourite poet?
W. B. Yeats.

Which play do you like best?
Shaw's "Arms and the Man."

Which role, new to you, would you like to play?
Juno Boyle in "Juno and the Paycock."

What is your greatest ambition?
To see the whole of Ireland free.

If you were not connected with the stage, what would you like to be?
Hairdresser.

What is your favourite hobby?
Knitting.

Favourite sport?
Basketball.

Favourite dish?
Tripe and onions.

What is your ideal holiday?
Vacation in West of Ireland.

Your pet aversion?
Spiders.

Which historical figure do you place highest?
Daniel O'Connell.

What character in fiction appeals to you most?
Stacey in Louis D'Alton's play, "The Devil a Saint Would Be."

Where would you prefer to live?
Dublin.

The 'Fiche Ceist', a twenty questions-type section of the *Evening Herald*. My grandmother's piece is from 1954. When reading this as an adult, I loved how strong my grandmother's personality was and how she appreciated fine arts and poetry.

My first birthday at my grandmother's house on the Howth Road in Dublin, 1980.

You can take the Libyan out of Libya, but not Libya out of the Libyan. My father feeding me watermelon, a staple of the Libyan diet, to my grandmother's surprise. Ballymun, Dublin 1980.

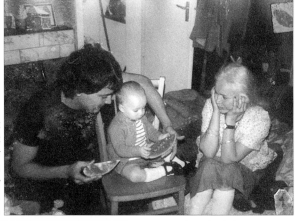

At my grandmother's house in Walkinstown after our return from Tripoli, 1992.

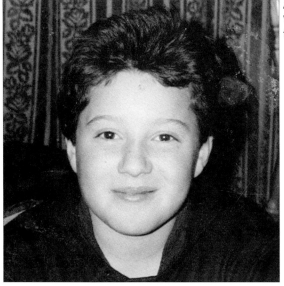

Playing with my sister outside my grandmother's house.
I always loved the military look, even as a twelve-year-old boy.

From left to right: Adil Essalhi, me and Hamza, during the Eid celebration, similar to the
Christian Christmas, Muslims dress up to celebrate the end of the Ramadan period.
Having friends from many backgrounds was a great cultural education as a child.

At the age of nine, I went on my first hunting trip with my cousin
in the forests of the Green Mountains in Libya. Soon after this picture was taken
I took my first shot and killed an owl.

Enjoying the tasty fresh game we hunted on our trip.
My cousin Ibraheem Farara is sitting behind me – he also taught me how
to drive at this time and was a great role model.

When I returned to Tripoli in 1999, I made many friends with whom I still keep in contact to this day. I always felt for my Libyan friends who, despite all the oppression set on them, were always modern and sophisticated. Tripoli Zoo, 1999.

From left to right: my cousin Abdu Fararra, me, my cousin Nabeel Najjair, Hatem Dwebi and Basem Dwebi. Martyrs' Square, Tripoli, 1999.

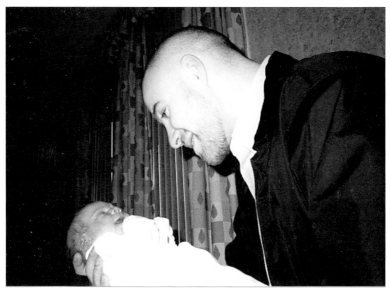

The look of a proud new father. Layla was born on 28 February 2002 at Craigavon Hospital and made me the happiest man alive.

Layla on St Patrick's Day, 2005, enjoying a ride on the carousel in Merrion Square.

A loving dad and his princess. Dublin, 2006.

From left to right: Ashraf Tamzeen, Salem Khamis, myself and Basem Mugbal
on the street where I live in Portobello, Dublin.

From left to right: Mustafa Wa'ar, Waleed Zumeet, myself and Mohamed Tayari (Che) when we first met in the resort in Hammamet, Tunisia, part of the future Lion Pack.

An emotional goodbye with my mother as I set off to take part in the Libyan Revolution. Also in the picture is Mehdi's son, Abdul Hameed. Hammamet, Tunisia, 2011.

trained in the aftermath of the 17 February revolution. I've heard you guys have even fought as far east as Brega. Mahdi, of course, I know and I have met with him many times. What I know about the brigade is that you are men of the highest calibre who have left Tripoli and will return to liberate what is essentially *your* city. I strongly believe that cities should liberate themselves, and that we are here to just help these transitions go ahead with as little bloodshed as possible.'

Meshrey asked, 'After seeing the brigade today, under the command of Mahdi al-Harati, how do you see us as a fighting military unit?'

Hariri replied, 'I always think it's amazing to see men like Mahdi in action, and I know some of you, leaving the comforts and safety of the various places you have come from, to fight with such determination … you don't need anyone's blessing, you are doing a great job already.'

Holy water

I decided I wanted to be to the fore in this battle a little more than I had been in Nalut, so I avoided Mahdi in the buildup. I had learned from the first battles that staying with him meant that I was held back and wasn't able to reach my full potential. I think he knew that too. I was still concerned for his security, of course, but I knew there were other people watching his back too, so I didn't have to be by his side at all times. I teamed up with Falolo, Isa, Kafu, Abdaroof Jojma and American Malek, guys I knew I could trust completely. They weren't going to turn around and run for the hills just because things got hairy.

Once the advance was ordered, we got back into our vehicles and were directed away from the road out down a different route, along a dirt track that led through the desert. To keep the element of surprise for as long as possible, we were making our way across scrubland towards the base until we got within range. The lads with me were in great spirits, singing songs and making jokes. I joined in a bit, but had to keep a close eye on the ground ahead all the time to watch for sudden drops and to avoid taking an impassable route. We had to cross a massive dried-up ravine at one stage and although it took a while to find a way across and it was tough on the jeep, we managed.

Our battlefield turned out to be a few acres of the same type of rocky scrubland, full of rifts and ridges and a few parched shrubs, just short of the town's military base. I could see it would be very easy to get lost in this terrain, so when I spotted a line of high-voltage pylons, I took note of them as a bearing, and they turned out to be very useful.

Directly in front of us in the distance was our target, the massive walled military compound of Tiji. Our mission was to take out whatever force was protecting it so that we could advance into the town and beyond. We couldn't see the compound itself from our early positions, but we knew we would hear from its forces very soon. A lot of the other brigades positioned themselves back on the main road, well away from the heat of the battle, but I wasn't aware of them at first.

We entered the battlefield from both the left and right. Within the walls of the compound ahead of us there was a massive mushroom-shaped water tank, about ten storeys high with a big dome at the top. *Perfect for snipers*, was my first thought. Between us and it was a huge gorge of some sort, the banks of which were impassable from our battlefield position, but which we could get into by going down a track off to our right. We could then travel along the length of the gorge, which would bring us right up within range of the compound. We moved our three tanks and two or three AA guns to a position as far forward in the fissure as possible, pointing at the barracks.

On the left side, closer to the barracks, there was a small shack of some sort, about five metres square with a flat roof, with an outhouse just beside it. These were the only structures providing cover within gun range of the barracks, and this is where most of the guys I was with ended up.

As we got closer, we could hear the sounds of gunfire starting up all over the battlefield. When they spotted us, the Gaddafi troops at the barracks began firing non-stop, spraying the area with whatever firepower they had. The other revolutionary brigades already in place started firing back with mortar rounds from their positions on the road.

Some of the guys I was with, apart from Housam Kafu, wanted to get out and continue as infantry, so I let them all off and they started making their way forwards, low to the ground and in proper military formation. I travelled on with Kafu over the jolting terrain. When we reached Mahdi, we jumped out of the jeep and got down beside him on our hunkers. He was positioned in a small dip near one of our 106 guns, as far forward as he could get. He was waiting on word from the tanks before launching an infantry assault, typically directing things from the heart of the battlefield. The tanks were taking it in turns to move out of the ravine, fire at the barracks and then pull back into cover. Our guys on the AA guns were taking on the AA guns from the barracks. Other infantry platoons were behind the heavy artillery, waiting for the order to advance.

There was nearly constant fire going on around us and it was scorching hot.

Looking around at the guys and seeing how white their lips

were getting, I realised they had been out in the sun for a long time and some were starting to suffer badly from dehydration. A few had draped T-shirts on little bushes in front of them and were crawling in under them to get as much shade on their bodies as possible. I wasn't feeling it myself, having been in the jeep and having the benefit of Kafu's battlefield water-cooling trick, where he wrapped a plastic bottle of water in a wet canvas and tied it to the side of the jeep to catch the draught – classic Arab/Berber ingenuity, much like the way we soaked our turbans. I told Mahdi that I was going to go out to the road to get a supply of water. 'The person who brings water to you on the battlefield is just as important as the fiercest fighter,' Mahdi had said to me before and it had stayed with me as a kind of ideal of humility.

After about half an hour over very rough terrain, I made it out to the road. To my surprise, there were a lot of cars and men there, keeping well back from the action, screened behind trees. They were from a different Tripoli Brigade and some mountain brigades. I ignored them, drove on to our support vehicles, loaded up the jeep from one of pick-ups and headed back. Unfortunately, I got a puncture on the way back and had to stop to change the tyre – my second wheel disaster of the campaign.

Once back on the battlefield, still with no advance underway, I started handing out water to our men, who were scattered all over the place. Wherever I went I tossed out a bottle of water, and guys later told me that it was dearer to them than gold at that moment in time.

I headed over to the gorge because I heard from some guys that a sniper was bothering them. I got out of the jeep to investigate. Instinctively, as I was heading for the slope of the ravine, I pulled up a plant, some kind of a dried-up shrub with a few leaves on it, and wrapped the branches in my turban so that they stood up over my head. It looked ridiculous and there were guys laughing at me as I passed, but at the same time they probably saw it was the right approach to take, considering what I was doing.

I made my way up the side of the gorge. From there, I was able to observe our tanks shooting at the tower, and it was amazing to watch them in action from such a close position. These were Nalutian tanks. Abul Waleed, one of the drivers who was aslo training the rest because he had been in the Libyan tank regiments, was a friend of my dad's from his Manchester days. Having served in the tank regiments of Gaddafi's army, he knew exactly how these old T-72s worked – how to fix them, how to use them and how to train the operators. I remember hearing that his two sons were fighting with him and thinking how unique and special that was, and how proud he must be.

One direct hit that I saw from the tanks went straight into the main body of the tower. I thought it was definitely going to collapse, but amazingly it didn't. I saw another shot land straight into the bowl of the reservoir, and I reckoned that would be the end of the sniping, but it wasn't.

We had a couple of machine gunners set up along the way, and they told me how they were being targeted by a sniper from somewhere over in the direction of the water tower. Every time they tried to come up to ground level to get off some shots, they were fired at, and it was single shots. I crawled prone all the way to the edge, remembering from my first experience of edges not to just keep my head down when approaching. Assessing the situation from there, I realised that ideally a sniper doesn't take on a sniper. I wasn't going to be able to spot this guy, and in fact if he was well dug in, nine times out of ten I'd just be killed trying. A heavy artillery team was what we needed to flush out or kill him.

Regardless, I got up to the edge, low to the ground, and even though I couldn't see much, I felt safe enough with my position and camouflage to empty two or three clips in the general direction of where I thought the sniper might be. There was no way of knowing what did the trick, but the shots eventually stopped, so I left and started making my way back down and out of the gorge.

On the way, I was asked to get ammo for one of the units, so I got back into the jeep and made my way to Mahdi, near the 106 cannon. I filled up the back of the jeep with crates of ammo and headed back to gorge. I had more trouble on this trip, as I got stuck on a sandbank and had to get somebody to come and nudge me off.

Once back in the gorge, I grabbed one of the crates and started walking across to the guys who had asked for the ammo. Suddenly, I heard the clear sound of a gun being fired in the distance and a bullet thudding into the sand ahead of me on the far bank. Having become accustomed to a certain amount of fire at this stage, this wasn't actually enough to cause me to duck and I just carried on, thinking it was chance. But then I heard another crack from a gun and the *pfoosh* sound right beside me, and I realised someone had a line of sight on me over a low part of the gorge, maybe the same shooter as before. I crouched and made my way, staying low to the ground.

I imagined the sniper's reaction. *You brave bastard!* I thought he'd be saying after the first shot missed and I didn't duck, before taking another shot with more determination. I reckoned he would have got me with a third one for sure. I told myself what a rubbish shot he must be.

I didn't see any point trying to follow up on it, so I gave the guys their ammo and went back to Mahdi. Apparently, in the meantime, the tanks had started running out of ammo too and

Mahdi had discovered that we had no more on the way. This meant that the tanks would be pulling back. We also heard that the volume of shots the AA guns were firing had caused their barrels to warp – some were left with only one barrel and others were left totally inoperative as they didn't have spares.

Mahdi told me that we would not be advancing.

As soon as he said it, I thought about my guys advancing on foot without support. I turned to Mahdi and said that I had to go and get them. Before he could respond, I gave him that look by which he knew there was no stopping me. He looked at me in turn and I knew he was worried, but understood.

Trap me if you can

Making my way with Kafu across the rugged terrain, I drove into a particular crevasse and, as I came up off the opposite side, we started taking a lot of AA fire from the barracks. With rounds designed to travel thousands of metres into the air and take down airplanes, I knew that if we got hit, it would rip the jeep apart entirely. In the next dip, I said to Kafu, 'As soon as I come up again, we are going to come under serious fire, so if you want to bail this is your chance.'

'No,' he said. 'I'm with you all the way.'

Just as I'd said, they started giving us everything they had. We couldn't see clearly enough to be able to make out the barracks – it was kind of a blur in the distance – but from the bullets we knew exactly where it was. While I was moving, I was using my initiative, thinking that the more I make the AA gunmen work their cranks, the better, so I started to weave back and forth at high speed, frantically looking for the next dip to get out of the line of fire.

While I was taking all these evasive manoeuvres, I was continually whispering the Muslim *shahada,* or creed, 'I declare there is no God but Allah and Muhammad is His messenger.' This is something all Muslims learn from a young age, the first Pillar of Islam, something you would say at dangerous times or to give yourself strength. This was the first time I had said it in a life-threatening situation, knowing I could be killed at any moment and that these could be my last words. Just one round would have done it.

As I got closer to the barracks, I could see my guys standing in behind the shack, crouching behind the wall on the far side from the barracks. I sped forwards and pulled in beside them. As well as my guys, there were two other young fellas of about seventeen or eighteen years of age with an RPG. Falolo told me that they were under serious pressure. He described how he had been hunkered down at the corner of the outhouse just a few feet away, trying to get off some shots, but that he was pinned down by so much machine gun fire that he could hardly even get back behind the bungalow.

Knowing that the tanks were retreating, I was worried about Gaddafi's troops advancing and flanking us to the point that we wouldn't be able to retreat. But having survived the drive up, and having such a strong unit around me, I wanted to see if we could gain some advantage from this location and maybe even finally turn things in our favour. We were way ahead of everyone else on the battlefield, and I felt it was worth a try. At the same time, we all knew an RPG could take out the entire building protecting us at any moment. We were on borrowed time.

On our side of the building, there were two shuttered windows with steel bars in them. I could see through them to the door on the side facing the compound and could see a huge hole in the wall, probably the result of a previous missile or mortar. I got the crazy idea that if I could get around at speed and in there, I might be able to get into a good shooting position beside the hole.

As a first step, I ran across to the outhouse. As soon as I took a look around the edge of the wall, shots were fired at me and one or two of them came so close I got a face-full of concrete dust. I ducked back, realising just how closely they were watching us. I shouted over to Abdarouf that I needed cover. Brave soldier that he is, he immediately stepped out with his PKT and a belt of ammo. He widened his stance and started blasting in the direction of the compound. It was brilliant to see him in action like that. I ran for it, heart pounding and adrenaline pumping. By the time I had kicked in the door, the place was getting showered with rounds.

As soon as I got inside I knew I was trapped and that it had been a bad plan. With the amount of firepower being let loose at the front of the building, not only was I not going to be able to take up a decent offensive position, but I also knew I wouldn't make it back the way I had come in. Now the odd bullet was starting to get through the wall. I shouted through the windows at the back, 'I have to get the hell out of here.'

I grabbed hold of the window bars and, lifting myself up, with my two feet on the sill, I started hauling and shaking at the bars with all my might. Having been a builder for so long, I knew how the bars would be sitting in the concrete. I could feel a loose movement that told me they would give way eventually – I was so desperate to get out that I even used the hollow butt of my precious gun a few times, cracking it against the concrete. The guys outside were also trying to weaken the blocks; the typical white chalk blocks used in Libya are very dense and weigh about fifty kilograms each. Finally, I gave it a big mighty tug with my full weight and the whole thing came out and I fell back off the sill onto the ground, window frame and all. With bullets now coming through the front wall easily, I got up as quick as I could and climbed out of the window.

I knew then that it was time to get out of there. I told Isa and Hisham about the tanks and they were clued-in enough to realise the danger that meant. We agreed to retreat. It was only the young fellas with the RPG who gave me a bit of grief about it, saying, 'No. We've come this far. We're not moving back after all we've been through. We're going forwards. That's what we're here for.'

I replied, 'Look, I can see you have heart, but you don't have to prove anything here. An RPG unit can't take on that compound alone.'

As I was talking to them, I saw two or three shots hit the ground near us, kicking up sand. Given that we were at the rear of the building, I knew this meant my fears of an advance were being realised. Gaddafi's troops must have understood that our tanks and AA guns were withdrawing and had started moving out from the compound. We didn't have much time.

The AA gunners said to me afterwards that they could see us way out ahead of the rest of the brigade but couldn't provide any cover for us with their damaged barrels. I shouted to everyone to get into the jeep. There were about ten of us, literally on top of each other. I think we must have left while Gaddafi's troops were manoeuvring because even though we took a bit of fire, it was nothing as intense as it had been on the way in.

Just before we got back to the rest of the brigade, a mortar round struck the 106 canon near where Mahdi was stationed, decapitating one of our guys and injuring two or three others. There were mortar rounds landing all over the battlefield all the time, and shots whizzing through the air. We were coming under serious pressure right across the front and it seemed to me that we would soon be surrounded if we didn't get some back-up. Even though retreat was on our minds, we really didn't want to give up. I told Mahdi I was going to see if I could persuade the brigades in the rear to advance and help us hold our position.

A blessing in disguise

I went with Mahdi's driver, Lukmann, in the Cherokee and left my jeep parked up. Using the high-voltage wires as our guide, we got back to the main road quite quickly. There was a bunch from another Tripoli brigade firing up over our positions in the direction of the barracks. I felt this was a total waste – these guys were just too far back. It was more like they were pretending to be in a battle rather than actually trying to win it. I jumped out of the jeep and walked over to a mortar unit.

'What are you doing? You're wasting your time here,' I said. 'Would you not advance with us? We could do with the help.'

I explained our situation and also told them to be careful not to land any of their mortars near us. They didn't receive my pleas too well. Even though some of them knew Mahdi personally, they still brushed me off. I was sickened by it.

We drove on another track to where the commander of all these troops was hanging out at a cabin in an orchard. It was a lovely spot, and there were guys sitting around eating. I burst in and made a desperate plea: 'Please don't let us get caught in a pincer manoeuvre out there. We need you guys or we're going to lose this position and lose men.'

They brushed me off as well. Maybe they were waiting to see how we got on before joining in. I'll never know what their thinking was. Having failed to get support, I grabbed a load more water and other supplies and got back in the jeep to head back to Mahdi.

Unfortunately, while I'd been away chaos had descended on the battlefield in the form of a sudden sandstorm. Once we moved off-road, it was impossible to see beyond a few metres, and, without being able to catch sight of the power lines, we soon lost our bearings. We tried to backtrack over the nightmare terrain of rifts and rocky hollows, but it was impossible to find our way in the blizzard of sand and dust. We came across places that we thought we recognised, but we just couldn't be sure and so remained lost. We were afraid of overshooting the frontline and ending up in enemy territory, but we refused to give up. We struggled on. I cursed the whole damn thing, wondering how we were going to find everyone.

Eventually, we saw a lot of jeeps filled with troops on the move and realised this was a full-scale retreat. I shouted out to anyone we passed, 'Have you seen Mahdi?', but no one knew where he was.

I was getting really worried at this stage, wondering how far we could advance to search for Mahdi without coming face to face with Gaddafi's troops. After seeing maybe ten or fifteen of our vehicles, we realised one of two things had happened. Either Mahdi was sending these vehicles back and planning to be the last one out himself, or he was already heading back to the road and we had missed him. I had to make a decision.

We had started picking up some of the infantry guys who were wandering about lost in the sandstorm, and pretty soon the jeep was full. We found our way to another building but there was still no word or sign of Mahdi. The guys in the back were saying, 'Don't go back in, just wait here for him!' Even Lukmann said we should wait and hope he emerged. I got very frustrated with all this. One guy came out of the house with a pot, saying, 'Look, we could probably make something to eat with this.'

'You waster,' I said, 'what the hell do you think this is? I am going to get Mahdi right now.'

Lukmann jumped in with me and we drove off, leaving the other guys to their pots. Finally, someone we met as we were driving told me he had seen Mahdi on his way out to the main road. Relieved, I turned around and we made our way back to the farm where I had seen some of the commanders.

'Where were you? Mahdi has been looking for you,' Marwan said to me.

It turned out that all the time I was searching for Mahdi, he was trying to track me down. Even though I had told him where I was going when I had last left him, he hadn't taken it in. I understood his concern because he didn't know, but it was terribly frustrating because I had clearly told him what I was up to. That's the confusion of battle, or, as we hear in movies, 'the fog of war'.

❖

Everyone eventually gathered at the farm and we made our retreat, downhearted. We drove the half an hour back to the barracks licking our wounds. The Pajero just about made it. The chassis had taken such a beating on the jagged terrain and with all my to-ing and fro-ing that it had nothing more to give. Farewell, Pajero!

Even though it messed us up in a big way, the sandstorm, biblical-like, was probably a blessing in that it saved us from being attacked full-on by a better-armed force. Based on my reports to Mahdi about the brigades that didn't respond to my pleas, he didn't trust anyone after that. He learned the lesson from that not to rely on the back-up of other brigades. The damage done to our 14.5-mm guns made us realise we needed a lot more by way of weaponry and ammunition to advance successfully. As I told a reporter around this time, 'They have ammunition to burn. We have barely any.'

❖

The next day was the first day of Ramadan, and I was on scouting duty near Tiji to follow up on the battle. Reconnaissance requires stealth, courage and patience. Firstly, we would spend a good amount of time finding the right places to use, making sure they were safe and that we could not be spotted from them. Then, we'd move in quietly. There, we would spend hours observing movements through the binoculars, identifying different types of vehicles and recording the whole thing on camcorder. Obviously the closer you got, the more dangerous it was, but also the more useful the information you could acquire. It was important because it could provide the intelligence that would make all the difference in an assault.

The fact that our checkpoints were now set up on the roads meant we could come down from the mountains easily enough. This changed the whole dynamic of our activities and gave us a great sense of progress, but it didn't mean we weren't in danger or on high alert.

Just before Tiji there were farmlands and abandoned farm dwellings that we were able to access. We spent the day there, adjusting to the fasting, recovering from the day before and monitoring the movements around Tiji.

Back at the barracks that night, I managed to get a short rest before the eagerly awaited breaking of the fast. The first day of Ramadan is always particularly difficult as your body adjusts to going without food, caffeine and cigarettes.

Over the next few days, we built up our resources again and prepared ourselves through more training. Every day I saw more troops, more pick-ups, more weapons and gained more confidence.

Ramadan

In 2011, Ramadan lasted for the month of August. It was very tough. The fasting and going without cigarettes was bad enough, but with the extreme dry heat and no air conditioning as well, it was a test for us all. I found it harder than everything else and did battle with my old self right through it. I wrote in my notebook one day:

> I'm getting sick of this place. Screw this. I'm just not in the mood for most of them anymore. It's doing my head in.

When I felt like this, I just stayed away from everyone as much as possible and did my own thing, but even at that, I was having rows with people. Some people were at me constantly: 'Are you OK? What's wrong with you?'

The sense that it wouldn't be long before we'd be on our way into battle helped me through. As did writing down how I felt and venting my anger on the page. It surprises me that I was able to write at all given the mood I was in. Back in Dublin, I definitely wouldn't have, but with absolutely nothing else to do, I put the pen to paper and let the words come out. And I'm glad I did.

❖

At one stage, the new recruits who had finished their course with the Tunisian trainer did an exercise out on the mountain to show off their new skills. Mahdi kicked things off by throwing a grenade as the sign to start. One group of graduates was up on high ground with an RPG, and another group came down and attacked a particular spot while the RPG team did their thing.

Our battlefield commander, Bashir Mekki, travelled with me in the jeep to see the exercise. I had had no contact with him up to this point, but I realised he was known by some of the lads and they showed him a lot of respect. In my innocence, I asked him how long he had been with the brigade.

'Oh, I've been with the brigade for quite a while.'

'Why haven't I seen you around?' I asked.

'You'll have to ask Mahdi about that,' he answered cryptically.

It turned out that Mahdi had sent him on a delicate mission to another brigade to act as Mahdi's eyes and ears on the ground, and to make sure we weren't being excluded from plans. How modest Mekki was.

After the graduation exercise, when they were all singing and celebrating, he and I went over to their targets to take a few shots ourselves, and I was able to witness close up how gentle a man he was and the amazing way he conducted himself. After a while, he began helping another fella who was there, an administrator who just wanted to have a go. He was so encouraging and calm, and such a great teacher. The admin guy hadn't a clue and, at one stage, shot frighteningly close to us, and yet Mekki didn't so much as flinch. You could see courage, calmness and strength in everything he did.

On one of the occasions that some dignitaries were visiting the barracks, there was a special breaking of the fast meal put on for them in a building away from the rest of us who were just eating the usual stuff. All of our top brass were in with the dignitaries enjoying the nice food. As I was on security detail, I went in to check on things at one stage, and saw Mekki not partaking in the food.

'Come on,' I said to him, 'tuck in.'

'I'm not having it if the rest of the brigade isn't.'

I said something to him about how he deserved it – and needed it – and I fetched a bowl of the soup for him. Even then, although he still hadn't broken his fast at all, he didn't touch it. At that stage, you'd expect someone to change their mind about something like that, but Mekki had such strong principles. He was something very special and rare.

For fridges' sake

Another time, our observance of Ramadan got us into trouble. It's hard to imagine how important food had become in the barracks. Physically, it becomes an obsession and religiously it takes on a greater significance. For the break of fast, we always wanted to have something special to eat, and one day, we decided to take the matter into our own hands.

With Falolo, Hisham, Isa and my room-mate Sami, we came up with the idea of going to the nearby town of Huamid to get some fridges from an abandoned housing development on the edge of the town that had been designed for the workers of a huge electricity plant.

The guys guarding the electricity plant, who were revolutionaries from a local brigade, didn't say anything to us as we passed and we drove into the development. The place was very fancy. It had a swimming pool, a canteen, a gym, the whole lot, but it was very eerie driving through all this salubrious real estate with no one around. It was like a ghost town. It had clearly been ransacked by Gaddafi's troops and I could see the signs that loyalist looters had been through the apartments looking for money and robbing anything valuable. I got the sense of people's lives being abandoned as they left suddenly – a hairbrush left on a hall table, a book on a bed, a mobile phone on a counter, rancid food in a fridge. I didn't feel like an intruder so much as an observer of history, of normality being interrupted by events outside the control of ordinary people.

Bizarrely, the loyalist looters had decided to commemorate their visit. On one mirror, the words 'Gaddafi Forever Die All NATO Rats' had been scrawled in lipstick, and on another 'God, Gaddafi And Libya Only' had been sprayed in shaving foam.

To have the chance of a decent meal, we were looking for a fridge or two that didn't contain mouldy old food. When we'd found what we wanted, we took the fridges to where we had parked. In the restaurant area, we found a few Pepsi fridges that we decided to bring as well to share with the brigade. We picked up a few other bits and pieces, like basins and some cutlery, that would be of use to us back in the barracks. We had nothing at all ourselves, of course, so even such simple things were a luxury.

We loaded everything into the pick-up and I led the way back to the barracks in the jeep, taking off at my usual fast speed along the mountain road. When I looked in the rear-view mirror, I wondered when the lads in the pick-up were going to catch up because I could see they had stopped at the exit. Eventually, I turned around and drove back only to find them in the middle of a row with the security guys from the electricity plant.

The security lads were accusing us of stealing. We tried to explain that, in fact, we were desperate and rather than leave the fridges and food to be looted or destroyed by loyalists, or go to waste, we were treating some inconsequential items as the spoils of war. We told them we would put them to good use, helping the brigade to regain its strength and morale. The big Pepsi fridges were the ones sticking out most from the pick-up and I pointed to them and said, 'Look, these were from the canteen in the common area, which means they are government property anyhow.'

To be fair to the security guards, they didn't know us at all, and probably saw us as nothing more than opportunistic looters. No matter what we said, though, we couldn't make them understand that the things we were taking were for a good cause, and the row became more heated. Of course, it was Ramadan and so nerves were on edge. Things got really stupid when one of them jumped up behind a 14.5-mm gun and started rolling it down to point at us. I was fit to kill him and started shouting my head off, saying, 'Who do you think you are? Do you think you look tough or something? Don't point your gun at us, I tell you, unless you're ready to actually use it.'

It drove me mad that these guys thought they could order us around and couldn't see who we were. I was furious and ready to fight, but someone managed to intervene by saying not to break our fast. We unloaded the stuff and left it on the roadside for them to deal with. But with my blood still boiling and the fact that we had to undo all the hard work of the day, instead of gently lifting out the last fridge, I kicked it off the back. Of course the glass broke, and that seemed about right to me, I was in such bad form.

We headed back to the barracks, collecting a few containers of water from a natural well on the way. It was hard to swallow the irony of the fact that we had nearly had fridges and now all we had was water, and that if we hadn't stopped off to get the water, the barracks wouldn't have had any, as supply was so low at the time. We made it back just in time for the break of fast. Afterwards Isa, Hisham, Falolo and I went into Nalut to a recently reopened café. We were sitting there trying to act normal, but you could tell that what had happened with the fridges was on all our minds.

Eventually Falolo said out loud what we were all thinking. 'Those guys are still wrecking my head. We need to put them in their place.'

We decided to go back and have it out with them. So off we

drove down the mountain again and into the electricity complex. We strutted into the big security hut ready for confrontation, but it wasn't to be.

The first thing that struck us was the relief provided by the air-conditioning. I'd forgotten what it was like to have it. I'd become so used to having a thick layer of sweat clinging to me all the time, it was hard to believe there was any other state.

The next thing we noticed was a complete change in attitude from the guards. They were now all sugar and spice, welcoming us in, talking sweetly. Then they offered us cakes.

We couldn't hide the fact that these cakes were clearly the loveliest thing we'd seen in weeks. It all totally disarmed us – they might as well have been gifts sent from heaven. The guards even apologised before we'd had a chance to let off some steam about their bullshit earlier. 'Typical Libyan,' I said to myself, and just tucked in to tea and cherry cakes.

I got to meet Abdulla Hamedi, the military council leader of Huamid, while I was there and, having been introduced to him as Mahdi's brother-in-law, I chatted with him for a bit. It turned out he was keen to arrange co-operation between our brigades, and even said he had men who had been born and bred in Tripoli who wanted to join us. He also offered us a high-spec 110-mm mortar canon with ammo free of charge. This was all great news to be able to bring back to Mahdi.

And we got the fridges too – for our room and for the barracks.

Public relations

Among the journalists we came across around this time, there was an Italian guy called Paolo and two Spaniards, one of whom told me that his report would go out on a Brazilian channel. I did interviews with them at our media centre. I liked the idea of getting an anti-dictator message out to the Latin American media, thinking of how there was a tendency among some South Americans to support the likes of Gaddafi.

I also met a Reuters journalist from America whose head of security was Michael Gregory, a big stocky guy from Belfast with years of experience of working in warzones and lots of media contacts in the UK.

'I'm going to make you famous back home, man,' Michael said to me after we'd finished the report. It was from that interview that all the information about me came out in the papers in Ireland. 'The Irishman Who Swapped Dublin Nightlife For The Libyan Frontline' ran one of the headlines. As I would find out from my friends on Facebook, the item also ended up in *The Sun* and numerous other newspapers and blog sites internationally.

Down at the very back of the barracks, in a big gym hall where some of the classes were held, there was a dodgy old TV and lads would hang out there at different times watching whatever they could pick up on it. During Ramadan, nearly everyone would chill out there at night, chatting and messing about. When I walked down one night, some of them said they had seen me on television.

Even though the item just mentioned that I'd done a report with Reuters and summarised my back story over an image of me in uniform, it was a big deal for me because, although I was getting used to a certain amount of coverage abroad, I wasn't really expecting it in Libya. This was my first recognition from my own people and it was poignant for me being on Al-Hurra TV, the station set up by the famous martyr, 'Mo' Nabbous.

Also on that television, we watched Gaddafi giving his speeches denouncing us and calling on people to defy us. His famous '*Min entum*' ('Who are you?') speech from earlier in the revolution was still inspiring lots of replies. I wrote my own based on some of the comeback I had heard and from reflecting on how I felt about the Libyan people and their courage.

Who are you?

Do you not recognise who we are?
We are the cause of your worry,
Of you and your family leaving in a hurry.
Do you not recognise who we are?
We are those who leave you sleepless,
That screaming voice that never ceases.
Do you not recognise who we are?
We are warriors for a cause without any doubt,
The cause of your destruction, you dirty coward.
Men you could measure on every scale,
Not rats like you called us, our story will tell,
That you didn't recognise who we are.

We are Barca,
We're the flame that burns your heart and
That thorn in your side that
Will never surrender, you must deal with that fact.
Do you not recognise who we are?
We are Musrata,
We're those who broke your nose and humbled you.
We fight the brunt of your force, yet we proceed to conquer
   you.
We are your peers, and your plans are a trick,
The men we have lost are too many to think.

Do you not recognise who we are?
We are Rujbaan,
We'll only die with gun in hand, and
Not far from a battle to gain more land.
You will not rule again, not you or your clan.

Do you not recognise who we are?
We are Fezaan,
Who you have surrounded with your dirty plan,
Use tribalism against us, we see right through your scam.

Do you not recognise who we are?
We are Libyans!
Who like in Tripoli can't express their feelings,
Under your iron fist, she takes the beatings.
Do you not recognise who we are?
We are the ones who rose against you,
From Derna and Baida, we won't stop until we're free of
    you.
Benghazi forges men and I'd just like to see if you
Ever stopped to see who we are.

I said to one of the lads when we were listening to Gaddafi's various ranting speeches, 'He is our best ally. The more speeches he makes, the better.'

There were rap songs about the revolution going around too. One day, I was listening to one in the jeep when Mahdi was with me. He wouldn't be one for listening to music, but when he heard this he thought it was clever and got me to play it for him again.

Don't touch my gun

As predicted, my rifle and I had bonded very well since our first encounter, but it was a relationship destined to cause trouble. Mahdi had, of course, bought it for training, whereas I wanted it all to myself. It's true what you hear in movies about how attached men become to their gun in a situation where it is vital to their safety or their job. When you need it for your survival, you want it to be totally reliable, so you take care of it and check and double-check it. That's what I started doing with this rifle. I got to know it inside out. I was able to take it apart and put it back together in seconds. There's an added problem with sniper rifles in that the crosshairs have to be zeroed in for distance, and maintained that way, otherwise they're useless.

I just knew from experience that too many hands on this gun would ruin it, so I became extremely protective. There was this one Tunisian military trainer with us who'd been teaching all kinds of tactical stuff – how to besiege and take over a town, how to take prisoners, and things like that. On one of those sessions, they used my jeep for transport. Even though I wasn't happy about it, I let them have it. But, of course, some hot-headed eejit shot a hole through the sunroof for some reason, so that was then ruined. I managed to let it go without getting too worked up, but it taught me a lesson. When the same trainer later came looking for my rifle, I adopted a very different attitude.

The confrontation took place during Ramadan, which meant we were all fasting and not smoking during the day, so there were a lot of frayed nerves and shortened tempers around the place to start with. My rifle wasn't kept in the armoury with the rest of the guns, but in a series of rooms opposite, where Mahdi and a few other commanders had their quarters and where some of the more unique equipment was stored. This trainer guy approached me

140

and asked me about the rifle and what ammunition we had for it. I didn't like his 'we' attitude one little bit. I asked him why he wanted to know and he told me that he wanted to take it out on a training exercise. I told him that was not going to happen. He didn't reply, but started walking towards the guy in charge of the armoury. I followed him to check that he didn't get my rifle and heard the trainer bad-mouthing me. We exchanged words and, in the end, I said, 'I don't care what you say, I don't want anyone touching my gun and you're not going near it, you hear? End of story.'

To avoid breaking Ramadan by fighting, we left it at that, but later that day, having broken our fast at *Iftar*, I saw him talking to some guys and could tell he was at it again, bad-mouthing me. I shouted over, 'Hey, if you've got something to say, say it to my face.'

He got riled up, and started roaring and shouting at me. We started heading for each other across the room and there was a bit of a scuffle, with guys grabbing us and holding us back, and telling us to cool it.

When Mahdi got back to the barracks later from a trip to Tunisia, he was informed of what had happened and had to intervene. He called me into the office with an observer who we both respected, and told me about the reports he had received on my disrespectful behaviour, and complaints that I was being given special treatment. He gave me a good dressing down, saying that if I couldn't listen to orders, I was going to get into trouble.

'Look at how little time you have been here,' he said, 'and yet you have a jeep, a walkie-talkie direct to NATO, a sniper rifle. And yet there are guys who've been here much longer than you, who don't have anything like that.'

I suppose my connection with the commander was a problem

for some people, but only for the guys who wanted to make it an issue, those who had nothing better to think about and who didn't see me getting up at the crack of dawn, putting in the hours of physical training, volunteering to do errands and all the rest of it. It caused a bit of jealousy and the odd time you'd hear whispering around the place that would suddenly stop when I arrived, but it was all nonsense.

I didn't want to go through all that stuff with Mahdi, about all the hard work I had been doing and how I just needed certain things to be able do my job better for the good of the brigade. Instead, I decided to go through the motions and, one by one, I handed over everything. I unloaded my gun and put it and the bullets on the table, along with the two-way walkie-talkie and the jeep key.

'If my being related to you is going to hamper me here,' I said, 'it might be best if I go to another brigade.'

Of course, Mahdi actually wanted me to have the gun, knowing that I was the right person for it, but he also had to be very careful not to show favouritism towards me. Rightly so. He was very alert to things like that, as they were the kinds of thing Gaddafi's regime had been doing. It was a catch-22 situation for both of us.

I left everything and walked out. After I broke the fast, I went back to my room, empty-handed and feeling pretty shit about things.

Later, I wrote in my notebook:

I slept all day today because I don't want to see anyone. I'm just sick of the whole lot and I'm nearly going to pack it in. I don't want to be part of the liberation of this country for some of these assholes. Anyway, just going to keep my distance from them. My head's all done in. I need a battle or something. This is like being locked up and is a real test of my patience. Damn you, Gaddafi. I stayed away from most everyone today, and even broke my fast outside of the brigade just to have a little peace. I heard also that there might be a battle tomorrow so this might be the last instalment in this diary. God only knows.

In the end, after a cooling-down period, things got back to normal bit by bit, and Mahdi just said to make sure I stayed in line. Fortunately, maybe because they knew there'd be trouble if they did, no one ever tried to take my sniper rifle again.

Rapid progress

On 2 August, I was woken by Marwan, telling me to get a team together. We were going to Bir al-Ghanem on the plains to meet up with the other platoons of our brigade – the ones that had left soon after I arrived in Nalut. We were to locate a building in that town into which we could move the entire brigade when the town had been fully liberated. Marwan explained to me on the way that this was one of the possible strategies being discussed – to bypass the Tiji route altogether and join with the progress being made by the other Tripoli Brigade platoons farther east.

Our group included Marwan, Mekki, Mahdi, Tabuni, Yusef Hamed (our strategist in the later planning), Majedy, Anis and Tayari, travelling in three different jeeps. When we got to Bir al-Ghanem after travelling for three hours, we were surprised to find that it had already been liberated and our forces had moved on.

As we made our way around in search of a new base, we followed our training and worked in teams, covering each other's backs, looking through a few government buildings and schools. One of the schools that was most promising was right beside a building that had been struck by NATO – a totally clean strike on a four-storey building that had simply dropped to the ground. It was so impressive what they could do with guided missiles. I decided to take a closer look at the strike, despite there still being sporadic enemy fire from the last remaining troops. As we were coming down some steps through the rubble, I slipped and fell head-first right out into the street into the line of enemy fire. Putting his own life at stake, Mekki came immediately to my aid and dragged me out of danger – a response typical of him that would resonate with later events.

Eventually we got back on the road to try to catch up with our platoons. It turned out they had actually gone all the way to Zawiya, about fifty kilometres north, which was amazing progress, and only about forty kilometres west of Tripoli. The feeling as we drove northwards on their trail, always at high speed because of the risk of being fired at, was heart-stopping – everywhere freshly liberated, petrol stations still in flames, loyalists being arrested, pick-ups full of revolutionaries zooming by, civilians being directed to safety. Towns and neighbourhoods were being liberated right before our eyes, and it was my first experience of urban warfare. There was a strange mixture of fighting and celebration all together.

We stopped off at one small town on the outskirts of Zawiya. The local council was just being set up in some civic building. There was a guy at a table trying to put some kind of official order on the chaos.

While Mahdi was introducing himself to local leaders, Tabuni and I had a look around. There were temporary cells inside where arrested Gaddafi troops were locked up. The local guys showed us around. One inmate we saw was a woman from Niger, extremely tall, wrapped in a blanket. We were told she was known to be a major sniper and had killed many revolutionaries: this was the first time we had come across one of Gaddafi's notorious female soldiers. We asked about another prisoner who was just being locked up, and were told that he was a known rapist. Tabuni reacted instantly. He had only recently taken off the brace from his arm, and yet without thinking, in a burst of the anger we all felt against rapists, he hit this guy a full whack with his damaged hand.

The encounter made us remember exactly where we were. We had heard awful stories of rapes in this area following the retaking of Zawiya by loyalist forces after it had liberated itself very early on in the revolution. The retribution that the Gaddafi thugs were directed to take on the people reached such awful levels that we all felt the urge for revenge on behalf of the victims, particularly the innocent women and girls who had been abused.

First arrest

Anis, Tayari and I went outside to wait for Mahdi. Suddenly, a spray of bullets hit close to us and brought us to our senses. We jumped in behind a wall. One of the rounds came very close to hitting me, and a sense of my worst nightmare flashed through me – being shot by some unseen sniper, leaving me with nothing to show for it, no chance to at least die fighting.

We spotted where the shots had come from and decided to do a flanking manoeuvre on the building. Anis stayed put and covered us with occasional bursts from his PKT to give the impression we were still there, while Tayari and I started making our way in a wide arc towards the farmhouse. When we reached the building, a run-down, uninhabited house, we went up quietly around the back and found the door was ajar. I stepped in slowly. Everything was dusty and a complete mess. I could see an opening across the room partly covered with a raggedy cloth hanging on a nail and waving in the breeze. We edged over slowly. I was able to peek through and could see the snipers in the room. There were three of them, one of them still at the window.

Signalling to Tayari, I stepped quickly and quietly into the room and as per our training, I covered the blind spot behind the entrance while Tiyari moved in at the same time, covering me. We shouted at them full force to stay where they were, keeping our guns high and pointed straight at the them while we rounded up their weapons. Their barrels were still hot. I could see immediately that they were the worst kind of thugs, right up to that minute delighted with themselves to have the opportunity to throw their weight around and exercise some power over the local people without any questions being asked. Looking at them, I found myself imagining how they might have abused that power, and started to feel the pain of the victims and the terror these guys inflicted on the local people. I started to feel a burning anger grow inside me.

The thugs knew their game was up and two of them became quite desperate. One was pleading with me, 'I swear, I wasn't—'

My anger swelled up inside, and next thing I hit him a punch and told him not to open his mouth again. I was soon to learn that one strike is never enough to silence these types, as fear and desperation take over in them and their instinct is to start up again.

'I swear to you—' he said.

I hit him again and said with a viciousness that surprised me, 'Don't you even open your mouth you scumbag.'

'But I swear—'

Whack!

146

It took one more strike before he got the message. Eventually, I silenced them and started walking up and down, searching for some way to get some kind of justice for their victims. Meanwhile, Anis arrived and he and Tayari gathered up the loyalists' personal papers and phones. While I looked through their papers, I started lecturing them, my jaw and voice tightening up with the anger. 'So was it worth it? Did you get so much from him that you don't mind this being the end? Look at you now, you dogs, and he doesn't give a shit about you.'

I noticed one guy was very quiet compared to the other two, and was keeping his head down. I reckoned he was the one who nearly got me through the window, and I reckoned he wished he had. I caught him looking very uneasily at the mobile phones, as if he was considering something. I decided to focus on him.

'You!' I shouted at him.

He looked up at me. Just that one look at him and all I could see in him was evil, something twisted, and he was looking back at me as if he knew what I saw. He was filthy dirty and grubby and the thought of him firing the bullet that nearly killed me made me ache.

'And what's your story?' I asked, piercing him with my voice, heading for the mobile phones.

'I raped,' he said defiantly, looking straight at me. The evil in his eyes seemed to add, *and I enjoyed every minute and there's nothing you can do about it.*

Something shifted in my head suddenly; I felt dizzy and weak. Time slowed down. I reacted quickly to put him in his place. Some other force had taken over, and I seemed to be acting out its will rather than my own. Then I just kept going as if nothing had happened. I turned and shouted at the third guy, 'What's your story then?'

He was in tears and screaming, 'I didn't do anything like that. I didn't do anything like that. I swear, I swear I didn't.'

I walked away.

It turned out that the phone showed what I had seen in his eyes: that he was a rapist and a sadist and a pervert of the worst kind. To me, it was as if in him I had suddenly come face to face with all the evil that had brought me to Libya in the first place, that evil I had witnessed back in Dublin on the internet and heard about here through first-hand accounts of the atrocities of the regime, an evil that had now been given a face for the first time. I was glad to get out of there and let the local revolutionaries deal with the thugs.

❖

Back out on the road, roadblocks were being set up with anything that was to hand – trucks, concrete bollards – and as we approached them, we were having to slow down from extremely high speeds to chicane through. We saw a blown-up tank and heard later that it had been driven by revolutionaries but was hit by NATO because its turret was pointing away from Tripoli and they had mistaken it for a Gaddafi vehicle on a counter-attack.

Mahdi wanted to go all the way to the front to see what was happening – it was history in the making, after all. Eventually, we saw a motorway flyover up ahead, under which some revolutionary brigades had gathered. A local told us not to go down under the flyover because it had just been hit. The Gaddafi forces had allowed the revolutionaries to gather there and think they were safe enough, and had then let loose on it. Even though the brigades were getting out of there as fast as they could, large numbers had been killed, and that was the point at which we arrived.

While we couldn't join the fight because we weren't armed for it, with bullets whizzing by us all the time, we knew we'd made it all the way to the frontline. Overall, Mahdi was impressed with the progress the brigades had made, but knew that there was still a lot of fighting to be done at this place before an advance on the capital would become a realistic possibility. We were also very conscious that our brigade needed another consignment of weapons before we would be ready to join in the final push.

The final piece in the jigsaw

Finally, some days later, back at base we got news that the weapons we'd been waiting so long for were on the way. 'The steel has arrived, the steel has arrived' was the call of the day. Our weapons were not, as later reported in a France 24 documentary, parachuted in by the French and English, but were organised by us, and arrived in four container-loads at Wazin.

The brigade had been screaming for months for these containers to be delivered from Benghazi, where they had been secured, but Mahdi had encountered nothing but hindrances. Some months back, a temporary runway had been set up on one of the main thoroughfares in Jadu to enable Hercules planes to land. Even Mustafa Abdul Jalil, the Chairman of the National Transition Council, had used it to visit the area. Mahdi had been trying to arrange with other brigades and councils to get one of those planes to deliver our containers. We had even tried to get the Americans to help out. At first they had said they'd try, but nothing came of it. It was all to do with the politics of the area. Whatever about our co-operation, we just weren't locals, and no other forces in the area wanted us to get so powerful that we could do it alone.

In the end, Mahdi had to arrange for them to be sent by boat to Tunisia, from where they were driven south to cross the border at

Wazin. Mahdi's brother, Abdel Ilah, travelled with the containers the whole way to the border, and I was put on security to make sure they got from there to the barracks safely. I was also told that some VIPs from Tripoli would be arriving in secret at the same time and that we were to escort them to the barracks as well. I was put on bodyguard duty for their visit.

Needless to say, we had to wait around the whole day for the weapons to arrive, which is what happens when you need to be secretive about movements. There was nothing much for us to do except observe the movement of people back and forth across the border and witness the delays and the arguments, all in the blistering heat. To add to our trouble, we were fasting and by the time the trucks arrived, I was fit to scream. As luck would have it, we encountered a problem that was like a spark for my mood. Apparently, the truck had one container that was to be delivered somewhere else, and the driver wanted to go there first and then come back to us. I was having none of it.

I walked over and let out a big roar, 'You must be joking. These trucks are going to Nalut first. Don't even think about defying us.'

He didn't like my attitude and a big ruckus ensued.

'See these twenty men?' I said. 'We're here with only one purpose – to make sure these containers get to Nalut. And see these guns?' I added, patting my rifle. 'They're here to make sure we fulfil that purpose. So unless you're going to take us on, get back in that truck and follow us.'

He got into the truck all right, but instead of sitting down quietly behind the wheel and submitting, he got an AK out and was shouting at me. 'Well, you see my gun …'

And then a few other guns came out and there was the sound of someone loading and locking. Luckily, the lads with me intervened. 'Come on, Housam, we don't have time for this.'

Knowing I was in no state to handle the situation calmly, I did the wise thing and stepped away to let them work it out without me. Sure enough, in the end the containers went to Nalut first, the final pieces in the jigsaw of our brigade.

We got another team to come out and escort the trucks, and us Special Forces guys took responsibility for the VIPs – some of the leading political figures from Tripoli. While the liberated towns were organising under their local councils, and as official institutions were getting support from the National Transition Council, unliberated Tripoli had no council because its leaders were scattered and, as yet, had no access to their own territory. However, they had begun forming a council secretly, appointing the figures they thought would be best, namely Abdur Raheem al-Keeb, later the interim Prime Minister, and Abdul Razzak Buhajir, later the head of the Tripoli Council.

Wanting to leave nothing to chance, I set up the convoy and instructed everyone, using the techniques I'd picked up from the Americans. It was great to see how Isa handled the mounted Dushka, or DShk, the Soviet equivalent of the American Browning 12.7 mm. He could have just stood there looking serious behind his hardcore gun, but he focused completely on covering the convoy, moving his barrel every time he spotted something that could provide cover to the enemy. This was how we rolled.

The timing of the visit from the leaders was perfect because, that night back at the barracks, we found out that we and the Nalutians were hitting Tiji again the following day, 15 August. The leaders gave a few morale-boosting speeches before I escorted them on to the town of Rujbaan.

By the time I got back that night, there was no time for sleep. In preparation for the battle, I printed out some Google satellite maps of the area as a reference for myself.

Tiji again – cursed with car trouble

With such short notice and now such a big brigade to assemble and arm, it was late the next morning by the time we took off. I was assigned to drive some of the commanders, including Mahdi, in his V8 Cherokee jeep. Not only was it a luxury compared to mine, with leather seats, air con and all kinds of other comforts, it was fantastically powerful. I could handle it, though, and loved driving it.

On our way down the mountain, even though I'd warned everyone not to speed or overtake, one of the young fellas driving a pick-up lost control. He had about ten other guys in the back and two in the front and if it wasn't for the gun tripod mounted on the back pole-vaulting the vehicle over, who knows what would have happened to them when it flipped. Mahdi decided we should go back to the barracks and get an ambulance and a mechanic out, while the rest of the brigade was pulled in waiting for orders.

While I was up at the barracks, I met Khalid Buzakari, one of Mahdi's trusted advisers, whose wife and family back in Ireland were close friends of mine. He was more of an office guy but I convinced him to join us for the battle. 'Come on, man, this is it,' I said. 'This is why we're here.'

He said he'd like to but that he didn't have a gun.

'We'll find you one.' Sure enough, he hopped in bravely.

Eventually, we came down the mountainside again, went by the turn for Ghazaia again, but this time kept going past the turn-off for the farm we had stationed ourselves at on the previous assault. We kept going straight towards the town, through all the roadblocks and barricades, because by this time, the Nalutians, who were leading again, were tearing up the loyalist defences in Tiji itself.

The first place we came to was Tiji General Hospital. It was chaotic in the area, with bullets flying everywhere and debris all over the place. Just as I pulled in off the main road, I heard this massive *pssshhhhhh* sound, and immediately cursed another puncture. My third! Mahdi jumped out with the other commanders and entered the hospital.

I tried to get the wheel changed in a hurry, but only ended up rounding a bolt so I couldn't get the fecking thing off at all. There were people coming up trying to help, knowing that it was Mahdi's vehicle, and eventually I let another guy take over, locked the jeep and entered the hospital to see what was going on. I was always a little worried about Mahdi in situations like this, when I knew things could happen out of the blue.

Inside it reminded me of something from a creepy sci-fi film: eerie, dark corridors, blinking lights, bed curtains blowing in the wind, even the odd wail coming out of a room. I started running up and down the hallways, screaming for Mahdi. Finally, I saw him coming back with the other commanders, heading out of the hospital. We came across a Russian or Eastern European doctor who seemed to have been injured when a stray bullet hit him in the hip. Even though my usual reaction would be to personally assist anyone I found in pain, I could see this guy was just another one of the many money-grabbing Gaddafi-regime servants, who was only in the country for the money he could make – so I didn't want to waste time on him. I got someone else to take care of him and moved on.

Outside, a big crowd made up of our brigade and other fighters was gathering. It was a bit worrying for me to see Mahdi so out in the open in the chaos, and if the jeep had been fixed, I would have bundled him in it and driven off.

Two or three young fellas had jumped onto the roof of the hospital and were pulling down the loyalist green flag. What followed was very bizarre. One of the Nalutian high-ranking officers started freaking out about this, almost like he had flipped or had sunstroke. He started screaming, 'Get down off the roof. There is more important work to do. Get down. The stupid thing has been there for forty years, it's not that important.'

Then he starting firing his gun in the air, spraying bullets all over the place, a few even hit the top of the building. We all shouted at him to stop, but Mahdi actually broke away from me and went right up to him.

'Muhammad, relax,' he said. 'What's wrong with you?'

I followed immediately, looking at the situation from a bodyguard point of view. To me, it seemed like the fella had completely lost it; his eyes weren't focusing on anything. He had taken off his headscarf and considering the scorching heat, I concluded he must be delusional.

As he lifted his gun again and started waving it around and firing it in the air, I immediately cut across Mahdi, grabbed the man's gun and with all my might yanked it away from him. He came after me and was staring at me so intensely that I stepped away as calmly as I could. He was a fighter after all, so I knew how he'd be feeling about having had his gun taken from him. I left others to calm him down and went over to a security hut at the edge of the hospital. I said to one of his men, 'There's his gun. Make sure he gets it when he's back to his senses.'

Still with a flat tyre, I drove with Madhi across the road, where I had spotted a few tyre repair shops. I busted one open by shooting through the lock and went in looking for an air gun wrench. I couldn't find one, so I made do with a lump hammer, a spike and a few wrenches instead. When they failed and I couldn't even chisel the bolt off, I decided to shoot it off. 'Step back!' I shouted, cocking my gun, but Mahdi stopped me. I knew he was right. I could have broken a cable and done more damage, or it might have ricocheted back. But I was just so frustrated knowing that Mahdi should be moving forwards, as well as wanting to be doing something constructive myself. I was lumping away at it, but losing energy and I asked somebody else to take over. I looked around again and realised that there was another wheel place down the road.

Meanwhile, our guys brought over two prisoners and put them in the jeep. Mahdi was interrogating them, though a little too gently by my reckoning.

I shouted at them, 'Tell him where the guns are or you'll regret it. Talk!'

Mahdi cut in, 'Don't hit them. It's not Islamic.' Then he said to them, 'You don't want me to let him loose on you, I'm telling you. He is vicious.'

When the threats didn't work, I gave one of them a slap. He started pleading, 'I don't know, I swear. I'm just a doctor.'

One of our guys pointed out that he was wearing a white coat, but you could tell he had just put it on over his other clothes.

I turned on him and said, 'If you're a doctor, say some medical terms in English.'

He had nothing to offer.

'Don't you lie to me, you hear? Where's the armoury?' I shouted as aggressively as possible, cocking my gun and pointing it at his chest to add to the fear.

Three older Se'aanians were also brought over to us, and even though they were in very good shape and without doubt full of useful information, nobody touched them. That respect for elders was always there.

Leaving them for others to deal with, I got back to the wheel problem, exhausting myself as I cracked the bolt, and then split it in two. I then hammered the spike into the split and tried to hit it at the side to cause it to flip around. Still no luck. I got everyone out of the jeep and drove out onto the main road doing crazy donut turns, hoping that the force would break it off. I was getting crazy with frustration, thinking about all the time that was being wasted. In the end, Mahdi got into another car and I decided to keep driving. One of our guys got in beside me to keep an eye on the prisoners. He shoved his gun right in the so-called doctor's chest and said to him, 'I don't even want to hear you breathe, Doc.'

Just after we got on our way, I noticed that the V8 was overheating with the pressure on the wheel. I spotted American Adam in a pick-up and flagged him down. I told him what had happened and said straight up, 'I have to take your car. Will you come with me?' I then said to Anis, 'I need you to get these prisoners to the base and drop the V8 back to the mechanic. Can you take care of that?'

I knew I was pushing it and probably nine times out of ten he would have said no way, but for whatever reason he was OK about it on this occasion.

Melons from the market

I finally got to make my way into the action, into the centre of the town. Tiji is basically one dusty highway with a number of roundabouts, smaller roads, and laneways of chalk-brick buildings running off it. I saw all the houses that had been painted green and the green flags flying outside shops and homes.

Coming under fire from loyalists up ahead, I pulled into a square where a lot of other revolutionary vehicles were parked. There was a large mosque on the other side of the road, and shops around the square and little lanes going off it in different directions. We had a tank at the corner of the square facing up the road and I parked behind it. I sat down with some of the guys from the brigade to catch up on how the battle was going. They were regrouping here after some serious fighting and letting the artillery units hold the ground.

I went over to the corner of the square near the tank just to see for myself how things were. Bullets whizzed past the odd time, which told me there was still fighting being done, so I dashed behind a pillar-like structure on the road and started scoping around with my sniper rifle. Bullets were coming very close all the time and one of them clipped the pillar just over my head. I decided sniping wasn't what the battle needed at that moment and went back to the safety of the square.

I saw some guys shooting off clips at the doors of the bank, banging at it and eventually getting in. With one or two of our lads, I went in and had a look around. There were upturned desks and tables all over the place, as well as glass everywhere. We came across one of those enormous safe rooms but couldn't get past the massive steel door. I found some paperwork on local people in one of the offices. I grabbed loads of files and outside handed them to our deputy commander, Hashem Bashir, saying, 'You might need these later.' I also came across sets of keys, big huge ones, and said to myself, 'Maybe, just maybe …'

I went back to the safe doors with thoughts of money for the brigade, but unfortunately they didn't fit.

Back outside, somebody said there was a fruit market just off the square worth checking out, so myself and a few others went around to have a look. The stalls were still laden with melons and all kinds of fruit. The traders had clearly just run off when the revolutionaries started arriving, but we still had to be careful. We grabbed armfuls of melons and started bringing them back to the square to fill up the cars, going back and forth a few times. One of the lads split one open, a particularly huge one, and it was so refreshing just digging our hands into the flesh and eating it straight. We were so dusty and parched it felt nearly as good as having a shower.

Two guys from the brigade came with me and we started combing through a laneway just off the fruit market. At the other end of the laneway, an old man stepped out from his creaking door holding a Smith and Wesson snub nose at his side.

I immediately had him targeted and we shouted at him, 'Put your weapon down! Put your gun down now, or we will shoot.'

He walked into the middle of the lane slowly, but we weren't too worried because we had him covered. Then he called to us, 'I'll die before Muammar dies.'

One of the others really screamed at him, 'Don't do it, Haj, don't raise your gun! We will have to shoot you.' ('Haj' is a respectful word we use for an older man.)

But he raised it, effectively committing suicide, and instantly met his end. As I said to an Associated Press journalist, 'These people's blood runs green.'

Our troops were starting to relax at this stage, as Marwan had ordered all infantry personnel to sit tight. Because I had no jeep and the pick-up would have been too slow to take into battle, I was infantry now.

There were a lot guys not connected with us going around looting at this stage, lane by lane, house by house, room by room. I tagged along with some of them, not for the looting, but to see if I could find anything significant from a military point of view.

I didn't care about the looting at that stage. I felt the people of Tiji had had plenty of warning that revolutionaries were on the way and time to surrender, but they had remained loyal to the regime and were blind to what was happening.

The miracle of the man from Morocco

I gathered about four or five guys, including a new recruit called Salah Baruni (considered one of the Lion Pack), who weren't doing anything and said we should use the time to do something useful. They were happy to come with me because they knew me to be very professional and liked to see how I did things. We started working our way systematically through the buildings down one of the laneways off the square to see if we could discover anything. I was training them as we went, first of all telling them to keep right up against the walls to stay out of sight, and out of the direct sun just to stay cool.

These were small, shanty-like houses, with basic unplastered chalk-brick walls and flimsy metal doors. Sometimes we'd find the door open and just walk in carefully. Other doors would be shut tight and I showed them the procedure to follow. We would shout out, 'Surrender and you'll be safe.' Then, having paused to listen for any answer (and not getting one), we'd shoot in through the door, shoot the lock, kick in the door, advance carefully and move inside. At one of them, when I shot through the door red liquid started oozing out of the holes. At first I thought it was blood, but when we kicked in the door we found someone had cans of tomato paste stacked up against it as some kind of barricade.

Inside the houses, we came across mostly unremarkable personal belongings, but also huge pictures of Gaddafi hidden under mattresses and behind wardrobes, and other such signs of the loyalty these people had to Gaddafi. In one house, I saw the mattress had a blanket on it that looked like there was somebody underneath. Shouting warnings, I went over and realised it wasn't a person at all. Worried it might be a booby trap, I very carefully lifted back the blanket. Underneath was a full range of military gear, minus the guns, left behind by somebody in their rush to flee. Among it all was a decent AK-bayonet-style dagger that I appropriated as a spoil of war and which became my knife for the rest of the campaign.

After maybe a half dozen more houses, we had come across nothing significant and we were picking up speed, but for some strange reason, I felt different about the next house I approached. I decided not to shoot in the door and just kicked it in instead. As the door flew open, there, lying down in front of the door, exactly where I would have been shooting, was an old man. While the other old men I'd come across so far were clearly Se'aanian, and to me represented the last days of a dying regime, this fella turned out to be Moroccan, I reckoned a helper or a caretaker of some sort. He was wearing a long Arabic-style white cotton shirt with matching loose white trousers. I walked in.

'What the hell are you doing here, Haj?'

He started mumbling to me, 'I don't know, my son. I'm old, I don't know what to do. I have nothing. I don't know what to do.'

'We'd better get you out of here before you get hurt. I nearly shot in the door, you know.'

'I don't want to go.'

'Sorry, Haj,' I said, 'you don't have a choice. You are leaving now with me for your own safety. I won't hurt you but I can't promise that the next guy that comes in here won't, so you're better off coming with me.'

We led him out to the square, where I spotted a Libyan camera crew. *This is a good story*, I thought to myself, and I called them over and said I wanted them to record this. Straight to camera I said, 'I want everyone to see. This is a Moroccan non-national who we have captured and will keep safe and free from harm.'

I told the man to tell the people his name, where he was from. 'Have we treated you well?' I asked.

He didn't say much, but it was enough to show that he was comfortable with me and for the story to work. Then I brought him across to the mosque, running across the road and making sure not to attract fire. I told him he'd be safe there inside the mosque. There was a bunch of old men outside and I asked them to look after him.

It was only later when I thought about it that I realised it was really a miracle that I didn't shoot him – lucky for him, but also for me. If we had found him dead on the other side of the door after I'd shot through it, I think it would have been on my conscience and made me overly cautious for the rest of the advance. I don't think I would have been able to live with the guilt either.

❖

Anis came back with the jeep all fixed up, and myself and Salah jumped in. Ali Arrara was also with us. By this stage, the last of the loyalist resistance was giving way, the military complex that had pinned us down last time was now under our control, and our tanks and the AA guns had moved forwards. We decided to get out in front to get a sense of what lay ahead.

We stopped off at a few villas on the other side of the town, just scouting, and we came across some hidden military equipment – signs of Gaddafi loyalists trying to cover up their association with the regime. I'd seen on the news how once NATO had begun to target all military installations, Gaddafi had instructed the military in places like this to stockpile weapons in greenhouses and sheds. We found a Caterpillar bulldozer, a garage full of electronics, a quad bike, weapons of various kinds and some ammunition. We got others to start taking it all back to the barracks and we kept going as far beyond the town as we could go.

Mostly everything was so basic that I wondered what kept these people loyal at all. It was a shock to me to see how little they had. I remember saying to myself constantly, 'Why in the name of God do they stand by him? It's not like they have been living in luxury.'

Guys were handing me passports and family papers they had found, and I got my answer in the fact that, in many cases, the place of birth listed was Tunisia: these were Se'aan planters, pawns in Gaddafi's bizarre sense of nationality.

Our infantry were finishing up their house-by-house searches on the outskirts of the town. When I was told that they had let mothers with youngsters go, I made it clear that I thought that all young men should have been rounded up and questioned. My view was that lots of the gear we were finding probably belonged to those families and we might find out more about our enemy from them. But it was too late and we didn't have a lot of time at this stage.

Our tanks and AA guns were holding the line up ahead, and by now it was getting dark, so without night-vision equipment, we finished up and headed back.

❖

That night, we had a massive celebration – everyone was in great spirits, singing and cheering. As we pulled up at the barracks in the jeep, Atif climbed up on top and called out for everyone's attention as if he had something important to announce. We all fell quiet and Atif shouted out, 'I have one thing to say.'

We all held our breaths.

And then he bellowed out, with a desperation we all recognised, 'Is there water for our showers or what?'

'Where are your dollars now?'

It was mid-August and the days that followed the liberation of Tiji were taken up with preparations of all kinds for our move to Zawiya and the final push on to Tripoli. Yusef Hamed gave a few talks in preparation for our assault on Tripoli, outlining how it might unfold, and how we needed to operate and act in order to be effective in the city, which was a very different battleground from the ones we were used to. The brigade was growing rapidly and there was hardly time to check up on all the new volunteers who were joining us. I was very busy going back and forth from Nalut to Zawiya and elsewhere, transporting people, collecting things and organising security. I must have driven about 3,000 or 4,000 kilometres, on about two or three hours' sleep a day.

On a trip to Zintan to do another arms deal, the Toyota Hilux I was in with Tabuni and Mahdi started sputtering so badly that we fell behind the convoy and just about made it to the base in Zintan before it collapsed altogether. We swapped it for a shiny new gold Pajero, with chrome trimmings, tinted windows and a V6, three-litre petrol engine, a massive step up from my old, sluggish, diesel navy one. 'We've traded in for a younger model,' I said. 'Perfect for Tripoli!'

On one of these days, we headed off through the mountains to the town of Gharyan, which had just been liberated. Mahdi wanted to make sure we got to buy a share of the arms spoils there. The road was long and dangerous and one wrong turn down the mountain and we'd be in the hands of loyalists. We were in a convoy of three jeeps driving well into the night over 400 kilometres or so over a winding mountainous road. We had to bring petrol reserves with us because the area was so far from our barracks and so unpopulated. In the end, it got so late and risky that we decided to break the journey.

We came across an old man with revolutionary connections who showed us to an empty, eerie town called Kikla, saying we would be better spending the night there and heading off in the morning. Having been introduced to the guy running the local brigade, we set up for the night in a school right on the edge of the mountainside. We rested near their mosque with our guns beside us, taking turns to get some sleep before dawn prayer. The odd person came over to say hello to us and introduce himself. At prayer-time, one of the lads spotted a prisoner wandering around and pointed him out to me. I was taken aback, grabbed my gun and told Mahdi. I went over to some of the brigade leaders and asked about it.

'Oh, we let them walk around openly,' he told me. 'It's so remote and barren, they wouldn't last long even if they did escape. We keep military prisoners locked up, but these are civilian loyalists you're seeing walking around.'

After prayer, I looked around with a few of the lads and found the whole set-up very peculiar. I didn't think the place was being well run and was very relieved to leave.

Gharyan, which we reached later that morning, was beautiful, unlike anywhere else in Libya that I knew, with a lushness and greenness that reminded me of Ireland. I had been to Gharyan about ten years earlier, camping with friends, and so this was the first place in the liberation that I recognised and had a personal connection with. It was another universe compared to the dry, barren, sandy world I had been inhabiting for the past few weeks.

We visited the town's barracks, which had been in revolutionaries' hands since the retreat of the Sahbaan Brigade, the group that had controlled the area since the revolution began. They had given way to the revolutionaries a few days before we arrived, adding to our confidence and sense of victory being close.

This photograph was taken just before we mobilised for the first battle for Tiji.
It shows the unity amongst men from many different backgrounds and shines bright
with the faces of many martyrs.

My personal arsenal after the liberation of Tripoli, from left to right: my sniper rifle, which was my most prized possession in the revolution; my HK USP 45. sidearm, one of the best handguns on the market, which I seized from a regime spy in a dawn raid; my AK, which I confiscated from a group of men pretending to be revolutionaries and carrying out a carjacking; and my Beretta SMG, which I took as a secondary weapon on the push for Tripoli. In the bottom left of the photograph is the Quran, which is my prized spoil of war from the battle of Tekut and Ghazaia.

At the barracks in Nalut, standing in front of a pickup with a rocket launcher welded to the back.

Housam Kafu and I about an hour before entering the battle of Tekut and Ghazaia.
Note the water canister covered in canvas.

From left to right: myself, Mahdi Harati and our battlefield commander Marwan Jamhoor. This photo was taken on our trip to Rujban to try and unite the Tripoli brigades under one leadership before the liberation of the capital.

Post-liberation and after the capture and killing of Gaddafi, this was at a celebration set up in Martyrs' Square to recognise the efforts of the Tripoli Revolution Brigade as well as commemorate those who had lost their lives for the cause.

In Tripoli, post-liberation. This was a very dangerous time when Mahdi would have been considered a very high-class target to the remnants of the regime and so I was always on high alert when out in public places.

Returning to Matiga military airport on a plane chartered by the WFP humanitarian NGO. I was back in Tripoli in the space of hours to make sure I was there for the proceedings and celebrations.

My meeting with Abdur Raheem al-Keeb after the liberation of Tripoli. This was weeks after our chat in the mountains when the prospect of a free Libya was still just a dream.

31 October 2011. I was asked to represent the revolutionaries at a ceremony to mark the end of the NATO mission and had the chance to thank Anders Fogh Rasmussen for the help NATO gave the Libyan people to end the nightmare they endured under the Gaddafi regime.

On a trip to the Amazigh town of Zwara in November 2011, where the locals were celebrating the liberation of the country. Seeing the beautiful smiles on the children, I couldn't help but think that all our efforts were not for our benefit but for this new generation who would live and grow in a atmosphere free of the regime's indoctrination.

From left to right: Saber Emsalati, an old friend of mine from my travel agency days in Tripoli; Alexandra Renard, camera woman for France 24; Matthieu Mabin, reporter for France 24 and a dear friend after our experiences together on the battlefield; and myself. At the Rixos hotel, Tripoli, ready to greet the General Secretary of NATO.

After the declaration of Libya was announced on the 23 October 2011, just eight months after the revolution began, Libya was set to shine once again. Even if it took years of uncertainty and instability, I knew that one day we as Libyans would overcome all obstacles and be able to enjoy the sights and smells of our beautiful country.

Mahdi and myself on the Syrian battlefield in the summer of 2012.

While Madhi had discussions about weapons, I visited the prison where they were holding large numbers of mercenaries from countries such as Ghana, Mali and Chad. The guards let me in to have a look around. I went into my lecturing mode, thinking of all my fellow Libyans whose lives had been ended by these murdering, marauding opportunists. I wanted the dead to have a voice through me, and in English started shouting at the prisoners.

'You low-lives, taking Gaddafi dollars to come here to our country and kill decent Libyans. Where are your dollars now? Was it worth it?'

Preparations for Tripoli – sincerity and sarcasm

From Gharyan, we went straight on to Zawiya, arriving at sunset. We passed the school where a few regiments of our brigade had already set up, and kept going towards the front to get a full sense of how things stood. The city centre was still bedlam. It was still being liberated and was in bits, with debris everywhere, holes in the road and buildings still on fire. But nonetheless, the locals were joyous – you could see on their faces how amazed and delighted they were to have such huge numbers of anti-Gaddafi forces in their town, well equipped and ready for battle. They welcomed us as liberators and were helpful to us as we set up, bringing food and supplies, and directing us around the city.

We got as far as the same overpass we had seen from a distance on our last visit – still the frontline essentially, as Mahdi had predicted. We were turning a corner at one stage and the next thing, we realised we were being fired at. Bullets hit the body of the car and windows, scattering shards of glass on us. Mohammed Jamhoor, who was sitting directly behind me, was bleeding from his head, we thought at first from a bullet, but in fact it was from a flying fragment of glass.

As quickly as they'd started, the bullets stopped while I was pulling away from the line of fire. It turned out that it was a local Zawiyan revolutionary who had shot at us, thinking, with our uniforms and convoy formation, that we must be loyalists. One of the guys he was with recognised the Tripoli Brigade emblem on the back of my jeep and stopped him, otherwise the gunner would have emptied the full clip at us.

Mahdi decided there was no point in hanging around in this chaos, so we headed back to the new barracks. On the way, a local Zawiyan suggested a more suitable school building for use as a barracks and we decided to occupy it. I instructed the troops who were already in the other building that they were to move and arranged the convoy. On one of the many trips over, at all hours of the morning, we were stopped in the street by a bunch of revolutionaries we didn't know.

'Who are you?' the guy in charge asked.

'We are the Tripoli Revolutionary Brigade,' I said. 'This is Madhi al-Harati's convoy.'

'Well, I've been put here by the NTC as the chief of the land here, and I don't like the way you're moving around without permission.'

'Chief of the land?' I said. 'I've never heard of such a thing.'

My position was that this was a free land, so who was this guy to be trying to stop us? I knew what it was about: it was another example of the agenda in the other brigades to try to hold us back. They were intimidated by our rapid growth when the big prize of the capital was so close. He started going on about them having provided one school already for the brigade, and he was clearly pissed off that we'd found and moved to another location.

166

'You won't be coming through here anymore.'

'Listen,' I said, 'you see this flood of men? This is only a fraction of what's coming, so you better get used to us going through here damn quick unless you want to risk a local war.'

Eventually, he let us through, but added, 'Tell Mahdi to come and speak to me.'

'Of course I will, man,' I managed to say without too much sarcasm.

❖

That night turned out to be one of the busiest nights of my life, and perhaps the most important up to that point. Not only did Mahdi task me with securing our new barracks to make it safe for the thousand-plus men who would be based there, he also put me in charge of preparations for the advance.

I set up proper checkpoints at each intersection in the roads and laneways around the building's perimeter. I brought a local man around with me in the jeep to get a complete understanding of the road network around the building. Then, I selected teams of guys to set up the barricades and man each checkpoint, and I instructed them how to do it properly. Of course, it was still Ramadan and some of the guys were giving out that it was time for *Iftar*, but I told them they had to start their shifts immediately. However, I made it my business to get food from inside and drive it around to each checkpoint so they couldn't complain. Only then did I get to break my own fast.

We assembled as much petrol as we could for all the vehicles, and, again, the locals were very obliging, giving us access to a tanker of fuel that was parked not far down the road. I organised hundreds of vehicles to go down in twos and threes to fill up under protection from other vehicles. It was non-stop. We had recently taken possession of twenty new Mitsubishi pick-ups, but they were indistinguishable from Gaddafi's. Yusef came up with the idea of painting Ns, as in NATO, on the roofs. Again with help from locals, I got paint and organised all the painting.

On the downside, I lost the keys for two vehicles, including one of the 14.5-mm AA pick-up trucks. It was a disaster, as every weapon was so crucial. After I gave up looking, I started trying to break in to them so we could hotwire them – but even that was a problem. Whatever type of glass they had, we couldn't smash it with either rifle butts or bricks, and in the end had to shoot through.

At some stage during all the frenzy of preparations, Mahdi introduced me to the television journalist Matthieu Mabin and his crew from France 24, and we agreed that I would help them make their report. I drove him back to where they had been staying so they could get themselves sorted – on the way, we discussed the dangers involved. I told him I wouldn't be able to take a full team, as I needed my men with me in the jeep to be effective. Matthieu got back to me later by phone and said he'd go with us alone. He came over to the barracks and started filming our preparations and interviewing some of us.

Atif told him on camera, 'I'm from Tripoli … beside Bab al-Azizia, near this murderer. Now we are preparing ourselves to get inside, to make Tripoli free.'

Our latest weapons shipment, three pick-ups full of AKs for the new recruits, arrived in a convoy. With Matthieu's camera following me around, we started our preparations for the advance. There were guns of all kinds going every which way, being checked and changed, ammunition being sorted and distributed, supplies of all sorts being unpacked and piled up. There was a great air of excitement about the place, as we all chatted and wished each other well for the great day ahead. It was quite dark inside the school building and there were a lot of people milling around, but because I had done a thorough job on setting up our security, I was actually quite relaxed.

I cleaned my PKT, and I swapped the new AK I'd been issued with for a handy 9-mm Beretta SMG for short-range indoor combat. I got all my ammo together – a few cartons of 9-mm bullets and bullets for my sniper rifle. I filled up my water canister and made sure I had a good pair of binoculars, my dagger, hand-cuffs, maps, a satellite phone, car chargers for the walkie-talkies and a few other bits and pieces.

One small problem that took on bigger significance later was when Atif was offered some petrol and poured it into his own little white Hyundai. Whatever was in the can caused it to start spluttering like mad and he had to hop in with someone else. 'If I don't make it, man,' he said to me, 'do me a favour. Sell this crock and all my stuff and give my mother the money so she can go on the pilgrimage of Hajj. She has always wanted to do that.'

'I will, man, I promise.'

Commander Najjair

Finally, well into the morning at around 3 a.m. on 20 August, with guys sitting around cleaning weapons and chatting, I got to lie down under a tree outside the school in the company of Mahdi, Yusef and a few of the other leaders. I suppose this was the point at which I was fully accepted into the ranks of the commanders.

I asked Yusef what we were to prepare for, and he took me into his full confidence and explained our plans in detail. The operation, called Mermaid Dawn, had been organised by our brigade leaders. I had been at some of the meetings, but this was the first time it was laid out in full for me.

The key to it all was momentum. Although we could have based ourselves in Zawiya for a time, and run incursions into the capital from there, we were actually proceeding with a full assault on the city that very day. At the same time, our revolutionary comrades within the city were going to attack along key routes, and as the Gaddafi defences came out of the woodwork, NATO forces would provide support from the air.

One reason for the need for urgency was that, apparently, Gaddafi had realised we were smuggling arms into the capital. Our contacts were informing us that reprisal arrests and killings by the regime were becoming more and more intense. Too many of our people were being taken – and no doubt some killed – for us to sit by any longer.

So this was it. The brigade's day had finally come.

The speed with which the final push was going to be made was amazing news to me. The previous days had been incredibly intense in terms of movement and organisation for me and the rest of the Lion Pack, but I hadn't expected things to culminate so quickly in the assault on Tripoli. When I pictured it in my head, I saw this massive force making its way rapidly up through the country, bearing down on Tripoli, drawing ever closer to the source of all the problems, to the site where so many innocent people were losing their lives every day because of one man's terror.

I rested for maybe two hours, though I couldn't sleep because of the level of anticipation in the air. Everyone was excited about the idea of Tripoli finally being liberated – I was too, of course, but inside I was also coming to terms with the fact that I might never see it myself. 'If that's what it takes,' I told myself, 'I'm now happy to die for it.'

Then, at the crack of dawn, for the first time since I joined the fighting, I heard the distinct sound of Apaches firing missiles and knew that it was time to get ready.

❖

The order came for us to prepare to roll out and I took control of setting up the convoy. With more guys from Zawiya and Tripoli joining us all the time, there were about 1,400 of us. The latest volunteers had their own cars, and all these vehicles – which I guessed numbered close to 200 – were starting to gather out on the side road.

Still in darkness, I started making my way down the road from the barracks to the end of the convoy, which took about fifteen minutes. I was telling everyone where to position themselves, what part they were to take, civilian vehicles to the left, military vehicles to the right. And everyone was responding. I was no longer just taking orders, I was giving them as well, with confidence, and they were being followed. I was freed from the association with Mahdi and had become accepted as a leader in my own right, recognised for all the work I had put in.

When I got to the top of the convoy, I turned around and made my way back again, telling everyone, 'Stay in position … No lights … No overtaking … This is not a race … This is not a wedding … Stay behind the car in front of you … Civilian vehicles stay to the back …' The message went all the way down the line.

As a faint light came into the sky, the full extent of the force became clear to me and I was amazed. 'Who can stop us now?' I asked myself.

Mahdi wanted me to stay towards the back at this early stage, to make sure everyone stayed in formation. Ali Arara, Abdulla Shegur and Mohammed Jamhoor were with me in the new gold Pajero. I'd fought alongside them in previous battles and I trusted them –

they had become some of my preferred crew. They respected me for my proactive attitude and seriousness.

And then we started moving.

❖

The convoy moved in an orderly fashion out onto the main road, the dual carriageway to Tripoli – heavy artillery out in front, military vehicles behind that, followed by the civilian vehicles and support bringing up the rear. There were also some local civilians and other revolutionaries out on the streets celebrating and wishing us well.

Some way up the road, past where we had been shot at by friendly fire the day before, everything came to a stop and I drove on up to the top to see what was going on. The leaders were gathered at a mosque and were letting the heavy artillery move ahead a little to soften up the Gaddafi positions before advancing.

Rather than hanging around, I joined the clear-up operation that was still going on in the neighbourhoods of Zawiya.

A man came running over to me suddenly, saying, 'Housam, come on, there's something you've got to deal with over here.'

I followed with my team to a farmhouse where there was an innocent family in complete terror from what was going on all around them. The old men were outside trying to protect the women inside. Feeling for them, and worried for their safety because they were black, I decided immediately that we would get them out of there, and I set up an escort. They drove in their own cars and we led them back into Zawiya centre and found some people to look after them.

Annoyingly, while we were making our way back to the front, just as we were catching up with the rear of the convoy where the journalists and support teams were, I got another puncture.

I felt plagued. And, yet again, it got complicated. The lock-bolt on the spare in the back of the Pajero wouldn't open no matter what I tried to do to get it off. I couldn't believe it. I debated using the gun for a while and eventually did. I opened the rear door to protect myself and shot the lock from the side. That worked and we got going again.

As we advanced towards the front, I made sure to drive tight to the side of the road, pulling in for cover when we needed to, before coming back out, taking shots and then swinging back in again. We were also under threat from the occasional mortar landing near us, but we made relatively good progress considering all the starting and stopping, covering about two kilometres in twenty minutes.

First direct hits

When we got to the very front of the infantry section, with only the heavy artillery ahead of us, we joined a platoon that was pinned down on the road, unable to move because of firing coming from up ahead. They were talking about having to do a flanking manoeuvre, but I felt that'd be a waste of time.

'What are you talking about?' I said. 'Forget about it.' I started crossing the road, aggressive and confident.

'Housam, get into cover or you'll get hit.'

There are different levels of courage. There's the courage of just being near a battle as a journalist or an ambulance driver. There's the courage of being armed and having to take cover just to avoid being in the line of fire. And then there's the courage of getting into that line of fire with your chest out, your life on the line and firing back. I didn't feel like I was better than anyone else just because I had that level of courage – and there were many others just like me – but I knew that I was able for the extremes of battle, and realised that the brigade badly needed as many guys as possible who were. I was starting to disregard the danger of getting shot, not because I didn't think it could happen, but because I didn't mind if it did. I was in full-on battle mode, focused on advancing and pushing on the other guys. I saw it as my job, and if I got shot doing it, so be it.

❖

While the others took cover behind a wall, I got down on one knee on the side of the road and looked through my scope. There was a Gaddafi jeep up ahead with some guy in it. He didn't seem to know what was going on and I thought maybe he'd been hit already and was passing out or something. Beyond him, there were buildings where one of the lads had told me there was a sniper on the roof. I was trying to get a fix on the sniper and started firing off shots now and again. In this situation, I felt it was an effective way of at least silencing the bastards because even though you might not see the target, if you hit even near them, often that was enough. Then I saw that the guy back at the jeep was now moving around. I couldn't figure out what exactly he was at but was worried that he might be about to get hold of a gun or a grenade or something, so I shot him.

There was no time to reflect on my feelings, neither pride nor remorse, about my first direct hit – within seconds, a mortar round landed just behind us and as I ran back across the road to the jeep, another projectile that would have killed me if it had landed whizzed by and prompted Matthieu, who had been following me, to jump for cover. Isa, who had joined me by this stage, said it was a mortar, but I reckoned it was a Milan missile. All I knew was that the fighting had suddenly got a lot more personal.

❖

After more fighting on the route, we went back to Mahdi and the others, and were able to sit down and take a short break. We restocked our ammunition and reloaded our gear. We were all sweating like mad in the intense heat of the direct sun and with all our gear on us, but we couldn't drink because of Ramadan. Atif suddenly arrived with fresh cotton vests and aftershave. 'Smell good, courtesy of Gaddafi,' he said.

Typical, I thought, smiling at my friend's crazy ideas.

Then there was a bit of a panic as the sound of gunfire intensified ahead of us. We got news from guys up ahead that there was a major stand-off taking place. Gaddafi troops were dug in inside a school building and ripping into anything that tried to get by. Two of our pick-ups, one full of ammunition, had just been taken out by RPGs and the people inside killed. I informed Mahdi that I was going to need two RPG teams and my crew to flank this school.

I'll never forget the mixture of excitement and willingness to die that I felt as I stepped across the road. With the Irishness in me coming out, I shouted in English, and knowing fully that no one understood me, 'Who wants to go on a mission?'

I left Mahdi behind and jumped in the jeep with my team. As we drove forwards, we saw one of the pick-ups in flames, black smoke rising from it, and the driver's charred body seated at the wheel as if he was still alive. 'He would have had no idea what was about to happen to him,' I said to myself.

I pulled into a laneway and took command. We met with a local who said he could help us get around the school into a better position. I got my platoon together and organised a stealth assault on the building.

When we were in position on the far side of the school, we rested up a little, and had some cold water, juice and food to boost our energy levels. Fasting to the point of self-harm is not Islamic, and that was the point we had reached. We got into our positions and I gave the order to attack. We started with missiles fired from pick-ups on the road, then opened fire from our various positions all around the building.

At one stage, I took up a very exposed position to get some shots off from a better angle and ended up getting myself pinned down by fire. One bullet hit the wall so close to me that a piece of cement ricocheted off and hit my forehead. There was nothing for me to do but take proper cover and I was totally immobilised for a few minutes. It was so intense that I lay down on my back and stayed still for a few minutes, thinking the worst.

Adil came to mind. I knew that if he had been there with me, I'd have been able to shout out to him and he'd have unloaded at them for me, until I could get free. Of course, all the guys in the Pack were there for me 100 per cent … when we were together, but we weren't always together. They had their own teams and took on their own missions. With Adil, it had been different. We would have always stuck together, I knew that, and I longed for that kind of connection. *If you're wounded, I'm gonna carry you. I'm not leaving your side.*

Eventually I got free and managed to snipe from a different position. In the end we totally overwhelmed the place, flushed out the RPG unit, and were able to get the brigade moving again on the main road.

We saw our two tanks, with Abul Waleed in one of them, moving forwards to the frontline after a reloading. They moved ahead with the AA guns, which were also doing their thing against the Gaddafi-defensive positions.

Next, I saw one of the tanks coming back towards us at full

tilt. As I was looking at it, wondering, then the AA-gun pick-ups started turning around and coming back as well. 'What have they seen?' I wondered.

I sped off in their direction to try and figure out what had happened. I pulled alongside the tank and was shouting as loud as I could to Abul Waleed. With the noise of the thing, I couldn't hear exactly what he was saying but I think because I knew him I at least got the gist from the way he was pointing that something had happened to the barrel. It turned out a shell had got jammed in the barrel and become welded to the pipe inside. But the lads in the AAs and heavy artillery vehicles had seen this almighty hulk of a tank suddenly speeding off away from the frontline and had got scared. It was a total mix-up.

Our other tank was taken out of action because of engine failure, which meant we would have to do without their power up front. We got whatever we had left organised for another advance. Unfortunately it wasn't enough against the loyalist artillery and we soon found ourselves at an impasse.

So that Matthieu could get a second perspective on events, I got him to stay with Madhi for the next while. I was relieved about this because, even though he was well able to look after himself, being ex-military, I was always worried about him. It also enabled me to get Atif into the jeep with Isa. Abdulla jumped out at this stage because, although he was brave, he wasn't as comfortable with my ways as the other lads. He was always telling me to pull in and to stay in when I was driving in the line of fire!

Mortars on Camp 27

It was at that stage that somebody came to me, a local fella, and asked if we were planning an assault on the Khamis Brigade's military base a few kilometres up the road, known as Camp 27. I had only just realised there was a base up ahead and started wondering myself about how well fortified it might be.

The Khamis Brigade, formally called the 32nd Reinforced Brigade of the Armed People, was named after Gaddafi's youngest son and was said to be a very powerful force and very loyal to Gaddafi. This local guy told me he could show me a way of getting within two kilometres of it without being spotted. I recognised immediately that this might be a way of evening things up a little for us and maybe getting us moving again.

I started preparing immediately. I guessed that mortars would be best in such a situation and immediately thought of a guy I knew to be very handy with canons. I went back to the ammunition truck at the very rear of the convoy, jumped in and started hauling out what I figured we'd need, though I wasn't totally sure. I got the guys around to help fill up the back of the pick-up and the jeep. I spotted a guy we'd nicknamed Obama (based on his resemblance) driving a pick-up. I knew he had been in the brigade from the start, so I reckoned he must be good, though I'd never seen him in action. He turned out to be more of an administrator than a fighter, but I didn't know that when I asked him to join me on this mission.

I couldn't find my mortar expert, so had to go without him in the end, even though I'd never fired a mortar myself. I knew the basics of how they worked from the training sessions with Wa'el – and anyway, at this stage, I was starting to let God's will take over. I allowed myself to be guided by whatever happened. Yes, there were difficulties and obstacles, but the fact that we hadn't encountered a significant Gaddafi force at this stage made me feel like God was on our side in this.

I told Obama to stick with me, that we'd be going up past the rest of the convoy, would have to take on fire, but that we'd be pulling off the road then, into a laneway on the right-hand side, and from there we'd be out of the line of fire.

When we were out past our forward positions, where the assault on the base was in full swing, you could feel the increased danger immediately from all the rounds being fired directly at us – including some massive 23-mm, mineral bottle-sized bullets. Even though I stayed in to the verge of the road as tightly as possible, it was very hairy, and when I checked in the mirror, I could see that Obama was way behind. I got around the corner, parked up and waited, every second feeling like a minute and every minute like an hour. I soon concluded that he was actually staying back down the road, and I cursed him, realising that I'd have to turn around and go back through that firing to see what was going on.

When I pulled up alongside him, I bellowed at him, with only the minimum of respect necessary to acknowledge that he was one of ours, 'If you can't handle it, let someone else take over the driving. I have to get those weapons up there, you're delaying the whole mission.'

He was in an awkward position now as I'd put it up to him and he said he'd go for it this time. I got another fella I knew, Fadel, who happened to be there in another pick-up, with a DShk gun on the back and huge metal plates welded out front like something out of *Mad Max*, to join us.

This time, we made it through the shower of bullets and into the laneway. We took a whole series of turns along winding little roads up and around to the right of the military base. With all the firepower of the Gaddafi force aimed in another direction, we found ourselves in a clearing, undetected and within mortar range of the base. It was brilliant. I spotted a villa a few storeys high and because I felt this was my mission, even though he was my equal and my elder, I asked Isa to take the binoculars over to it to see if he could get a view of the base. Meanwhile, I got the guy who'd directed us there to point out to me where he thought the base was relative to our position.

We set up the mortar, put the tripod into the ground, and I gauged what angle to fire it at – nearly perpendicular, I reckoned, considering it was only one or two kilometres to the base. I was reading the labels on the ammo and came across smoke rounds, which I figured would be perfect for pinpointing how close to the base we were getting. I shouted up to Isa to tell him I was firing a smoke round. I said a prayer, 'O please God, direct our bullets well!' We were always looking for God's intervention.

I dropped the round in the muzzle and heard the metallic swoosh sound as it slid down the barrel. It exploded off on its way and we waited for the impact. But nothing happened for a few seconds, again seconds that felt like minutes. I figured it must have landed in soft ground or water. But then suddenly a big cloud of smoke rose up over the trees. Isa shouted down encouragement, 'It's a hit', along with directions to aim a little to the right. I adjusted the tripod and started dropping in the TNT rounds in quick succession, changing the trajectory slightly after every three shells.

Meanwhile, the guys around me were starting to get jittery. Fadel kept on pointing out how unsafe we were so far from the rest of the brigade. We started arguing about it and when my own guys started to side with him, saying that we were putting ourselves at risk without any back-up, I lost my temper, kicked the tripod and threw everything to the ground, saying that they could deal with the mess. Isa calmed me down, and we eventually headed back to the main road.

❖

We found that the convoy had moved forwards a little, helped I hoped by our mortar attack, but it was still under intense fire from the base. I was desperate to find some way to break the stand-off. I met up with American Adam, the munitions guy, driving a big Ford pick-up with our only 106-mm cannon on the back of it. This one-hit-wonder, with rounds about a foot long, including armour-piercing ones, was so big we'd had to cut off the roof to get the boom of the cannon to fit. Unfortunately, we were out of ammo for it, and none of us had ever used one. Atif had done some training on them, but with our lack of ammo for practice, we'd never actually fired it.

Someone told me there was a bunch of 105-mm bullets somewhere, and we wondered if they would work. I went back and asked the guys who had been driving the tanks. They were recuperating, covered in the soot and grime that had stuck to them in the course of their operations through the day. I told them the problem and they said they'd give it a try. Unfortunately, it didn't work but Adam managed to dig up some 106-mm rounds from somewhere and we decided to get even farther forward so that we could make as much impact as possible with the beast.

Myself, Atif and Isa were in my jeep, while Adam and a few other lads were in the pick-up. As we got to the very front, about 800 metres away from the base, we were attacked with some enormous fire, including those explosive 23-mms. It was touch and go for a while.

I spotted a huge gate to the right, jumped out of the jeep, shot the lock and hauled the gate back. It was a compound of some sort. I drove the jeep in while Adam positioned the pick-up in the entrance. Seeing us out front gave a few others behind us the confidence to move forwards, and we soon had all the 14.5-mms coming in. This in itself was a breakthrough, in that it was the first advance we'd made in a while.

People used the opportunity of just being off the road and having a bit of cover to take a break, to get some water and reload. Atif and Adam positioned the 106-mm at the gateway and readied it to fire. They were aiming for just over a flyover, short of the base, to a spot where we gauged the Gaddafi 23-mm artillery might be coming from. They started firing off a few rounds but the end results weren't clear to us. I checked the aim through the actual barrel for myself and felt they had it right. The results of the next one, though, were more visible – a bull's-eye just at the edge of the flyover, which I reckoned took out the tank.

'Come on,' I said to Adam, 'let's move forward.' I was wondering what was keeping him, but he just looked back at me despondently and told me the Ford wasn't going anywhere. It was banjaxed – the dashboard was like something from a comic strip, with bits and pieces coming out of it in all directions. It turned out that they'd set up the cannon in a way that the blast was too close to the dash and it had blown all the electrics, leaving the vehicle unusable.

❖

Despite our mortar assault from the woods, and despite our efforts to take out the tank beyond the flyover, the Gaddafi base still managed to keep us pinned down with constant fire.

'How long is this going to go on?' I asked myself. 'Are we going to be stuck here for days or what?'

We had no idea what we were up against, how many of them were behind the walls of Camp 27. Maybe there were thousands. We were operating blind.

As I paused to take a drink of water, it struck me again just how hot the day was, and how long it had been since I'd eaten anything or slept properly. Every movement suddenly seemed impossible. Yet, I was able to keep going. At this stage, I was only running on adrenaline, but I also felt that God was helping me along, making the impossible possible for me.

I decided to try and get a closer look at the base from outside the gate of the compound. Every now and again, we were rolling a 14.5-mm out and firing off rounds, and other guys would go out with the heavier machine guns giving it everything they had. I just took my sniper rifle. I was completely bullet-hardened at this stage. It's not that I expected to get hit, but I felt that if it was my fate, so be it.

With the sound of bullets whizzing all around me, I took up my usual crouching position and started looking through the scope, desperately trying to catch a glimpse of something going on up there. I saw the odd glare suggesting movement and some muzzle flare coming from below the base, but I couldn't spot anything specific that would explain the amount of fire around me. As the firing became heavier, I reckoned I'd been spotted and decided to move. I was just about to pull back into the compound when I heard and then saw two massive explosions up at the base. Two missiles had struck. One had hit the entrance, the other had hit the road just in front of it. The explosions were huge, easily twenty or thirty times anything that we were capable of producing. I realised it must be NATO backing us up from the air.

Everyone was delighted. We shouted at the tops of our voices, 'Allah Akbar, Allah Akbar, God is great.'

I looked again through the scope and could see a few of Gaddafi's troops moving unsteadily around outside the barracks onto the road. I hit one of them in the leg and saw him lose his balance and fall. The other guy made it to cover before I could get him. Through my scope, I could tell that they were both shell-shocked and it occurred to me that the after-effects of the bomb represented a perfect opportunity for us – though how to take that opportunity, I wasn't sure. There was no sign of the convoy advancing, obviously as they couldn't see what I was seeing through the scope, so I felt it was up to me to do something.

With no clear plan in mind, I got Atif and Isa into the jeep and we sped off out of the compound heading straight for the camp.

Not prepared to risk driving straight at the base, I turned right off the dual-carriageway and headed up the flyover slip road opposite the base. We were taking fire from the trees beyond the road, but I ignored it and kept going. I did a U-turn and parked right in the middle of the bridge. I jumped out of the jeep, took our flag with me and headed straight for the side of the bridge. On YouTube, I had seen people in Tripoli hanging the flag from bridges as an act of resistance, so I suppose I started to think along those lines. I stood there looking back towards our convoy – hundreds of troops on foot and in vehicles stretching a few kilometres back, stalled by a mixture of exhaustion and fear. I don't think I was even aware of the firing from the trees at this stage; something helped me to just ignore it. I raised the flag up over my head and started shouting at the top of my voice, screaming out to the convoy below with every fibre of my body, 'Allah Akbar, Allah Akbar', and pumping the flag into the air at the same time. I wanted to shout courage into them. I wanted to convince them we could do this.

A few cars and infantry started moving towards the flyover, and then the entire convoy seemed to be chanting and waving and taking photographs of me on the flyover as they passed right underneath me, finally moving towards Tripoli again. It was the most exhilarating feeling I had ever had in my life.

❖

Isa and I tied the flag to the bridge and headed back to the jeep. It was only then that I appreciated how heavy the firing was. It was so bad, I slammed the jeep into reverse and backed the whole way down the other slip road, scraping off the steel barriers as I went. When we made it down onto the main road, the three of us jumped out and started celebrating. Atif and I were looking at each other and next thing we just ended up giving each other a full head-butt.

'I can't believe it, man,' he said. 'I've finally met someone just as crazy as me.'

I asked one of the guys where Mahdi was, still unsure of what we should be doing. I heard someone say we needed to stop for the night, but I felt the momentum was in our favour and that we should keep going.

Atif is hit

While the convoy was turning into the gate where the NATO airstrike had hit, I decided, still in extreme recon mode, to keep going a little farther down the road to the next corner, where there was another entrance into the site. When we got inside the perimeter, the scene changed. I could see that we were now dealing with a very different terrain – a dense-forest battlefield. I knew we could be shot at by someone here and have no idea where it was coming from. I was suddenly more on edge.

I spotted two very fancy military tents and decided to check them out. Atif and Isa ran off in the other direction, looking for a decent vehicle that would get us to Tripoli. Some spoils of war, maybe ones vital to the success of our campaign, could be waiting for us as long as we could stay alive.

I ran through the trees towards the tents, firing off the SMG in an arc ahead of me all the time. I shot a few more rounds into the first tent before taking a quick look in – nothing; same at the second tent. I went in and rummaged around. Jackpot – I found a full crate of AK bullets, and even though I didn't even use a Kalashnikov, I couldn't leave all that precious ammo behind. The crate was one of those rectangular wooden ones, with a handle on either end, designed for two people to carry. I had the rifle strapped on my back and the automatic in my left hand, so with my free hand, I just grabbed a handle and somehow managed to lift the thing clean off the ground.

As I started back towards the jeep, I thought of my friend Adil, picturing him there with me being able to take the other handle so we could carry it together. Without him, I don't know where else the strength to carry that load could have come from, other than God, with all I was already carrying, and all I'd already done that day. As I got closer to the jeep, I could feel the pull of the weight on my arm practically tugging my shoulder out of its socket, and I was saying to myself, 'Am I really carrying this?'

I managed to get the crate into the jeep just as Atif and Isa arrived back. We met two other revolutionaries from the convoy, though not from our brigade – 'floaters' as they were known. They had AK weapons, and I reckoned the more automatic firepower we had on board in the trees, the better, so I got them to jump onto our jeep's sidebars, hanging on inside with one hand and holding onto their guns with the other, fingers on the triggers. Atif stood up on the two back seats sticking out through the super-sized sunroof with his gun at the ready.

We drove through the base on a track that was parallel to the main route through the site. As we were moving, I was looking across through all the silver birch trees to the other road, and spotted a military truck heading in the same direction. It looked too official to be one of ours, so I thought it might be Gaddafi troops on the run. I took the next left and called out to the boys, 'Keep an eye on that truck. Keep an eye on it.'

I figured if I kept up our speed, we would come out right on top of them from the side road. Just as we were reaching the junction, we saw that our comrades had already stormed it. So instead of an assault, I took a right-hand turn onto the road and we found ourselves looking straight out onto the most breathtaking scene of the sun setting on the Mediterranean Sea. It was such a beautiful site, it lifted our spirits even more.

We were delighted to have made it so far. I was saying as we drove towards it, 'This is it, lads, this is as far north as we go. Now it's east along the coast to Tripoli. This is really happening.'

As I said those words, we passed a few revolutionary vehicles that had pulled in off the road and suddenly out of nowhere a spray of bullets, like so many others, came across the front of the jeep. I instinctively floored the jeep and swung to the left as sharply as I could to get away from it. The guys on the sidebars must have been hanging on for dear life. As we were coming out of the swerve, I heard Isa saying, 'Oh my God. It's Atif, it's Atif. He's hit.'

I turned my head quickly to take a look and I could see that he'd taken a shot to the head. Even though I knew it was much more than just a wound, and I knew he didn't stand a chance, I still wanted to try to do something for him. I could hear him choking on his own blood in the back, still trying to breathe. I sped back towards the main road but quickly came up against the convoy coming against us. I was freaking out trying to get through the crowd. Everyone was all happy and cheering, but I was beeping and the other guys were shouting at people, 'Get out of the way. Out of the way.'

I was nearly running people over just to get through, and when we eventually got back to the main road, it was even more chaotic, with crowds of revolutionaries and locals everywhere. I drove right over kerbs and debris, desperate to get across to the ambulances, but we got stuck in the crowd. We got out and lifted Atif out of the back, his lifeless body feeling extra heavy. Once we had him in an ambulance, Isa and I broke down and burst into tears.

'I can't believe it,' I repeated over and over.

It was one of the worst feelings I had ever had in my life – the first of our Lion Pack to be killed, one of the people I had felt closest to since arriving back in Libya was now gone.

People were hugging me, telling me not to be sad, to be happy for him because he was happy in paradise. 'Come on, we need to finish the mission', I heard someone say. But I was still angry – so angry that I smashed my fist clean through one of the windows in the jeep.

I heard a commotion in the distance and knew something odd was going on. Someone came running up to me, shouting at me, 'You shouldn't have done that. It's wrong.'

I was dazed and didn't take any notice of it, but just got back in the jeep with Isa and Abdulla. It turned out someone had thought that I had shot the guy suspected of having killed Atif.

❖

We stopped a few kilometres up the road and did what we could to recuperate. With help from some local young fellas, we removed the rear seats from the car and cleaned up the rest as best we could. We washed, ate and prayed. They say there are only two things that would keep a true revolutionary from the battlefront – running out of ammo or shedding a tear for a fallen comrade. I knew it wasn't the time to mourn Atif, I knew I had to keep going and I knew, in fact, that I needed something to boost my morale.

The way Atif had died made it even more clear to me that if a bullet is meant for me, it's meant for me from the moment it comes off the conveyor-belt at the factory. There is no way of escaping it. His death helped me lose all my remaining fear of dying. I was ready to take the convoy forward single-handedly if needs be. Luckily, just the thing to help with that and distract me came our way.

It was a munitions warehouse near the military base, the size of which made the eyes pop out of our heads. I would never again wonder where all Libya's oil money had gone. The warehouse stretched for as far as the eye could see with high-quality arms and ammunition. Now that it was ours, it made me all the more confident that we would be victorious. There was no point gloating about it, though, so we just took what we needed for now and moved on.

To Martyrs' Square

The terrain at this stage was suburban roads and dual-carriageways. After Camp 27, there was no more concentrated resistance to our advance. As we moved forwards, the infantry cleared out the surrounding buildings and made sure we didn't leave ourselves exposed to attack from the rear.

I was at the head of the convoy at this stage, taking reconnaissance to its most extreme form. I still felt no fear and didn't care what happened to me. I said to myself, 'If Atif is gone, I can go at any time. Maybe I'm not meant to reach Tripoli.'

We were coming across abandoned posts and isolated pockets of Gaddafi troops still holding on, and we had to shoot up a few different buildings as we went along, including a police station. Despite the fact that things were still very dangerous, civilians were starting to venture out into the streets. I was screaming out to people from time to time to stay in their houses. 'Get away from the windows! We will shoot. Get off the roof!'

With all the shouting I did, it is no wonder I had no voice left by the time we got to Tripoli.

I noticed civilian cars starting to join us, their hazards blinking as if they were at a wedding. They were starting to get in the way of the big guns, so I knew I had to control them. I organised a row of brigade vehicles to act as a roadblock to the rest of the convoy at the entrance to Tripoli along the main road. Some of the more enthusiastic ones were starting to shout at us to let them by, but I was having none of it – only revolutionaries were going to get through and travel with us.

At some point on the way into the capital, I was delighted to hear news of my father's part of the city being shouted out: 'Souk al Juma has liberated itself! They've set up checkpoints in Tajura!' This not only filled me with joy but also with pride.

We re-established the convoy and headed over the flyover bridge at Janzoor junction. Just as the AA guns were heading over it, they were shot at from somewhere below and I immediately stopped the entire convoy. On top of that bridge, I knew we were totally out in the open, like sitting ducks. I took one other guy with me and went to investigate. We got shot at from the same position in a nearby car park. I jumped out of the jeep and the lad I was with flushed the group out with a blast from his AK. As they moved, I picked them up in my scope, shot the first guy at the first attempt and took three shots to get the second guy.

I didn't want to delay the convoy's advance any more than was necessary because the chances of our guys being shot or even bombed were considerably higher while we were slow or stationary. So I drove back up and around the flyover at full speed, spinning the car as I pulled on the brakes at the top and signalled to the convoy to advance. It was getting dark now. We needed to push forwards.

Unfortunately, we had to park up again a few kilometres farther down the road to re-form. I stepped out of the jeep to talk to some guys and suddenly from a road to our right, a shower of bullets came our way, hitting my jeep and a guy standing right beside me. He fell to the ground. I took cover behind the engine of the car and laid my rifle across the bonnet. I could see people in two cars parked up the road some distance, under a street lamp, but I didn't open fire in case they weren't the troops who had fired. In my mind, I had the idea that it could be a family fleeing and the actual shooter might be in one of the buildings on the street. I held my nerve, but focused carefully on them through the scope. The cars started to move slowly forward towards us and then more shots came our way. I still held off. Suddenly, they started burning rubber as if they were about to run at us – and I opened fire, taking about five shots. I saw windows and lights shattering. One car stopped and the other sped off.

I barely had time to catch my breath and make sure the guy who had been shot was taken care of before someone came up to me asking whether we were going to Martyrs' Square or Bab al-Azizia, Gaddafi's compound. I was a little surprised to be asked this question, though considering the way I'd been leading the convoy I suppose it wouldn't have appeared strange to some people to ask me.

For a moment, I was about to tell him to go back and ask the commanders, but I decided there wasn't time and that I could probably guess what they would say anyway. I took the responsibility and decided on Martyrs' Square. I knew the symbolic victory lay there, and that it was the safer option for now, considering how dark it was getting, how tired we were and how well defended Gaddafi's main military compound would be.

As we hit Omar Mukhtar Street, I started picking up speed. My heart rate started picking up speed too. The thought of the brigade being only minutes from Martyrs' Square, in the heart of Tripoli, like a life-saving syringe being injected into a dying patient, sent my adrenaline levels rocketing. I drove faster and faster towards the square. I was on my own in the jeep. To my right, Omar Akarmy, one of our best AA gunners, was in the back of an AA vehicle, and Amur Jurnazi, a Nalutian who I knew as having led the quad-bike platoon in the early battles, was in a Toyota Landcruiser with missile launcher to his right. We drove neck and neck right to the edge of the square, the first three vehicles of the convoy to arrive.

The first thing I noticed was the scaffolding towers all over the place, seemingly erected solely to display a massive image of Gaddafi. Under normal circumstances, I would have laughed at the irony, but these were not normal circumstances. I was too busy looking out for snipers hiding on the scaffold.

I glanced down to street level and spotted three uniformed soldiers, armed. I got out of the jeep and from behind the door shouted at them to drop their weapons or I'd shoot. I could have done with an AK in these circumstances, as the SMG range is so short, but I had my sniper rifle and trained it on them. As the guy closest to me took in who I was, the expression on his face was a great sight – a picture of complete disbelief. Of course, Gaddafi's commanders had probably kept infantry guys like these entirely in the dark about our progress into the city. Shocked, the three of them started to run away out of the square. I managed to hit the nearest guy in the leg before he got away.

Somehow or other, I got a sense of trouble in the air, some kind of response to our arrival, big guns being cranked up for action at the realisation that we were in Martyrs' Square. I couldn't see or hear anything, but I felt we couldn't stick around.

Sure enough, a major barrage of 14.5-mm bullets soon came pouring down on Martyrs' Square and particularly around the Omar Mukhtar Street opening, probably killing the Gaddafi guys who had been retreating. I just about managed to jump into the jeep and reverse it away from the square, but the firing was so intense, I couldn't even stay in the jeep. I immediately bailed while it was still rolling and jumped in behind the pillars of the archways on Omar Mukhtar Street. The jeep bumped into another car and came to a stop. One of the vehicles that had been partly barricading the road exploded into pieces nearby.

Battle for Martyrs' Square

I watched our Caterpillar bulldozer push its way through the wreckage all the way up to the mouth of the square, taking on more and more fire all the time. The driver raised the blade in front to cover his cab, but bullets started to get through and he had no choice but to jump ship and run for cover. Meanwhile, another car nearby took a direct hit from a 106-mm cannon and blew up right in front of us, lighting up the place in glowing red.

As Gaddafi's troops ratcheted up the firing, I looked back up the street and could see the marble cladding on the pillars shattering like glass and falling away in pieces, and men ducking and diving their way towards us, smashing street lights and sending dust into the air.

Next, I felt an intensifying heat building up on the back of my calf just inside my boot. The pain of it hit me full on then, and I thought I'd been shot. I reached down expecting to feel the damp of blood oozing through the fabric, but it was actually a roasting hot .23 bullet that must have ricocheted off a wall and landed in my boot. I had to drop it instantly before my skin sizzled.

I watched, almost without believing it, as Amur, in position at his AA gun in the back of the pick-up, was reversed right into the square, braving all the bullet fire.

The most amazing showdown of AA gunfire followed. Gaddafi's somewhere north towards the port; ours now in the middle of Martyrs' Square.

It was very dark by this time, but I could see the tracer rounds travelling in both directions through the sky, getting nearer and nearer to direct hits. It was down to who was cranking faster to adjust the trajectory. God was clearly on our side – Amur got there first. The other gun fell silent.

Not stopping there, Amur looked up to the roofs of the surrounding buildings, spotted another source of firing and began winding furiously. Lit up by the flare from the muzzle, I could see his face and goggles momentarily as each round was fired, and then darkness again and then lit up again. *What a lion!* I thought to myself. I was pinned down by fire and unable to do anything to help. Amur was cracking off rounds up at the edge of the roof of one of the buildings and making slight adjustments until a whole chunk of the building came away and a sniper fell to the ground. In their private language of banging on the cab, Amur was able to tell the driver to get out of there. The driver duly floored it and sped out into a nearby lane.

I then tried to advance into the square myself, keeping tight to the wall, in a line with some other young fellas. When the guy directly in front of me got hit and dropped dead at my feet, I decided to take a different approach. I checked his vital signs to confirm what I suspected, kissed him on the forehead as a mark of respect and turned around.

As I moved back, I met American Adam. He introduced me to a local who was offering us access to the roof of his building, which overlooked the area. My intuition told me I could trust this guy, so I took the opportunity and followed.

I can't recall exactly how, but around this time we got hold of a Gaddafi sniper and when Tabuni started questioning him, we realised we could get a lot of vital information from this guy. We didn't hold anything back during the interrogation. We found out that there were twelve snipers in place around the square and an AA gun down near the port firing in our direction – *Maybe the one Amur had just taken out*, I thought.

It was at this stage that my tank ran dry. Punching the sniper totally emptied my reserves and I started falling back against the wall myself after the hits. Another loyalist, a non-military Matoa (a Libyan mercenary, of sorts – civilians who thought it would be quick money to join the loyalist ranks) was brought to me, but trying to interrogate him was just too much. I asked the guy who owned the house if he could do me a big favour.

'What?' he asked, probably expecting something risky.

'Can you lend me a pair of clean socks?' I asked. With the sweat and extremes of the day, I had burst blisters galore all over my feet, and the discomfort was unbearable.

In fresh socks, I tried to keep going. I went back up to the roof and started scoping around for more targets. But I started hearing a voice in my head telling me to rest. I had no energy left in me, my vision was becoming blurry and the pains in my muscles were intensifying. I knew that if I wanted to stay alive, I should stop now and give in to all the signals from my body.

But I just couldn't. The thought of all the innocent lives being lost that very minute out on the streets as Gaddafi's forces came out to take us on was too much for my conscience. I could hear their voices clearly in the street right below me. 'I am a fighter, so I'm going out to fight,' I said to myself.

Not heeding anyone, I struggled down the stairs, leaning against the wall the odd time for support. Not really able to see clearly, I left the building and headed up the street under the archways towards Martyrs' Square. As I got closer, I prepared myself for the worst, raising my gun, ready to kill whoever I could before I got killed.

'Right, Housam, now is your moment. You've come this far. You've seen Tripoli. Be ready,' I said to myself. 'There is only one God and Mohammed is His messenger.'

I truly believed that this was the end of me, but I wasn't afraid. I embraced the thought and entered the square ready to die.

But it was not the end. I did not die. Instead, the most amazing thing happened. Two of our guys came over to me, overflowing with joy, grabbing me, hugging me, squeezing me.

'What's happening?' I asked.

'It's liberated, Housam. Tripoli is free.'

'Are you sure?

'Yes, come on, come and see.'

I walked farther into the square, aware that if I'd done this any earlier, I'd have been riddled with bullets by now. Amazingly, I saw a few people standing around and they seemed to be relaxed. I went into a kind of trance, everything slowed down and sounds became muffled. I walked over to a palm tree and let go of all the tension inside me. I threw the SMG to the ground, and realising that all that I had dreamed of and all that I had strived for and all that I had prayed for was coming true, I fell to my knees and gave thanks to God with a *sajdah shukr* prayer (prostration of thanksgiving).

When I tried to get up, I just couldn't find the energy, and some guys came over to help me to my feet. I walked back towards Omar Mukhtar Street and met Matthieu from France 24.

'We meet again,' I said to the world, my voice shredded to bits, 'and this time we meet in Tripoli. Finally, after six months of fighting, pure fighting, we eventually made it. And the Gaddafi regime is over. It's finished.'

Part IV

Cats on the Streets

September 2011

The three-day war

In Gaddafi's hour-long speech after the protests in February 2011, he'd said that they would hunt down the rebels 'inch by inch, house by house, home by home, alley by alley' (*'shebr shebr, beit beit, dar dar, zenga zenga'*). His words were turned against him and people made fun of them on the internet. When we arrived in Tripoli on 21 August, he made another speech, this time from a secret location, no doubt far from the city, in which he appealed to his followers in the city, 'Don't leave Tripoli for the rats. Fight them and kill them.'

I wrote my answer to him in my journal:

Well the 'rats' have arrived, Muammar, and we're taking back the streets of Tripoli, alley by alley, house by house, inch by inch. But the truth is we're not the rats, we are cats come to rid Tripoli of your rats, to run them out and give the streets back to the people.

Patrolling the streets

In the days immediately following our entry into Tripoli, even though there was a lot of joy and celebrating on the streets, the city was still a dangerous place. We felt that things could turn against us at any time, both individually and as a force. Our taking of Martyrs' Square did not amount to an outright victory by any means. While other brigades made a fuss of themselves and started celebrating openly, our brigade's ethos was to get on with the job, and continue with the follow-up work that remained to be done. Not only was there an expectation that we would have a major showdown battle at some point with Gaddafi's forces in the city, we were also constantly on alert for sudden one-off strikes.

My main focus immediately after the Martyrs' Square victory became security. Even that night, despite the exhaustion and the atmosphere of celebration, with monarchy flags taking over from images of Gaddafi, I got back in the jeep and patrolled the area around the square to make sure we were setting up properly to keep a firm hold on the area. There was still the odd mortar landing, and a good deal of directed gunfire (as opposed to celebratory) could be heard, but there was no sign of a loyalist army.

'Libya is free,' I told Matthieu on camera. 'I am absolutely destroyed mentally and physically, but inside I am screaming with joy.' I then headed off to silence the remaining pockets of loyalist fighters around the square.

Tabuni must have seen on my face how wrecked I was. He insisted I stop and spend the night at his family home in the inner city. American Adam joined us. As soon as I was introduced to Tabuni's family, I immediately knew I could trust them and their friends – that instant reading of people that I had started to develop showed them to be lovely people. The locals had secured the street nearby with checkpoints, and I slept easy. For the first time in days, I was able to get out of my clothes and take a shower. What a change that made, let me tell you!

I was up again by about nine the next morning and off patrolling immediately. Getting into the jeep, I noticed on the driver's side that the last of my windows wouldn't open or close thanks to a bullet that had gone through the door. Upon examination, I discovered that the bullet had ended up in the steering column, and I could tell from the trajectory that it must have passed just by my knee. In fact, I then looked and found a tear in my combats that corresponded exactly. Another lucky escape. I decided the window was going to be a nuisance so I jumped out in the middle of traffic on Martyrs' Square to deal with it. The guy behind me started beeping until he saw me taking out my rifle. I just smashed the glass with the butt of it. Passers-by were looking at me funnily, and I thought, *Well, it's not the kind of thing you'd do on an average afternoon on O'Connell Street.*

In those early days after our arrival, I also started noticing the good wishes from the people of Tripoli. We were constantly being given blessings from passers-by: 'May God protect you, the real revolutionaries.' If I ever wondered how we made it that far and how so many of us survived, that was my answer – the prayers of the people.

In the first few days, understandably, there were very few civilians to be seen out and about outside the city centre. Once the celebrations actually started, our work became very different, and we had to negotiate our way around and through the crowds more sensitively. Of course, I never had a chance to join in with the people, but I was very happy and proud to see them out enjoying the streets of their city again, with a great sense of liberty and optimism. I was particularly chuffed one day when a shopkeeper refused to take money off me for a few things I was buying. 'A token of appreciation for what you have done for Tripoli,' he said.

❖

Checkpoints were being set up and I was able to talk to various groups of revolutionaries, some from our brigade, to get updates from them. I asked about Mahdi but no one I met had any news of him at that stage, though I later found out that with a few others he had split off from the convoy the night before to apprehend Mohamed Gaddafi, one of the sons whose house was not far from our route to the capital. I continued with my patrolling, knowing that things would be a bit uncertain for a while and that I would be relying on my initiative. I was alert at all times, aware of the danger of being attacked.

I had taken a phone from the guy on the roof we'd arrested the previous night and had started giving out the number. I got a phone call from one of our guys who said he had intelligence on a particularly nasty 'Gaddafi head'. He was one of the many recently hired 'guns' brought in to fill up the depleted Gaddafi ranks. This guy was known to have been involved in the torturing of protesters, and we had plenty of evidence. Most of these types had been very loud in expressing their loyalty to Gaddafi and what they were doing for the regime, so it wasn't hard to track them down and gather evidence against them.

With Adam, who had established the house off Martyrs' Square as a temporary prison, and a few others, we went to the address we'd been given. I banged on the door. Eventually, the man's sister came to an upstairs window and I shouted up asking if Mohammed was in the building. At first, she said he wasn't and refused to open up, but when I threatened to shoot through the door, and then fired off a couple of shots in the air, she came down to us. She and another sister were in visible shock to have revolutionaries come into their house. I knew the impression they'd have of the likes of us from years of being brainwashed by the regime, but I wasn't going to live up to that image. I wasn't even aggressive with them. But I didn't want to waste valuable time either, so I was firm. I knew from the reports that he had a gun, so when I got hold of him, it was the first thing I asked him about.

'I haven't got a gun.'

'Listen,' I said, 'I don't want to start beating you in front of your family, but I will if you don't tell me where the gun is.'

The sisters joined in the denial just before Adam, who had been going through the house with the other guys, appeared with a fancy new black AK47 that he'd found under the bed. We knew that since the revolution started, this particular gun had been issued to loyalists to use in 'whatever way necessary to stamp out the trouble-makers'. To show the guy what I knew about this and to show him I wouldn't take any more of his nonsense about being innocent, I hit him a smack and started hauling him downstairs. He was a big enough guy, but I had reached a level of confidence in my strength that meant nothing was too much for me. He was trying to pull away all the time, but I was able to hold on to him and reef him forwards in front of me out the door to Adam.

This was my first arrest in Tripoli, the first of many over the next few weeks.

Our new barracks

By chance, I bumped into one of Mahdi's right-hand men, and he informed me that the brigade was about to occupy the Ali Uraith secondary school on Al Wady Street. I knew it well, having lived just around the corner from it when I was a child. In fact, one of the main reasons I was able to be so effective in this phase of the revolution was that I knew most of the city so well, back to front and inside out. The streets, the shops, the laneways, the people – it was all so familiar to me.

Coincidentally, when I reached the school, Mahdi and a convoy of jeeps and then lots of other brigade vehicles were arriving. I pulled up outside the school and entered the grounds. I could see waste ground and a graveyard behind a high wall on the opposite side of the road from the school. Ever conscious about security, I did my own quick sweep of the building, looking through the ground-floor windows to check that the rooms were empty, hugging close to the walls.

When I was satisfied that it was clear, I went over to the car gate. As I was about to shoot out the lock with my rifle, I heard gunfire coming from over the high wall opposite and bullets hitting the gate right beside me. I then felt a burning sensation on the front of my left leg and realised I'd been hit. By this time, I had support from other guys who had come into the car park and started firing back. I took cover and inspected the wound. The material of my combats was sopping wet. I tore off a piece so I could get a better look. It wasn't too bad, a shrapnel wound, I reckoned, so I could ignore it and carry on. Anyway, I didn't want to go to a doctor straight away, as I knew the medics were overwhelmed with much more serious cases. (The piece of shrapnel is still in my leg today. When I visited a doctor about it in Dublin, I was told that as it had been there for so long and hadn't become infected, there was no need to remove it.)

I shot out the lock on the gate, pushed it open and ran for one of the alcoves in the wall outside, seeing that the wall opposite was high enough to prevent the shooter from getting a line of sight on me again. While others kept an eye on the wall opposite, I scoped up the road and fired off a few warning shots. This once-lovely neighbourhood where I had lived as a child was now the frontline in our battle to liberate the city. It felt very strange to shoot into a setting that I knew so well from childhood.

❖

After we had secured the building and were starting to set up, I got a chance to meet with Mahdi for the first time in what seemed like ages – though it was actually only a day. It was great to be able to give him a few big hugs and share some of the emotion of the previous day with him. But he was being pulled in all directions, of course, so we didn't talk for long or discuss plans or anything. We both knew I was now experienced and clued in enough to be able to act alone.

Later on, I went with a few others, including Bashir Mekki and Waleed Fezan, to suss out a hotel next to the school. It was one of the tallest buildings in the area, so I knew its top floors would give us a good tactical vantage point on the surrounding area. Among the crowds that had gathered outside the school, we came across the owner of the hotel and got him to open up for us. I knew from local wisdom that many of the hotel owners were strongly loyal to Gaddafi, but this fella had no choice at this stage other than to let us in.

We got up to the very top apartment and started looking out through the mirrored windows over the graveyard – which was still causing us problems – and beyond. Very calmly and methodically, I started preparing to set up a sniper's nest to clear out the locality.

With one sweep of my arm I cleared off the kitchen table and pulled it over to the window. I placed my rifle on the table in front of me, along with bullets, binoculars, walkie-talkie, and so on. Step by step, I took apart the rifle, cleaned it and reassembled it. Bashir spent the time looking through binoculars, surveying the area and buildings around and up towards Bab al-Azizia, before I joined him.

About an hour after we'd been let into the building – which was just enough time for a rat to pass on our location to Gaddafi troops – the building suddenly shook. We realised it had been hit by something big, an RPG probably. After the initial shock, I jumped back into the centre of the room and shouted out to everyone, 'Get back from the windows!' We gathered our stuff quickly and ran out. On our way down, I could see the light dust of an explosion coming out of a door that was slightly ajar. It was the door of the room immediately beneath the one we had been in. I went over and opened it just enough to see that in fact the missile had struck in the exact position where Bashir and I had been standing up against the window, but one floor above.

Although I had my suspicions about who it was that had passed on our location, I had no way of proving it and no time to hunt down the owner of the hotel. Despite the fact that our new HQ was clearly in an area still full of Gaddafi forces, we stayed put – where else would we want to be but where the action was?

Eventually, we moved to a better building in the Matiga military airport complex that the Americans had built in the 1960s, but it was from the school that we launched our strike the next day against the heart of Gaddafi's power, Bab al-Azizia.

'Fish'

That night, Housam Kafu asked me to help him out on a mission to get medical supplies to a female medic who had turned her villa into a makeshift hospital. It was dark when we got going, and I knew it was going to be very risky given where she was based.

Even at the first checkpoint, a revolutionary one, we had trouble. As we approached it one of the local guys started shouting at us aggressively, 'What's the password? Say the password!'

But for the fact that he recognised the jeep as revolutionary, we might have been caught in a spray of so-called friendly fire. He hailed me over, asked who we were, and told us the password was 'fish'. For the rest of the drive, Kafu sat in the window, half outside the jeep, calling out, 'Allah Akbar … Fish … Allah Akbar!'

When we got to the makeshift medical centre, I let Kafu deal with the medical staff. I was given a cup of tea and was able to have a chat with some of the patients who were on stretchers outside, wishing them well and asking them how they were. I was very moved to hear that one of them was from Egypt and, in the spirit of the Arab Spring, had come all this way to help us rid Libya of its tyrant. I kissed him on the forehead and said a heartfelt thank you. He was barely conscious, so I asked if he'd be OK and was told, 'Just about.'

I loved this kind of work, loved the fact that we could help someone who was in turn helping others. It was very satisfying to be part of this impromptu co-operation that was emerging among the real people of Tripoli as they found ways to help each other and get through this difficult phase of change. Unfortunately, most of my work involved dealing with nasty characters in hostile situations.

Family blessings

After a couple of days, I decided it was time to head into Souk al Juma, my father's part of the city, to see my relatives. Patches of the city I had to go through to get there were still unsecured, so I drove on high alert all the time. I met up with a local fella at one of the checkpoints who suggested driving me in his car, as he knew the guys farther on and it would be safer. I trusted him, so I parked my jeep and took the lift. We took fire a few times on the route he chose, and eventually arrived at a checkpoint by the Radisson Blu hotel, which looked more and more suspect the closer we got to it. The guys on duty were not in the casual clothes we had seen at other spots, but were uniformed – and I didn't recognise the uniform – but it was too late to turn around.

We got as far as the first security guard and the driver said to him, 'Can we go through?'

The security guy shook his head slowly from side to side with a stony expression on his face. I knew I had to do something fast. I leaned across the driver, pressing his hand on the gearstick. 'Well thanks very much,' I said nicely. 'It's grand. Thank you.'

Out of the corner of my mouth, I said to the driver, 'Get out of here.' He responded and reversed quickly, picking up speed as we moved away.

This encounter scared me more than many of the other close shaves I'd had because I hated the thought of going out that way, so wastefully. I got back to my jeep and decided to try the main highway route on my own. I opened up full tilt and made it through to Souk al Juma safely and without incident.

The local checkpoints could see from the state of my vehicle that I was not Gaddafi material, so I got by most of them easily enough. After I told the guards at one checkpoint who I was, word spread down the line that there was a fella by the name of Najjair from the mountains on his way through and, eventually, my cousin, Emad, heard and came to greet me. We gave each other big hugs and celebrated the success. He jumped in and we drove on to my aunt's house.

Funnily enough, the particular part of Souk al Juma where my aunty lives is a very conservative community, and the locals would have had reservations about revolutionaries, but they were not violent people. My own relatives were very conservative too, but they were all delighted to see me now, whatever I stood for. I got a huge, friendly, warm welcome. It was such an amazing feeling to be with family again after such a life-changing period of time. I knew it was a challenging time for them, given their conservative nature and having connections with the old order, and yet here I was, a revolutionary, in their home. But fair play to them, blood is thick and they were very good to me. They knew too that if there was to be a new government in Libya, it was a blessing to have one of their own connected with it.

It was also amazing to be able to wash properly again, and get disinfectant and proper dressings on my wounds. I had a great sleep that night.

❖

I received some letters from home through a friend of the family's and was moved to tears reading the words of encouragement and love from my parents and my sister.

From my mother:

In the name Allah most gracious most merciful, salams and much love to you, my darling first-born son. No matter how much I write, the words would never be able to describe how much pride and love I feel in my heart for you, my beloved son.

I pray every day and ask my lord and creator to protect

and guide you in your honourable task. I ask Him to please, if it be His will, to return you safely to us. You have raised our heads high as I always knew you would.

Tell all of the Revolutionaries we are proud of them. Give Mahdi our best salams and tell him we love him and miss him. God willing, we will all meet soon in Tripoli.

Your father and I love you very, very much. Remember us in your prayers.

Your proud mother.

From my father, translated from Arabic:

In the name of God, the most gracious, the most merciful, and prayers be upon our beloved prophet Mohammed, peace be upon Him.

Warm regards full of love and respect towards you. I ask God to protect you from the evil of the tyrant's forces, you and the men among you, and may He strengthen and support your steps in the advance to liberate Libya and to cleanse it from the evil of the tyrant and his henchmen. And that Tripoli will be liberated by your hands so we will be proud of your actions.

My son, be patient for patience will bring victory, God willing.

May God open the way to your great cause, and we are all very proud of you, my courageous one. Every step and action that you take in the name of God will be counted for you in Heaven, God willing. Our hearts are with you. We will never surrender. We will win, or we will die.

Your father, Mohammed Najjair.

My sister, Zayneb, wrote a poem for me:

'O, you revolutionaries'

Salam Alaikum,
I hope all is well,
Can't wait to hear the stories
You've lived through to tell.
May Allah be with you
In all that you do
We're all smiling proudly
And so happy for you.

Come home to us safely
I shall kiss those hands
That fought for our freedom
And protected our lands.

My five-year-old niece sent me a drawing she had made of me,
bald head, long beard and gun in hand.

❖

I'm not sure when it was exactly, but at some stage during the
height of the fighting in Tripoli, when so many people I knew
were being killed, and so much was yet to be done, and I felt
certain that I was sure to die myself, I rang home.

I was in the jeep parked up in Martyrs' Square, having managed
to get away from everyone for a few moments. My mother
answered and was, of course, delighted to hear from me, to know
that I was alive. I told her how great it was to have reached Tripoli
and be so close to victory. But then I broke down. I told her how

fraught with danger it was and how I thought I might die at any time. Huge sobs and gushes of tears flooded out of me.

'Will you forgive me, Mam, if I do go?' I asked. She started crying herself, and told me how much she loved me and that God loved me and that I was *already* forgiven.

'I am so proud of you, Housam. Be strong! God is great.'

❖

I often felt that God was looking out for me, given all the strange coincidences that had happened to me. One incident involved yet another puncture, this time in Tripoli. There was nowhere to get my wheel repaired at the time, so I took one from an old police jeep we came across. It just happened to fit. Then when I got mine repaired properly, instead of getting rid of the other one, I left it in the back. Some days later in the midst of a battle, I heard this really nice Nalutian guy I knew, Sheikh Atif, going around in some panic asking if anyone knew where he could get a spare wheel for his vehicle – it was an important one, carrying a 14.5-mm gun. I couldn't believe it when I realised his was same type as the police vehicle and, of course, I called to him immediately and told him the good news.

Another instance of what seemed like divine intervention involved gas masks. I was out on a security mission at a huge army warehouse complex that had been completely flattened by NATO. There was military hardware and equipment scattered all over the place, much of it damaged or useless on its own, but I came across some gas masks that I just decided might come in handy at some stage, and threw them in the back of the jeep. I had been thinking more about our defence against chemical weapon attacks or suchlike. A few days later, I got a call from one of the brigade saying that a mass grave had been found in the city and the stench was so bad the guys couldn't deal with it.

'Do you know anywhere we might get better masks?' he asked.

It was unnerving.

'As a matter of fact …'

Assault on Bab al-Azizia

The next morning, 23 August, at about 9 a.m., I headed off again, out onto the war-torn streets. I met Emad at one of the checkpoints and he decided, having helped to with liberate Souk al Juma and set up the local checkpoints, that he wanted to go big and travel with me, even though I warned him it might get dangerous. He didn't have any battle experience or training, but I knew he was clued-in enough to make the right decision himself and be of help to the brigade.

I drove straight back to the base only to discover that the advance on Bab al-Azizia had already started. I also got an update on the death toll – between twenty and thirty of our brigade had been killed since we had arrived in Tripoli. This was not just saddening but also worrying. 'How many more?' I wondered. 'And who?'

As I headed off from the school towards Bab al-Azizia, up the same street where I had fired the warning shots the previous day, I spotted a few old friends of mine from the area. I jumped out of the jeep and greeted them warmly. They were amazed to see me back, completely out of the blue and ten years since my last visit, and this time dressed in combats of all things. We chatted briefly, but I told them I was in work mode and had to push on.

From that point on, the route to the military complex was very dangerous, both from snipers positioned in the surrounding buildings and from mortars coming from the base itself. This was also the area where many of the military from Bab al-Azizia lived and where, we had heard, Gaddafi had organised drug- and alcohol-fuelled parties for all sorts of thugs and then encouraged them to spread fear through the city in whatever ways they wished.

I decided to take advantage of my local knowledge and drove along the smaller side roads to keep away from the openness of the main route. We were hearing all kinds of sporadic gunfire the whole time. Some way on, I spotted a military truck with a rear-mounted 32-mm AA gun – the same calibre as the one that had caused us major trouble back in Camp 27. I felt it was something we couldn't just pass up. A military vehicle like this could prove decisive for us in many situations. It was near one of Gaddafi's notorious orphanages, so I knew the area was dangerous. I was on edge. Myself and Emad got out and were looking over the truck when an old man approached us from a laneway in behind where the truck was parked.

'Come with me, son,' he said. 'I have the batteries. When the Gaddafi troops abandoned it, I removed them and hid them away safely for you.'

I was concerned that this guy could be trying to lead us into a trap, like in some kind of a kid's fairy-tale, but I read him as being sincere and decided to follow. He was true to his word. Even with the batteries, though, the truck presented a problem in that hot-wiring it and driving it would have been beyond me. But, lo and behold, there was Emad, much better with trucks than me, and well able to figure out how to get it up and running. I was very proud of him and of this find.

I led the way back to the barracks in the jeep with our huge spoil of war in train. I beeped the horn as we got close to HQ, and we got loads of cheers and beeps back from the guys. At the barracks, I spent a good while trying to get the gun working and would definitely have taken it back out onto the streets around Bab al-Azazia if I'd succeeded, but it wasn't to be.

To me, these kinds of efforts were not wasted, even though this time it didn't work out. I felt every act in the service of the revolution was important. Mahdi's belief that the person that brings a bottle of water to you on the battlefield is just as important as the highest commander came back to me at times like these. I refocused and made my way back, with one other guy, in the direction of Bab al-Azizia. Meanwhile, unknown to me at the time, Mahdi and Bashir Mekki and others were heading towards the base, accompanied by the France 24 crew.

Because the orphanage we had passed earlier still hadn't been cleared and was a danger, I decided to concentrate on it for the time being and went back to look at it more closely. I first tried opening the big metal gates at the entrance, but they wouldn't budge. There was firing coming from somewhere inside the complex, though it wasn't getting anywhere near us. I lay down on my front and stuck my 9-mm under the gate, spraying a load of bullets through. By chance, Uncle Naji came upon us and he had an RPG, so he blew a hole in the gate for us. Unfortunately, the power of it sent shrapnel flying in all directions and a bit of it hit Naji in the leg. He screamed out and I ran over to him, fearing the worst. He was in a lot of pain for a while, but it turned out to be nothing serious in the end.

I went up and put my head through the hole, conscious that I could be shot but anxious to get in and get this building secured without any more delays. I got through, opened the gate for the others and ran to the wall for cover. SWAT-style, I led the others through a courtyard and into the main building. As we swept through the building, I spotted signs of sniper positions having been suddenly abandoned – binoculars, bullet-proof vests, ammo in heaps under windows.

As we didn't find anyone in the building, we made our way out again. Just as we were leaving, I spotted an older Libyan man running away surrounded by a ring of black mercenaries. I knew immediately that this was significant and opened fire with the AK I had with me in the jeep. A few of the bodyguard-like guys went down and the old guy stopped in panic while the other guys bolted. I got hold of the old man, pulled his dog-tag off him and threw him in the back of the jeep.

We drove him back to the barracks and handed him over to the prison guards. As I was leaving, one of the younger lads called over to me. 'Sheikh Housam,' he said, giving me the rank of leader. 'We have the fella who killed Sheik Eiftaysi in here.'

Sheikh Eiftaysi was the oldest member of our brigade. He had been with us from the start and was a gentleman and an inspiration. How he was killed was particularly distressing. He was one of a squad that was conducting a raid on a group of Gaddafi heads in an apartment. Sheikh Eiftaysi stepped in, shouting out, 'Surrender and you'll be safe! Put your weapons down and we won't shoot.'

The guys in front of him did so, but as Sheikh Eiftaysi entered and dropped his guard, another guy stepped out from behind a wall and opened fire. Sheikh Eiftaysi died instantly. A gunfight ensued, with the squad eventually having to fire an RPG into the room.

When I went to see the prisoner, I saw that he had a bandage around his head from an injury he'd received in that explosion. He was in a bad way generally. I could see by the look of him that he was a hardened criminal, I was guessing a rapist. I was getting to recognise the kind of 'soldier' Gaddafi had resorted to, towards the end to do his evil bidding.

'A man gave you a chance,' I shouted, 'and you went and murdered him.'

I was doing this for Sheikh Eftaysi. I hit the prisoner and flung him back against the wall and walked away. I felt sick just having to deal with such low-lifes.

Bab al-Azizia falls

Emad was still with me in the jeep when I drove back to Bab al-Azizia via a different route, dangerous as hell, full of mercenaries, debris, buildings on fire and non-stop firing all around. I found somewhere relatively safe to park and we tried approaching it on foot. The control towers of the triple-walled compound were raining down everything they had on the streets from their heavy-calibre guns. I moved forwards as tight to the wall as I could when suddenly I heard bullets hitting all around us and saw the guy right in front of me, a young fella I didn't recognise, drop. I realised the area was still way too hot for infantry, so I retreated and got back to the jeep. I decided to get more support, drove back to the barracks and got one of our AA gunners and a few others to join us.

I led them back to the same area. The plan was to drive in tight formation and at high speed – with the 14.5-mm on the back of a Toyota Landcruiser out front, then me in the jeep, and a pick-up at the rear – from the approach road straight onto the roundabout in front of the compound, aiming to get over to the other flank. I knew we could pull off into a side road at any time, so decided it was worth the risk.

With all our firepower turned towards the compound, we made it across without any problems, and reached the route into Bab al-Azizia by which Mahdi and the others had approached earlier.

Mahdi had actually been injured in the ankle while advancing on the compound, and although he was advised by the medics treating him to sit tight, he had gone back to fight and was leading his men as soon as he was bandaged up.

It was there, I found out later, that Bashir Mekki had a team trying to take out the control towers nearest them. They had taken cover in a small laneway off another laneway near the walls of the compound. The control towers were particularly difficult targets because the only opening into them was a very narrow slit.

Nadir Rueben had an RPG on his shoulder. One of the squad loaded it for him and he stepped out into the bigger lane and fired a first shot up at the control tower. It hit the concrete below, but the hit posed no danger to the troops inside. He stepped in, reloaded, stepped out and fired again, but missed. When he stepped out to take a third shot, he was hit by a sniper in the chest and fell back onto the ground. He let the RPG fall to his side and he held his chest, gasping for air. Mekki was watching from the lane and without hesitation, just as he had done for me in Bir al-Ghanim, stepped out into the line of fire to help his friend, except this time he only got as far as taking Rueben by the hand when he too was shot, in the head, and fell back on the ground beside him. The two of them died side by side in the lane and for some time no one could get to them.

By the time I arrived, it was all over. The ambulance had just left and one of the squad, himself still in bits about the tragedy, told me what had happened. Because of the connection I felt with Mekki and the massive respect I'd built up for him, this was the saddest moment in the revolution for me. For a while I was just miserable and could do nothing. I realised that films depicting the damage done to morale when a group of soldiers loses their leader were, indeed, true to life.

❖

By the time we entered Bab al-Azizia, it was dark and the assault itself was over. We only went in out of curiosity, just to see what it was like. This was the most significant military symbol of the Gaddafi regime and now it belonged to the people. Having been bombed repeatedly by NATO since the start of the revolution, and shot up heavily during our offensive, the place was a mess: more rubble and ruins than imposing architecture.

The scene was chaotic, with men milling about in every direction, on foot and in vehicles, some with guns, firing them into the air, some without, just singing and chanting and dancing for joy. I made my way to the clenched-fist statue, the place where Gaddafi gave his famous '*Zenga Zenga*' speech, and with the hundreds of others celebrating, I screamed with joy and emptied a few clips into the air. The noise of all the celebratory gunfire was so strong that it was like a roar of thunder in my ears but I was too exhilarated and pumped full of adrenaline to have worried about it. To me, all sound was cancelled as the feeling of joy overwhelmed everything else.

There was some major looting going on too, of course, and I decided to get out of there and leave them to it. I didn't particularly like the fact that people were looting, but I understood the conditions that had led them to act in that way, so I was not motivated to try to stop it. I had no objection to them taking the possessions of the old regime up to a point, though with big items I would have preferred everything to go to the state.

In some situations, I did lecture a few people on it. 'Stick to the cause!' was my advice. I also used to say, though, 'As long as it's not innocent people's possessions, I'm not going to risk my life trying to protect it ... Opening the taps on the oil for one day will be enough to make up for these small losses. Money is not our problem.'

I imagined revolutionaries being killed just as they were taking their piece of the pie, negating everything they had done, and this was enough to make me avoid it altogether. Was my intention to liberate the country or get myself a luxury car? I actually did hear a story later about guys who were in a car accident after they had looted some place. Two of them died instantly, but the driver, who survived, was found with fancy gold bracelets down the whole length of his arms. He pleaded with the witnesses not to reveal what he had been up to. It all left a bad taste in my mouth.

❖

I headed back to the barracks, my heart still very low, thinking about Mekki and Rueben. I felt the best thing for me now was to get back out on the streets. Of course it was a great feeling to think that Bab al-Azizia had finally been conquered, but it wasn't the end of our problems by any means, and I didn't even stop to reflect on it or on my friends' deaths at the time.

Two massive challenges still faced us, one quite short term and one longer term.

The first, which we sorted in the space of another week or so, was the remaining Gaddafi troops, both mercenary and old guard, who continued to wage a war on us – a war without a front, without a focus, worse in some ways than a head-on battle because we had no idea where or when we might be targeted, and nowhere specific to concentrate our forces.

The second challenge, which took longer, was the flushing out of other lawless elements of the regime, those who were not actively targeting us as such, but who were a danger to the people more generally and a barrier to returning life in the city to relative normality. I was motivated all the time by the thought that this was our city and we needed to reclaim it fully on behalf of peace and on behalf of the people. I didn't feel that I could rest or celebrate or mourn or take a break or just go home until that was achieved.

And of course there was ongoing talk of Gaddafi assembling an army of Saharan and sub-Saharan mercenaries in the south. The bigger objective was always to make sure Libya stayed free.

In a sense, as one of the commanders later said to me, it might have been better if the war – the actual confrontation – had lasted longer. If we hadn't overwhelmed them so easily, the loyalists would have had to come out into the open more and we could have eradicated them fully that way. Instead, the regime crumbled easily and the loyalists had a chance to disperse or try to blend in and we had to flush them out bit by bit.

❖

I had met Matthieu from France 24 again by chance on the beach in Souk al-Jumma. Exhausted and barely able to hold back my tears, I told him about my promise to Atif.

> You know Atif … who lived near Bab al-Azizia. I have to go visit his family. Before he died, he told me that morning, when we left, he said to me, 'If I pass away, sell my car and stuff, and give it to my mother so she can travel and go on the pilgrimage of Hajj.' So, even if I can't find his car … I'll pay the money myself and I'll tell his mother how much of a lion he was in the desert. A lion.

Checkpoints

More depressing news was waiting for me when I finally arrived back at the barracks. Earlier on in the day, a group of our guys who had been on the roof of the school were hit by a mortar and Najmee Mahfood, one of our young recruits, was martyred and two others were seriously injured.

To my surprise, the American journalist Marie Colvin stayed the night in the building with us, having spent the day with Mahdi's platoon. Another reporter, Miles Amoore from *The Sunday Times*, who had travelled with them had been shot at and even got hit in the helmet. I was speaking to Marie for a little while and found her to be very professional and pleasant to deal with. She was certainly one of the bravest women of her generation.

❖

Back out on the streets, I came across a young fella at a checkpoint with a huge SAM-7 ground-to-air missile, the gun that the Americans had warned me about. It was strapped uselessly to his shoulder, without even a trigger, more of a danger to him than to his enemies. I told him I'd have to take it and at first he said no. I could tell he was curious about me, not looking totally Libyan.

'Listen,' I said, 'I've discussed this with NATO. We don't want these in our country because they could get into terrorist hands, do terrible damage and end up giving Libya a bad reputation. And anyway, it's useless to you. It's a heat-seeking missile.'

Eventually he agreed.

I didn't want to have the bare metal of the missile on the bare steel of the back of my jeep, which of course had no seats or floor mats since Atif's death, so I looked around on the ground and found a big rug tapestry portrait of Gaddafi and used that to protect it. I brought it back to the armoury in the school with strict instructions for it to be stored for Mahdi to deal with. In the meantime, I forgot all about the tapestry until later that night when I was stopped at a checkpoint in Souk al Juma and had to explain what the hell I was doing with a picture of Gaddafi in my jeep. The guard looked at me and back at the tapestry.

'It's a long story,' I said. 'Will you throw it out on the street for me before I forget?'

❖

The guys at local checkpoints took a little while to get used to us, at first wanting to exert their power and slow us down – but eventually realising that we were doing a bigger job and were better equipped to do it, so they started letting us through without question. Many even began passing on intelligence and some even apprehended suspects for us.

At one checkpoint, I was told to watch out for two women going around in full Islamic dress. Apparently they were carrying AKs and shooting at revolutionaries who approached them innocently with their guard down. You could be forgiven for becoming sceptical and even paranoid.

On another occasion, for instance, I spotted a girl on the side of the road crying. Without a second thought, I pulled in and jumped out to see what was wrong. Between her sobs, she managed to tell me what had happened. 'I was with a group of girls and all I said was that the revolution might be the best thing for everyone. They turned on me suddenly. Then they shoved me down on the ground and went off with my money.'

'Don't worry about them,' I said. 'Their day is over.' She was a young, good-looking girl and I knew she would be in danger on the lawless night-time streets, so I drove her home and gave her a few quid.

Prisoners of war

One day, I was handed two of Gaddafi's army men to bring in to prison and was told they were father and son. I had them in the back of the jeep and decided to dish out some of my own form of punishment to them.

'Look at the pair of ye,' I said with disgust. 'Like father, like son, I suppose. Well, you're both going to get what you deserve now.'

The father started pleading innocence, 'I swear—'

But I was having none of it. 'I don't want to hear a word out of you, do you hear?'

'But I swear, we were only following—'

I jammed on the brakes and turned around to him and yelled at him. 'Listen, don't make me slap you in front of your son. There were plenty of others who refused to fight against their own people and joined with us instead. You made your choice. Now I don't want to hear another word till we get to the prison, do you hear? And if you make me stop this jeep again you won't even make it to prison.'

'But we didn't realise who you were …'

His attempts at pleading ignorance infuriated me. I flicked open the pouch of my dagger, whipped it out and stuck it angrily into the dash of the jeep. With the knife still there, I turned around and gave him an almighty wallop that threw him sideways up against the other side of the jeep. He was silent for the rest of the journey apart from the odd whimper or moan, which I hoped was from a sense of regret.

❖

People started to recognise our professionalism – the uniforms, the tight teams, the equipment. I was being approached all the time by guys telling me about any number of regime loyalists and crooks and thugs who needed to be picked up.

I started to become more particular about who I would go after. 'I'll go after murderers and rapists, anyone who fought against us and large-scale embezzlers, but otherwise it'll have to wait,' I told them.

We even had 'high-class targets' giving themselves up to us, knowing that at least they'd be treated according to the law rather than face an uncertain fate with less scrupulous outfits who might capture them for money.

I got a strange call at one stage from two characters who could have been a bit dodgy, but since the collapse of the regime they had set up a security office and were starting to help us track down figures from Gaddafi's regime. They tipped me off about the location of a member of the inner circle of Saadi, one of Gaddafi's sons. This man was the first loyalist I'd become involved with who was well turned out. I brought him to Mahdi first, and, of course, Mahdi was pleased to have him in custody. He got two of his top guys to do the interrogation and I stayed on to observe.

Afterwards, I brought him to the jail and instructed the guards to keep him separate and safe. 'He's important to us, so we need him in good shape.'

They were a bit surprised but carried out the order.

❖

Whenever I passed through the barracks, I'd make a point of talking to the prison guards about the latest prisoners to have been brought in, particularly the ones they were having trouble with. One low-life the guards told me about apparently used to go around the morgues stealing dead bodies. His job was then to bring the bodies to faked bomb sites which the Gaddafi propaganda machine would film and photograph. They then used such material to accuse NATO of bombing civilian areas and killing innocent people. In fact, one of our lads saw footage of a fake burial ceremony for the fake victims and spotted a kid in the footage who'd obviously got a whiff of the decayed morgue bodies and ran off holding his nose.

I felt an anger inside me on behalf of all those who had died, which I directed against the low-lifes like this man who had helped take them from us.

At times, this anger demanded action. Through it, I sensed a way to help in interrogations, to make the prisoners afraid quickly, and hopefully get information or confessions, or both, out of them efficiently.

I surprised myself by how naturally it all came to me. Putting me in a room with dodgy characters who had killed or abused innocent people just set me off. Every time I even walked down the corridor of the prison area, I found myself shouting at them aggressively, 'Look down, you scumbags! Don't you dare look at me! If you look at me one more time, you'll regret it.'

And if they did look up, I'd react so forcefully that I'd soon have a roomful of them with their heads bowed down, shaking in fear.

When it came to soldiers in the army who had remained loyal to Gaddafi, I was equally angry. I would often think of the defection of Ali Obeidi, the officer who had left the army in April to join the revolution in Misrata. His words showed to any soldier who cared to think about it that it was clear what they needed to do. 'With words like Obedi's to inform them, how could any soldier justify standing by Gaddafi?' I asked myself.

'You don't have the right to eyeball me,' I'd say to them in Arabic, and quote verses from the Quran at them.

'Look at you,' I'd shout. 'How could you stand by him? How could you obey his orders to kill us? We are Libyan and yet you fired on us and killed us in our own streets. To me, you are no longer Libyan, nor are you Muslim, and your children and your children's children will forever know you as traitors of your country.'

I could see the effect this talk had on them. Some of them would even cry and break down on the spot. I could also tell that the guards saw that I had what it took to soften up the prisoners, especially the mercenaries.

Based on the techniques that I had learned in training, I knew that showing a prisoner even a hint of weakness immediately reduced your chances of getting what you needed from them. I was also of the view that every minute wasted on these low-lifes was time that could have been spent out on the streets saving innocent lives, the lives of people who were decent enough to refuse the Gaddafi dollar and yet suffered for it. My attitude was, *Let's get this over with.*

So, although it was never planned that way, and never a major part of my day, I did get a reputation for being able to make fellas talk, and was sometimes called in as 'the muscle' if I happened to be in the building when an interrogation had stalled.

❖

I was in our larger Matiga prison one day some weeks later and the guards told me that they had discovered that one of the prisoners I had brought in had burned two people alive. I froze on the spot, finding it hard to even comprehend the idea. The guard continued to talk to me about how they couldn't get all the details out of him about the two other guys involved, but my mind was frozen in on one emotion – revenge.

'Show me where he is,' I said, and followed down a long corridor between rooms full of the worst types of evil human beings you can imagine. I hated them. I looked at them and hated that I had to look at them. I shouted at them, told them not to look up.

My shithead prisoner was at the end of the corridor, and I told the guys to bring him out to me rather than me going in. I threw him up against the wall, grabbed him by the head and laid into him.

Once I had him reeling, hardly knowing what had hit him, I got him to the ground. I put my right foot on his face and pressed it sideways against the floor to keep his eyes from me. With my foot still on his face, I stood up calmly and took out my knife. He was straining his eyes to get a look at what I was doing.

As I brought the knife down towards him, I said, 'We can do this the easy way or the hard way – it's up to you. But if you don't co-operate, you better be prepared to be messed up.'

The other guys played along with some comments about how it took them ages to clean up the mess I left the last time.

'You see this knife? I'm going to start here at your ankle joint and cut into the bone … or maybe leave that and start here at the knee instead.'

I poked the knife firmly into his skin at different points, not hurting him but threatening to. He started shaking from fear, like an animal. Suddenly when I got to his eyeball, I saw him panic immediately and his breathing changed to a rapid panting. I placed the edge of the knife right into the corner of his eye with just enough pressure to feel it moving, and next thing he opened up like a dam – all the names and places and orders he had received came gushing out of him. I had to tell him to shut up so the guards could get a pen and paper to take down all the details.

It was the first time I had used the technique, but considering it was so successful from the fear factor alone, I thought it probably wouldn't be the last.

Of course, in a peaceful, civilised setting, it's difficult to describe such violence without feeling and causing unease. I don't like being seen as aggressive or dangerous, and it's tempting to leave out such stories, but I think it's important for people to understand the forces at work in such abnormal situations. In everyday life, I'm as far from aggressive and dangerous as you can get. Even if I have a small row with someone, I feel guilty afterwards and I want to make up immediately. But some of the things I encountered in Libya were so evil that I felt what I now think is a natural and protective urge to stomp out the evil immediately to remove those people from the world.

This prisoner, for instance, had actually set fire to people while they were still alive, and no doubt crying and pleading for mercy. And he felt so little remorse and showed so little understanding of the evil nature of his deeds that not only did he not plead for forgiveness, he wouldn't even give up his accomplices who were still roaming free.

In war, you fight fire with fire and open cans with knives. It's not pretty or flattering, but I can't say that I would do things any differently if I had to start all over again.

Initiative and assertiveness

Late on the first night in Tripoli, I had met Housam Kafu and we'd decided it would be a good idea to check out the port – one of the primary target areas that we'd identified with our strategist, Nadir Rueben. My thinking had been that if I were a mercenary and the tide had turned against my paymaster, I'd want to get out of the country and off the radar as quickly as possible – so the port would be a good place to head.

We'd driven out through the laneways of the Old City to the port area. It was all hours of the morning and we'd had to pass the hotel strip where there were still snipers active, so we'd been on edge. We met up with a few squads of local guys and, in convoy, we'd driven with them through the darkness and silence of the port, the only light being the occasional yellowy neon street lamp, the only sounds our engines and the roll of our wheels.

It was a typical port, with crane towers at regular intervals and mazes of containers. We drove up and down each row, guns at the ready, expecting trouble. I'd pictured a container bursting open suddenly and a gang of mercenaries opening fire on us. In fact, not only were we not attacked, we didn't even come across anyone. I'd seen all the fancy yachts, jet skis, speedboats and so on, but no mercenaries.

More importantly, though, we did find what I thought was the AA gun that had caused us so many problems hours before in Martyrs' Square, the one that Amur had taken out. The local guys took it off to see if they could get it working again and put it to better use.

Some days after my brief visit that night, the brigade returned to the port officially to do a clear out, with news crews in tow, Marie Colvin among them. We drove out to the end of the port road and worked our way back boat by boat, wharf by wharf.

As we were about to board the very first ship, we realised there were some other people inside. I called to Mahdi to stay back and jumped on with two or three lads. With the narrow corridors, small doors and tight spaces, it all felt very movie-like, but we had a job to do and did it seriously. I burst through the first door and started shouting, 'Give yourself up and you'll be saved.'

The first man I came across was visibly shocked to see me. I grabbed him quickly and turned him face forward in front of me as a shield. 'How many people are on the boat?' I demanded quietly in his ear as we moved through the ship. 'Where are they? If they're going to shoot, you'll be first to go, so you better co-operate.'

He was shitting it and blubbering out answers as quickly as he could. 'There's only a few, downstairs, but we haven't done anything wrong, I swear.'

And he spoke the truth. As it turned out, they were just a bunch of Egyptian boatmen who'd been stuck in the port since we arrived in the city, but that's what such security operations were all about – making sure everything was normal.

Again I saw the expensive yachts, this time in the daylight, and I saw in the gigantic containers with all the fancy gear and equipment for the wealthy. There was certainly a lot of money floating around in Tripoli, I concluded again.

When I saw an enormous lever-crane after our job was done, I got this mad idea and decided to go through with it. I grabbed a monarchy flag out of my jeep, climbed to the top of the crane with two other guys and we hung it there, maybe 100 metres up. Of course, I did it for the photo opportunity, but it wasn't about me – it was about the flag and letting people know who was in charge.

It was also on that visit that I first noticed the gas tankers in the bay, though they didn't worry me at the time, with the port being closed and under our control. After a while, people started going back to work and the port became a little busier. I received a phone call from the guys at port security, saying how they were overwhelmed by having to search every person and vehicle coming into the area. They hoped there was something I could do to help.

I arranged a meeting with the manager of the port and as well as discussing the security issues, I asked him about the gas tankers. It occurred to me that they could be accidentally hit by celebratory fire (workers at the port had told me they could hear the bullets clanging off containers regularly) or they might be the target of a loyalist attack.

I rang our explosives guy with the details of what the ships were carrying and he gave me the blast radius. I asked the manager if they had an anchorage area at least two kilometres outside the port where these ships could be taken to. He hummed and hawed a little at first, but in the end it was done, and I felt I had made the city a safer place.

❖

In the second week after the liberation of Tripoli, I woke up with the Foreign Ministry on my mind – another of the target buildings we had identified in our planning. I knew a lot of important information would be kept in that building, in records of one form or another. Abdu and our friend Mohamed Sakali came with me. This was the start of us three working together as a team around the city. The other two weren't used to gunfire and when I drove towards the sound rather than away from it, they thought I was a little mad. Abdu joked about wanting to get out.

'This is how I roll, guys,' I said. 'You better get used to it.'

Later while on patrol, I disarmed a bunch of thugs in a car and gave a weapon each from their stash to Abdu and Mohammed. 'Look after them,' I said.

When I got to the Foreign Ministry, I was glad I had decided to check it out – the only protection on the building was a young local fella on the door. I got a team together to secure the place properly, and we worked our way through the building methodically. I came across someone from the ministry, who tried to pull rank on me, saying he had a letter from Abdelhakim Belhaj, the leader of the Tripoli Council, giving him authority over the offices.

'Hang on a second,' I said. 'See that letter? Let's put that aside for the moment. It's not that I don't accept what's in it, but I am now head of security in Tripoli, and what I am saying to you is that you are not allowed in these offices until I say so.'

It's true that Falolo was Head of Special Forces, but when we arrived in Tripoli, he was absent for a while and I was appointed to the position.

I could tell this guy was a product of the old regime and I was concerned that he might be destroying records in an effort to cover things up. The letter he had may have been legitimate, but I knew I'd be able to override it, and so I did. I was aware that people like Belhaj and Mahdi were being pulled in all directions and pressed by guys like this to let them handle certain aspects of the state while things were still so uncertain. I had time to check up on his claims, so I forced him to wait and do things my way.

Tip-offs and arrests

I spent a lot of my time during the first few weeks in Tripoli responding to information about loyalists, and gathering them up into our prisons. It was not a task I particularly wanted to do – although I did enjoy seeing these people brought to justice – but it was necessary to bring stability and peace to Tripoli.

On one occasion, my friend from the Martyrs' Square building who had lent me the pair of socks rang to tell me about an awful character who had ratted out loads of people to the regime since the start of the unrest in Tripoli. Of course, it's more than likely true that those he had informed on would have been picked up, imprisoned and either tortured or killed.

When I saw this man, I was taken aback by how old he was. Then, as we were taking him with us, some locals got involved and started accusing us of being disrespectful to our elders. The situation got seriously out of hand, with more and more shouting and aggression. I was forced to jump up on the bonnet of the jeep to try and bring some calm to the situation.

'Listen to me, you lot!' I shouted. 'We're here doing a job and you've got to let us get on with it. If I have to stop like this every time we're arresting someone and listen to everyone's opinions, the city will never get back to normal.'

Some of the crowd went along with me in this, but others still gave out about the fact that this was an old man. I just had to ignore them, and I threw him into the back of the jeep. He was there with a nasty smirk on his face, thinking he was going to get away with it – he was obviously used to being untouchable – but I was having none of it and brought him with me, just like all the others.

❖

However, I wasn't indiscriminate about bringing people in. I knew what they faced and did my best to be fair.

Salah Baruni asked me to do some work out in his neighbourhood of Ghot Shaal. He knew there were loyalists still hiding there and, in particular, one guy he really wanted to have picked up and arrested – one of the most active local loyalists in the backlash against and disappearance of demonstrators in Tripoli, a really nasty piece of work.

I got a group together and set up a security cordon around the two buildings that Salah identified as being owned by the guy. We went through the first house where he was staying but only found evidence, not the man. Clearly, he was a highly trained, active sniper and henchman. We took out all the military gear and paperwork, and headed for the second premises.

After some planning and organising, we entered the building in full assault mode. The house apparently lodged many mercenaries, and I knew it could be trouble, but I took up the lead, scaling the wall without a sound, and running for the house. As I burst through the front door, AK up at eye level and ready to fire, I began shouting at the top of my voice telling everyone to get down.

I got to one of them very quickly and grabbed hold of him by the scruff of the neck. 'Is there anyone else in the building? Where are the others?'

He became hysterical, squealing, 'I don't know. I don't know.'

I dropped him, realising that he wasn't a danger, and left him for the guys coming in behind to deal with.

While Salah and two other guys were grabbing others, I pushed on through the house and into the courtyard at the back, where I found another fella trying to escape via a flat roof. I pointed my rifle at him and shouted that if he didn't come down I would shoot. He did the wise thing and made his way back to me with his hands up, and I dragged him into the house.

We rounded them all up and put them into the main sitting room together; there were about fifteen of them. I had one of the lads go out to the jeep and fetch a bunch of plastic cable tie clips and a magazine of blanks that I had set aside especially for such a situation. We restrained them all and I then asked each of them where they were from. There were some from Nigeria, Niger and Chad, and about eight from Mali. I took the Malians, who couldn't speak English, out into the courtyard and kept the rest, who did speak English, inside. The lads were bringing me passports and phones and paperwork and I started laying it on the Nigerians. 'I know you're mercenaries and I want to know the full story.'

I recognised one fella from some footage I'd seen on one of the phones that showed him mixing with Gaddafi troops and chanting anti-revolutionary slogans. I grabbed him and dragged him out with me into another room. I had his ties removed and put the magazine of blanks into the AK. I started by giving him a boot up against the wall and shouted at him to tell me about the video. He was playing all innocent, so I just raised the stakes and told him I wouldn't hesitate to kill him.

'To me you are nothing. My brothers are dead because of people like you. Do you think I'd care about killing you?' He still wasn't talking, so I said, 'Right, that's it, you're going down now.'

I kicked him again up against the wall and cocked the AK, pointed it at him and emptied three or four blanks at him. He was shaking like a leaf and checking himself to see if he'd been hit. I held him tight up against the wall and covered his mouth, gesturing at him to shut up. He was mumbling but I managed to keep him quiet and get another one of my guys to take over. 'Don't let him make a sound, OK?' I whispered.

Cool as a breeze, I went back into the other room and found the rest of them on the floor, petrified and shaking, thinking I had just shot a man.

One of them started crying and talking about how he had been brought here by his master, and by the way he was talking I became convinced he was innocent. When I realised there were also three African women in the house, it occurred to me that these weren't all mercenaries. No mercenary would bring his wife with him, of course. I also knew that we didn't have a legal system in place that would sort this out any time soon, so I decided to take extra care to make sure to separate the innocent from the guilty, and not just wholesale them to jail because they weren't Libyan.

To get to the bottom of it all, I went outside where a bit of a crowd had gathered and I asked for someone who was a neighbour to help out. One person came forward and I briefed him on what I wanted him to do. He came in and I asked him if there was anyone in the room whom he recognised before the revolution. He pointed out a panel beater who worked in the local garage, a painter and another lad he knew, all of whom I then took to be innocent people being used as a kind of cover, and I let them be, along with the women and – once I'd verified their claims using photographs – their partners.

The rest of them were arrested and taken to prison. That little bit of extra effort saved a few innocent people from who knows how many months of prison, or worse. The guys I was with were impressed too, and possibly influenced by it. Libyans tend to lump a lot of immigrants into one second-class category and it would be unusual for them to see someone going to an effort to treat them civilly.

Outside, we found a brand-new Toyota Camry in the garage and I told Salah to take it for his official vehicle. On our way home, racing each other through the night-time streets, I caught a glimpse of what looked like a body on the side of the road. I jammed on the brakes and flashed the headlights at Salah to stop. I walked over to the lifeless form only to discover when I turned him round that it was a guy passed out drunk, reeking of alcohol and mumbling nonsense. I was furious at him, not so much for drinking, which is his problem, but for getting so drunk at a time when others were still suffering so much and being killed out on the streets. I just found it very irresponsible of him to be in this state. I put cuffs on him and threw him into the back of my jeep and got one of my guys to keep an eye on him.

Soon the cool night air rushing in through the shot-out windows sobered him up a bit, and he started asking what was going on and where I was taking him. I told him he was going to spend the night in a cell and he started giving me lip. As we neared a busy checkpoint on the coast road, the rear door opened and the drunkard bailed, running for the guys manning the checkpoint. I had to run after him and explain to the suspicious checkpoint guards what was going on.

'He's a drunk and I'm bringing him in for the night to teach him a lesson,' I said, and it was enough.

❖

One night after I'd dropped Emad off at his place, a local guy came up to me and told me he knew of a house in Souk al Juma that had been rented by a group of foreigners who had only arrived at the start of Ramadan. I was immediately as suspicious as he was, and got him into the jeep with me to show me where the house was. I rang around and got a few of my guys to follow us, and a few of the local guys to meet us there.

We barged in with the usual formation and started sweeping through the house. I found three men in the first room I came to and trained the gun on them until the guys with me had them searched. There were two older men, retired military types, and one younger, in his thirties – a huge lump of a fella, exactly what I picture when I think of Russian military. I went over to him first.

'Do you speak English?'

'A little,' he said in a thick accent and deep voice.

With a tone of taking no shit I said, 'What are you doing here?'

'I'm here working for oil business.'

One of my guys had dug up their papers and there was this homemade business card among them with the name of some oil refinery on it. I studied it directly in front of him and then gave him the hardest slap I could. I bent down and drilled my stare deep into his eyes and spat out, 'What the hell are you doing here?'

'Oil,' he said again, and I slapped him again.

'What oil are you talking about? You only got here in July.'

The local guys were looking on, concerned, and one of them even whispered something about how I shouldn't be hitting him. I told him politely to stay quiet, and my men did the same.

'These shits [*smack*],' I told him, 'snuck into our country to murder our brothers and sisters for Gaddafi dollars, and they will talk and tell us what we need to know or they will pay with their lives.'

The mercenary was petrified at this stage, looking up at me.

'Look down!' I shouted at him. 'Now, what are you doing here?' I demanded again.

'Me no speak good English—'

Smack!

He raised his hands.

'Put your hands down and keep your eyes down and don't you dare lift them up again.' I went to hit him and he raised a hand again. 'I said down. One more time, if you raise your hands or your eyes one more time, I'll pull the trigger on this gun.'

I shoved the gun into his cheekbone. It gave him a little gash and a bit of blood started to run down his face, and while I asked again, I wiped his face with his shirtsleeve. 'Now, talk to me. What is your business here?'

One of the guys came in with a laptop he'd found and while I was waiting for it to start up I went to the two older men and asked them what their story was. They let on they didn't understand what was happening, and even though it felt very different because of their age, I knew I couldn't give them the impression that I would be soft on them.

I looked at the computer and found a file that wouldn't open. 'Open this file for me,' I said to the younger guy. 'Open it.' He looked confused, so I shouted at him, 'Don't waste my time!'

He opened the file and there it was, the evidence and proof of what I had guessed as soon as I saw them: a map of Libya, and in more detail of Tripoli and Misrata, marked with what were clearly trajectories and targets, including Tajura and Souk al Juma, and writing on the side showing serial numbers and types of missiles, including Scud.

I faced them and said with controlled anger, 'You … are … screwed. You will never see the Ukraine again. The day you entered this country to do Gaddafi's dirty work will haunt you for the rest of your lives.'

As well as saying stuff in English, I screamed at them in Arabic for the benefit of the guys there.

We brought them into the barracks and I handed the laptop over to our second-in-command, Hashim Bishir. Very pleased with the scale of this haul, he gave me a big hug and thanked me for the great work. For my own peace of mind, I kept their passports and the microchips, which I'd found cushioned in small silica bags.

A few days later, I asked about them at the prison and was told the story of how one of the guys bringing them their food happened to touch off the grill of the window and noticed that it was loose. When he examined it more closely, he found that the surround was just crumbled chalk that had been scraped out and put back in. Obviously aware that they were doomed, they had been planning to run, and were clearly highly trained in methods of escape.

A few weeks later in the Nadi Diplomacy, the diplomatic area of the capital, state-of-the-art Russian surface-to-surface missiles were found in their firing positions. I recalled Gaddafi's speech saying that if one revolutionary steps inside Tripoli, he would burn the whole city to the ground. On the news report that day, I smiled when the reporter stated, 'It is not known why these missiles were never fired.'

Abu Salim sleeper cell

The run-down district of Abu Salim near Bab al-Azizia was a problem spot for us, and for me. Based on the stories I had heard, I began to see Abu Salim as having been run down on purpose by Gaddafi so that he could use it as a recruiting ground. It was all high-rise tower blocks of overcrowded apartments. The place was rife with drugs and now also with snipers. When we took control of the city, many of the undesirables who had something to fear from us – murderers, rapists, mercenaries and so on – sought refuge in Abu Salim, and many of them were armed.

Unlike other districts where we could eventually concentrate on policing and arresting individuals as required, Abu Salim remained a battleground for some time. But the type of warfare it required was not to my liking, and not the Tripoli Brigade's specialty. My heart sighed with relief when I saw that the Misrata brigades were well able for it. Their experience earlier in the year in the intense urban battles of their own city proved to be invaluable to us in sorting out this area.

Many guys were being shot at by snipers from Abu Salim, with shots to the head, neck and chest the most common. I steered clear of the area and left it to the experts. The thought of going out like that freaked me out too much. Instead, I concentrated on other parts of the city, equally life-threatening but in a more open and confrontational way.

However, when I received reports of a bunch of snipers operating from a building on the edge of Abu Salim, I decided to take on the job myself. I literally had a little talk with myself when I'd decided to head there. 'Now, Housam, this is a different battleground, this is urban warfare. You have to pace yourself and control yourself. Don't be taking your time out in the open or trying to cover too much ground.'

I got together a team of guys in a few vehicles and we drove to a specific high-rise building. We knew the precise floor and room the loyalists were in, but I set up guys at various points outside and up through the building. We burst into the room and screamed them into a state of shock. We got the six of them together and my first impression was that they were good-for-nothing scumbags, filthy and unhealthy. To my mind, one of them, with long hair and in an AC Milan jersey, was clearly the ringleader. They had sniper rifles, AKs and a belt-fed machine gun for cover, which told me they were a proper military unit.

I was determined to get as much out of them as possible, so we brought them back to the barracks and had them put into a cell on their own.

One of the guards came up to me as I was approaching, saying, 'Sorry, sir, you can't go in there with a weapon.'

I told him, politely, to step aside.

There was one guy slouched in the corner of the room, whining about some kind of pain or other.

'It's not going to work with me,' I said, and hoisted him upright against the wall. It wasn't that I wanted to make him suffer for the hell of it, but that I knew this was the perfect way to show the others, particularly the guy in the AC Milan jersey, that I wasn't going to waste my time.

I went over and stood over the leader guy and when he looked up at me and said something or other, I hit him an almighty slap and yelled at him, 'Don't you dare look at me! Keep your eyes down! There's no point denying it. I know that you're in the military. I know you're a unit. Tell me everything I need to know!'

He tried to deny it.

I took hold of his arm and twisted it and I could see the trigger calluses on his index finger.

One of the guards called me out and introduced me to a guy who knew who this man was. 'He used to play football in our neighbourhood,' he informed me, 'and he used to tell everyone on the football field, "If anyone is not with Gaddafi, I'll personally see to it that they live out the rest of their lives in misery."'

I went back to the guy and said, 'You know you're screwed now because I know you're a murderer.'

Meanwhile, another witness to this fella's atrocities was brought to my attention. He was a local youngster, about seventeen years old, whose head was in bandages. I took him with me by the hand into the room and asked him if he recognised anyone. He picked out the same guy and said to me, 'Him and his sister bashed me to bits just before you all arrived in Tripoli. I've been in hospital ever since.'

I kneed the loyalist in the gut, causing him to pull back and drop his head. I then turned to the young fella and said, 'Right, he's yours if you want to get your own back on him.'

'No, I can't do it,' he said.

'That's grand, son. Don't worry. He's just a scumbag, anyhow. And now he is where he belongs and he'll get what he deserves.'

Female sniper

On another day in Abu Salim, I had my cousin Abdu and Mohamed Sakali with me, and we met up with a few others. We stopped at a particular building to secure the entrance while a platoon of Misrata guys were clearing it floor by floor.

I spotted someone at the back of the building struggling to get up off the ground, seemingly having jumped from a first-floor balcony above. I made my way over and discovered a girl, dressed in a loose robe and headscarf. She was short and very frail looking. I knew that we had already lifted large numbers of female snipers, so I didn't relax my guard in any way. She couldn't move easily anyway as she had hurt her hip.

I grabbed her and shouted, 'What have you done? What were you doing up there?'

'Nothing, I swear. Help me, I am in a lot of pain.'

I could see she was, so I brought her in the jeep to Matiga hospital and then just went about my business. As per our procedures, a day or two later, I got a call from the hospital explaining that she was a criminal all right, so I had to go and bring her from the hospital to the prison. When I got to the hospital, I heard from one of our guys who had interviewed her that she had confessed, without any pressure, to sixteen murders. I couldn't believe it. Sixteen innocent people! I was seething about it and wanted to give her a piece of my mind immediately.

On my way to see her, I came across a whole load of journalists in the corridor outside her room, apparently waiting to talk to her.

I hit the roof, knowing that she could say anything she liked about us and it would be impossible to repair the damage. I first gave out shit to the hospital staff who had made this situation possible, and then I walked up the corridor to sort it out myself. I was approached by a female journalist and her cameraman, but

I pushed past her and announced loudly to everyone, 'Excuse me. Can you all please leave the hospital right this minute? There will be nobody doing an interview with this girl. You're wasting your time here and blocking up the corridor.'

The same female journalist spoke up, claiming they had a right to talk to the prisoner.

'Excuse me. I say who has a right to talk to her and who doesn't. This is a security issue and I am head of security here.'

She had a smug smirk on her face as she replied, 'Well, there's already someone else getting an interview with her, so you're a little too late anyhow.'

At this, I pushed through the lot of them and stormed down the corridor saying to my guys behind me to get everyone out and close off the corridor. I opened the door of the room and found another female reporter and a male cameraman talking to the sniper. They got a shock when I burst in.

'You and you, out,' I said, pointing to each of them in turn.

The woman was very nice about it so I didn't lose my temper with her and instead just showed her I meant business. They left the room.

'Not another soul into this room,' I told the guy at the door.

So finally I got to confront this killer. There was me, her and the guy who had done the preliminary interview and got the confession. I was busting with rage. The faces of all the guys who I had seen killed by snipers filled my mind, especially Bashir Mekki and Nadir Rueben. I vented the huge anger I felt about it at her.

'Why did you do this? How could you do it?' I yelled.

'They put me in the window. I had no choice.'

'Why didn't you miss on purpose? Why did you kill so many of my brothers, who were coming here just to help the likes of you, to free you from this mess?'

She looked like a wounded animal. She was only nineteen, but nineteen years of poverty in Abu Salim made her look much older.

'I had no choice. They said kill or be killed. And at night, they would rape me and during the day I had to stay in the window and shoot anyone who passed who looked like a rebel.'

Her answers disarmed me. Something clicked in my mind and I suddenly became very calm. I realised all the anger I had inside me was not for her, but was only for Gaddafi and his circle. As much as this girl was guilty of terrible wrongs, she was herself a victim of this twisted regime. I could feel myself pull back all that anger and keep it for another time.

I told her to stand up, that I was taking her away. She started to get a little hysterical. 'Where am I going? Where am I going? I'm not going with you.'

The other guy told her to calm down. 'Don't worry! We're bringing you home.'

'Am I going to my mamma?' she asked in a pathetic voice.

I looked at the other guy and he winked. 'Yeah, yeah, we're going to take you home to your mamma.'

'All I want is to go home to my mamma. I don't want to be hurt any more.'

When I got to the jail, I saw truckloads of mercenaries who had just arrived and were waiting in the yard: rows upon rows of black Africans. I knew that some of them were probably innocent but had been picked up in the sweep because of the colour of their skin and because not all of the guys were thorough when they made their arrests. I knew it would be a long time before the innocent among them would get someone to listen to their stories and realise the mistakes. This made me sad, of course, but I knew I couldn't do everything, and that it was an inevitable consequence of our need to protect our citizens and get the country back to peace.

I registered the girl, explaining that I couldn't bring her home yet. She was upset but I told her she would be OK, that nothing bad would happen to her here, and she was calm. As I brought her to the cell, I wouldn't say I felt for her but I did feel saddened by the whole mess she was in.

Pulling back the cell door, I was surprised to see the room full of female snipers. I also noticed looks of recognition passing between her and two girls, who then welcomed her in and gave her a hug. I thought it was a little suspicious at the time, but reckoned they knew her from Abu Salim, and that all the snipers probably knew each other. I said across the room to her, 'Right, I'm going now.'

'Will you be back to take me home?'

'No,' I said. 'You're here with your friends now and the people here will deal with your case.' Then I left.

Some weeks later, I spotted her face in a photograph on Facebook, in uniform, head held high, and I realised that she had in fact been in the proper sniper regiments and an officer to boot.

❖

One day, I was called out to visit the gigantic complex that was the foreign security service. Many of the buildings across the site had been destroyed by NATO bombing, but one that was still standing was a prison. I met up with Mahdi there for the first time in a while and noticed that he had a new bodyguard unit, armed with four Fabrique Nationale F2000 weapons (part of a Gaddafi cache that I had previously uncovered) and so really looking the part.

One of Mahdi's inner circle, Shukre Mashaiykh – the guy we met in a villa in the mountains on our way over from Tunis – had been put in charge of this building and we were there to be briefed on various aspects of its security. Afterwards, we were taken on a tour of the place. When the first cell was opened up to be shown to us, I got quite a shock. It was like I was looking into death – pure blackness; walls, ceiling, door, floor all painted with a thick tarry black paint. Inside was a black female prisoner, one of Gaddafi's infamous female unit. Mahdi took the time to ask her if she was being treated well and even listened to the usual plea of innocence before moving on.

There were about eight or nine of these cells occupied, and some of the women I saw were just sobbing away in the corner of their cells. After a while, Mahdi left, but out of curiosity I decided to stay and look around some more. I slid back the door windows and looked inside, trying to imagine how desperate the place must have been for the innocent Libyans thrown in there by Gaddafi without explanation, never mind a trial or hope of release.

Police car convoy

I was one of the few people in the brigade who had a letter from the head of the Tripoli Council giving me the authority to impound property that was suspected of belonging to the state. 'Anything that belongs to the government returns to the government,' I used to say.

One day in late September, I got a call from Amur, the brave lion from the 14.5-mm in Martyrs' Square, to say there was an official government hangar on the airport road where there were a lot of cars in storage. 'The security on the cars is serious, so even the thieves haven't been able to get them started, but they're attracting a lot of attention. Will you get hold of your car fella and help us get them moved before they are destroyed?'

Within a few days of arriving in Tripoli, I realised that some of the work was going to involve reappropriating vehicles and through my cousin I got in touch with a guy who was good at starting cars. I soon developed a reputation as the go-to guy for vehicles.

When I got there, I saw four or five huge government coaches, forty-odd police cars, and loads of fancy new and vintage cars, including two of Gaddafi's green Cadillac limos with the standing platforms at the back for bodyguards. There were ten spy cars – the ones that had all the secret technology in secret compartments. They even had cameras hidden in the headrests.

In their efforts to siphon off petrol, the thieves who had got in before us had smashed the rear quarter glass of every car in the place. They had tried to get at car stereos and then, when they got frustrated, they had just scratched and broken what they could. On the bulletproof cars, you could see where the thieves had let off shots but still hadn't gained access.

The police cars gave us an idea. We got a bunch of guys together and organised one car each. I told them we were going to drive in convoy through the city heading for the barracks, but making sure the city of Tripoli saw us. As I had done on so many other occasions by this stage, I gave them strict instructions about the convoy – do not speed, do not overtake, stay safely behind the car in front of you, and so on. 'No problem, sir. Yes, Sheik Housam.' All was in order.

We got out on the main road and – *crash*! Two or three of them immediately ended up in a pile-up. Young fellas are impossible to command in revolutionary forces when there is no threat of punishment to hold over them, so I wasn't surprised. And it didn't take from the fact that this was the first time in a long time that the people of Tripoli had seen signs of a friendly police force on the streets – a great symbol of security and peace at last.

Trouble with other revolutionaries

Not all our problems were caused by the enemy. The manager of Palm City, a new five-star, beachfront resort on the outskirts of Tripoli, rang me one day. He informed me that some revolutionaries from Bayda (a town in the extreme east of the country) had 'secured' the place but had continued to stay put and were causing trouble, living it up in fancy accommodation, demanding room service and even having parties where they were shooting off guns.

I knew the resort was being used by diplomats and even some UN officials, and that this situation was not good for the image of a new Libya. I also knew there were a lot of very high-end regime vehicles in the car park there that I had been tasked by Belhaj to confiscate on behalf of the council.

I drove out with two other guys to meet the manager and find out how many cars there were. I didn't bring back-up with me because I considered it to be just a recon trip.

I asked the manager to bring me to the Baydans and discovered that he was actually afraid for his life because they had threatened to shoot him if he complained. Instead, I got him to show me where the vehicles were and we headed to the underground car park. The security guy on the gate tried to stop us going in, but I ignored him and, sure enough, we found a large number of very expensive cars, including a silver Austin Martin DB9, Escalades, Audi Q7s – in total about a million euro-worth of vehicles.

The security guy must have called it in, because very soon a bunch of hefty lads came roaring down after me shouting, 'Who the hell are you?'

I told them I had the authority to seize the vehicles, but realised immediately these guys were scumbags and were going to be trouble.

'Well, I don't know who you are,' one of them said, 'and I don't care about your letter. You're nothing to me. Now give me your gun and keys.'

'Listen,' I said, 'if you even touch my gun or my car, there's going to be war here.'

He went over to the car and managed to get the keys out before I pulled him away. He managed to grab hold of me and held on while trying to go for my gun. I heard my guys moving in and the Baydan guys' guns cocking. The red alert alarm went off in my head. I had managed to get my pistol out of its holster and held it just out his reach, but didn't cock it on purpose, as I knew already the kind of trouble that that could bring. He was a big fella and with about ten of them and only three of us I knew not to push things too far, so after a few minutes of wrestling with me, I eventually gave him the pistol.

One of the older guys, with some authority but clearly not complete control, arrived on the scene and I turned on him.

'You're letting this shit go on? You're letting this bunch push us around even though we're revolutionaries and you've fought alongside us? You don't even have control over them, do you? It's a damn disgrace.'

It remained a stand-off because I refused to leave without my stuff and they refused to return the pistol. But one of the lads had rung in for reinforcements and soon three of our brand-new Toyota Landcruisers arrived with fully armed men in uniform jumping out and addressing me, 'Are you OK, Sheik Housam? What's going on?'

Now I had a dozen or more armed men backing me up and, of course, the tide turned. They gave me back my papers and keys and started apologising.

'What about my pistol?' I said. 'Or have you sold it on already?'

I gave them as much shit as I could about their looting and betrayal of the revolution, until the guy who had the pistol came back with it and we left. I decided not to push it with the vehicles. I could have, but the situation was too volatile at that time so I just reported that the cars were there to be picked up, and left it at that.

I followed up on it afterwards and persuaded our commanders to put pressure on the Baydan commanders to get its soldiers under control, and as far as I know that was eventually done.

❖

About this time, towards the end of September, I got a phone call about a stockpile of missiles hidden in an abandoned factory. When I went to investigate, the guy at the security hut showed me to the warehouse where the missiles were stored. We pulled back the tarpaulin to examine them and saw about thirty-five or forty missiles encased in secure metal containers. I could see the emblem of the Italian factory where they had been made. At the base of each, there were two turbines. I got hold of our missiles expert and sent him some pictures over the phone. He recognised them as being extremely dangerous torpedoes.

I went back to the brigade and organised a HGV and a few support vehicles to head out with me. We couldn't get the HGV in over the sandbanks at the entrance. The unit next door was being protected by Zintani and I went over to tell them that we needed to get through to get access to the torpedoes. They said some shit about having orders not to let them be moved.

'Orders from who?' I asked.

'From Osama Al-Juwali.'

'Well, you better get on to someone, because I have an order to remove them to the airbase in Matiga, and we're here to do it. My order is from Abdelhakim Belhaj, the head of the Tripoli Council, and last I checked we were in Tripoli.'

I went back to the others and we started trying to organise a digger to remove the sandbanks. A Zintani arrived over and handed me a phone. It was Al-Juwali. I told him about my connection with Mahdi and that I'd met him in the mountains – but he wasn't at all friendly. He asked me coldly what I was doing out there, and I explained the plan.

'No, you can't do that,' he snapped. 'It would be dangerous to have all those weapons in one place in Tripoli. We are dealing with it.'

I knew well that he was spouting lies, but I rang our missiles guy again about it and he took Al-Juwali's number. They must have had a bit of an explosive conversation themselves because when I spoke to our guy again, he was a bit shaken and told me I should get out of there, because the situation was beyond our control and dangerous.

Al-Juwali rang me again, and I worked out how I could get at him.

'You do realise these are torpedoes, not missiles, don't you?' I asked.

'Yeah.'

'Well, as far as I remember from geography, there is no sea in Zintan.'

'Are you trying to be smart with me?' he shouted. 'I'm a military officer and don't have to put up with this from a civilian.'

'I'll tell you what,' I replied, 'you take the torpedoes if you want them so badly. I'll just report this back to the commanders and you can deal with them.'

A few days later, I asked the missiles guy about it and he told me they actually offered to give them in afterwards. It turned out that each one was worth about US$150,000.

I would have more serious trouble with Zitani later on, but I was well able for them by that stage.

Returning to Nalut and leaving Libya

Just for a break, one day in early October, when things were starting to calm down, I decided to take Abdu, Khayri (Abdu's cousin) and Sakali to see Nalut. I hadn't been back since the day we moved the brigade to Zawiya. So much had happened to me since then, all of which had started in Nalut, and I felt I wanted to go back and see the place. It wasn't much to look at as a town, apart from the amazing Berber beehive-like mud dwellings, but it had a special place in my heart now.

On the journey, as we passed all the landmarks of our advance on Tripoli – Camp 27, the overpass there, Zawiya, through the desert, and all the way to the mountains – I was able to go back over the whole story with my passengers. The interesting thing was being able to see the scars of battle from the other direction – the bullet holes from the Gaddafi ammo meant for us.

Despite the marks of war everywhere, the sense of this being a liberated countryside was much more important to me. The last time I had driven on this road, I was heading to Tripoli, to a city still in the hands of a tyrant who felt entitled to kill people who displeased him. Now it was just another road through the country. It was free.

On the winding road up the gorge to Nalut, the one that I knew so well from our assaults on the towns below, we stopped at a local spring behind a mosque. We performed *Wudu* and it was so refreshing I repeated it a good few times. The ravine and spring were very beautiful, and some nice stone work had been started around them to make it more attractive, but it had been left unfinished. My immediate response was how even a spot like this could be turned into a fantastic tourist attraction after the country was back on its feet.

When we arrived at the old barracks, I found it very emotional to walk around again and think of all the guys I had got to know there who were no longer with us. Our fridge was still in the room and it brought a smile to my face and gave me another excuse to tell the lads more stories. I showed them where my name was written on the wall amongst others, in large Arabic script, in a goodbye message:

Allah Akbar. God is great. To God we pray, and His messenger and all the faithful. Greetings from the revolutionaries of Kennedy Street and Omar Mukhtar Street, the Old City, and Ghotsha'al: Ahmed Falolo, Abdullah 'Gahwee' [coffee], Mohammed Jamhur, Hisham Breki, Isa Burqeeq, Salah Baruni, Housam Najjair, Housam Kafu, Tayari, Waleed Fezan, Zeyad Kafu [Housam's younger brother], Sami Bin Musa, and the martyr, if God wills, Aymen Krema.

❖

Back in Tripoli, I realised how totally exhausted I was from all the work I'd been doing and the crazy hours I'd been putting in. While I was giving the cause everything I had for no return, I could see others slacking off completely, giving less and less and taking more. This wasn't good for my morale, but ultimately I left because I just wanted to get away from the rats. Dealing with rapists, murderers, mercenaries and suchlike all the time was starting to get to me. As I told a journalist friend later, my problems weren't the after-effects of war but having to deal with all the visible horrors of the regime.

I also missed home. I'd had very intermittent access to Facebook and had only been able to phone home occasionally. I missed my family and friends more and more and I became excited about the idea of seeing everyone again. If I'm honest, I was also excited about the idea of that special homecoming for their 'hero' (as they were calling me!). I couldn't wait to tell them all my stories and let them share more in the excitement and the joy of Libya being free.

The day I made up my mind to leave, I called in to Mahdi in the hotel where the brigade commanders stayed. I was trying to move around the city unarmed, so when I went in without going through my usual routine of taking the magazine out of my pistol, cocking the gun to make sure it was empty and handing it over to the security guy, he said to me, 'What, no gun today, Housam?'

'No, I'm trying to leave it at home,' I said, 'to set an example.'

'I don't think that's a good idea, Housam. I'll tell you why. Some of the guys you have been arresting have been getting back out on the streets. So you need to have something to protect yourself.'

Poor Tripoli, I thought to myself, but I wasn't about to start worrying about possible assassination attempts. I'd heard it all already on Facebook and from friends, and we did hear about guys in our brigade going missing and being murdered, but I always said, both during and after the revolution, 'What's written for me is written for me. I'm not going to live in fear of retribution.'

Mahdi was exhausted, completely wrecked like myself from all the work he'd been doing to secure the city and help with the transition. His health had become a concern in the midst of the Tripoli clean-up – mainly because he was a diabetic, but hadn't had access to insulin since he went into the mountains. It had been months since his last injection in fact, but, strangely, he hadn't had any repercussions during the war. He told me at one stage that he hadn't felt so good in a long time and that he thought he had been given respite by God for the sake of the liberation. But in Tripoli, he'd started to feel some symptoms again and eventually agreed to see a doctor.

I had got to know the director of the Matiga hospital, so I went to him and explained that I wanted to get a doctor to see Mahdi but had to clear him first from a security perspective. The director introduced me to a Palestinian medic, and I immediately felt some comfort at his being from Palestine. Nonetheless, I sat in as he went about his work, not checking each vial or anything that strictly, but just keeping an eye on things.

In his hotel room, I told Mahdi I had to go home for a few weeks for a break. He gave me one of his looks. He and I communicated very well with one another after all this time, and he didn't need to say anything for me to know that he understood but was also keen to have me back as soon as possible. The country was starting to get back on its feet and some sense of normality was beginning to return to the streets, but Mahdi and I knew that as long as Gaddafi was still loose in Libya, it wasn't over.

❖

I decided to take my military vest with me to show everyone back home, but I had to put everything else away carefully. You might think that taking apart, cleaning, greasing and storing my rifle and AK would have been an ending for me, but because Gaddafi was still at large, I knew there was a good chance I'd be taking them out again in a few weeks when I got back, maybe for a final showdown with the old regime.

❖

Finally, in the first week of October, I left Libya for Ireland. With my friends Mohamed Sakali and Khairi Farara, I headed west along the coast for Tunisia, this time for the Ras Ajdir crossing. When we got to the border, there was a massive tailback but luckily I had a document from the council that gave me a kind of diplomatic privilege to be able to get through checkpoints without delay. On the Tunisian side, the guard decided to go through my stuff and even though I had been extra careful when I'd packed to get rid of anything that might cause me problems, I had missed one bullet in a fold of the military vest – a 5.6-mm for a F2000, a rare piece of ammunition. This was bad news. I had heard stories of guys being held for days just because the Tunisian border guards felt like flexing their muscles. This guy held the bullet on display in his hand and looked at me. I knew immediately that he wanted money, but I was having none of it.

'Look, you know well what the story is,' I said. 'You know we were in Libya and we are after being in the revolution. You're not getting any money out of me.'

'Well, this is Tunisia, not Libya. We've held some of you guys here for days for this kind of thing.'

'I won't be held here, I can tell you.'

He did his best to get some cash out of me, but I stood my ground and he eventually let us go through, probably because he could see that I wasn't the kind that was going to roll over easily.

Beyond the border, in the town of Ben Gardane, there was a group of what looked like local low-life gangsters standing around in dirty vests, with baseball bats, chains, bottles and massive chips on their shoulders, very obviously looking for trouble. By the looks of them, I guessed they were after revolutionaries, planning to get revenge for the loss of their patron, Gaddafi. They were hassling different people, verbally and physically.

I got out of the car to see how things lay and walked into the thick of it. I could see a car parked up ahead in the middle of the road with the old green Libyan reg – evidence of the cross-border nature of whatever corruption was at the heart of this place. I could hear them shouting things at people, like, 'Who do you think you are? Get the hell out of here. There's no place for you in Tunisia.' While other drivers in the queue were trying to hide anything they had that connected them with the revolution, I was wearing my revolutionary vest with the brigade symbol on it and wasn't about to hide it. I started talking to one of them.

'What's the story? Libya is free, is it?' he said sarcastically.

'Yeah, Libya is free. Do you not get it yet? I'm just back from Tripoli and Tripoli is now in the hands of revolutionaries. It's over. What do you think you are doing here?'

He didn't want to confront me on his own and walked off, sniggering, to get help from his pals. What really bothered me was that there were two armed Tunisian policemen outside a hut looking on at all this crap and tolerating it.

While I was walking back to our car, I could see some others turning around and going back in the other direction, and I saw a truck driver who had been hassled by the thugs just flooring it and speeding off down the road. I told Khairi to do the same if things got hairy once we'd made it close enough to the open laneway, even though I could see the loyalists stoning some cars up ahead that had got past them.

We drove up and another one of the gangsters stopped us. Khairi lowered the window and played it very cool, looking straight ahead as he chatted casually to the guy, nodding and smiling, and he even threw in a muttered Gaddafi slogan.

Next thing, the guy I had confronted came running over towards us to identify me and the guy starting asking us for our passports aggressively. When one of them went to open the back door on Sakali, I rasped to Khairi, 'Floor it!' He took off at whiplash speed.

We sped through the town and were talking about what a close shave the border had been when up ahead at the first junction we saw a bunch of Tunisian police, guns out and pointed at us. I figured we were OK, considering they were official. When we had stopped, they started shouting their heads off at us to get out of the car, really overdoing it. This was worrying. They yelled at us to get out of the car and forced us at gunpoint down on our knees with our hands behind our heads. They started looking through the car when the thugs we'd just escaped from drove up, screeching to a stop.

One of them came straight up to Khairi and clobbered him, and while Khairi retaliated another started towards me, but I got up off my knees before he could get at me.

The cop shouted at me to get back down, but I refused, saying, 'If you think I'm going to stay on my knees and let that thug hit me, you're sorely wrong. I'd rather risk getting shot.'

The cops eventually pulled the thugs away from us and got the situation under control, but not before Khairi had been hit some more, though it took a few of them to overwhelm him.

The cops brought us into the station and went through all our stuff. When I had identified the most senior-ranking guy and got the opportunity, I said quietly to him, 'Listen, you should know that I have dual nationality. I'm a European, so just be careful what you think you're going to do next, yeah?'

He responded very rapidly, leaving the room, talking to a few people and suddenly the whole atmosphere changed and we were let off on our way.

We drove on into Tunis. I said goodbye to the lads at the airport and was on my way back to Ireland.

❖

Back home in Ireland, I was mostly just glad to be able to see my family and friends again and to be able to tell my story, unlike so many others who never got the chance.

Being back in Ireland made everything I had experienced in Libya very surreal … and at the same time, paradoxically, more 'real' than my old life. Suddenly things that had excited me before the revolution just didn't interest me any more. I joked that the only thing that would give me a rush now would be a skydive or something life-risking like that. Of course, just being alive was a blessing, and I felt grateful to have a chance to start a new life, hopefully a better one than before. I knew I had a lot to look forward to, but there were still many loose ends to tidy up before I could move on.

Part V

In the Name of Justice

October–November 2011

War, a necessary evil

War is a terrible thing. Lawlessness, brutality, rape and killing are suddenly all around you. Guns and tanks are on the streets where there were people and cars. The sounds of gunfire and explosions fill the air instead of birdsong and conversation. Innocent people die or are injured or maimed. Lives are ruined, children are left without parents, families are devastated and communities are ripped apart. Countryside, cities, towns, homes and businesses are destroyed.

And yet even though it's that terrible, there is sadly always a war going on somewhere in the world, and most countries I know have had a few of their own in the course of history. Sometimes it's civil war, which is perhaps the worst of all.

If we're realistic about it, war seems to be a necessary evil in the world, and at certain times an almost inevitable step on a road to what we hope becomes a better situation.

Just as Ireland went through its War of Independence and Civil

War in the early twentieth century, so Libya is going through its own troubled times, and just as thousands of young Irish men and women, including a few of my own ancestors, were swept up in Ireland's struggle for freedom from British rule, in 2011 I found myself playing a part in Libya's upheaval against an oppressive regime.

Being half-Irish, I found myself very aware of such oppression and the long-term damage it does to a country. Being a Muslim growing up in Ireland, I became very sensitive to the experiences of minorities and underdogs, of innocent people being bullied or abused. Being half-Libyan and having spent many happy years in the country at different times in my life, I found my love for Libya drew me into its difficulties and convinced me to join the people's fight to free themselves from the tyranny and violence of Muammar Gaddafi's rule.

I never wanted it to happen. I never wanted to fight, and I was very close to not going at all, but I went – and once it was over, I thought it was important that the world should understand why regular people like me left the safety and comforts of home to risk and give our lives for this cause. Why we felt the burden of responsibility fell on our shoulders. I also thought people should see that though the revolution was full of ups and downs, joys and frustrations, successes and failures, overall, from my view of it at ground level, it was driven by something simple and pure and universal – a desire for freedom and justice.

Justice for Gaddafi

By 20 October, I had been back in Ireland for a few weeks. That morning, a friend rang me up and told me to switch on the news. Gaddafi had been captured. Within a few hours, I had arranged flights and was preparing to go to the airport. I wanted to celebrate with the people and be there for the actual end of the revolution.

I don't regret not being there when he was finally captured. I know I wouldn't have been able to lay a hand on him – I would have feared touching him because of the black magic he dealt in. One thing found in his possession when they got him was a curse of some sort written on a piece of paper and wrapped in tape. Apparently, the guy who pulled him out of the drainpipe was captured by loyalists, tortured and died from his wounds.

They say Gaddafi dealt in all kinds of dark arts, and when you think about how many assassination attempts he survived, you do wonder. In one famous instance, the assassins had even tested the grenades they were using beforehand, setting off a few to make sure they worked, but when it came to the one that they managed to land at Gaddafi's feet while he was on a walkabout … it didn't go off.

Anyway, I don't believe I would have made it that far in the search. I think I would have been killed early on if I had gone to Sirte. The dangers were multiplied on that campaign, as so many untrained and inexperienced guys, now finally free to leave Tripoli and join in the revolution, decided to take their chances in liberating Bani Waleed and Sirte. Some went just in the hope of getting their hands on valuables by looting, others wanted to play a part in the search for Gaddafi. Whatever their motivation, they dropped like flies under loyalist fire, some even from friendly fire.

I think I would have been so desperate to protect these new volunteers that I would have been caught out, probably by one of our own bullets.

❖

The brigade knew I was coming back, but I intentionally didn't give them any details so that I could avoid the fuss of a welcome party. I wanted to be just another Libyan now, arriving in the country at this historic time, and to experience things as a normal person. I didn't want to be this different guy, getting special treatment and loads of attention.

My main concern when I landed was getting a 'clean' taxi driver – one who was not being paid to kidnap unsuspecting revolutionaries and hand them over to loyalist cells. I was relieved that the guy I got was on our side and very happy with Gadaffi's capture.

I made my way to Martyrs' Square and found the place absolutely jammed from one side to the other with people from all over Libya gathered to celebrate the end of Gaddafi. I was delighted to finally be able to join in celebrations. My cousin Abdu and I went up on top of one of the buildings and looked out over this great scene of pure joy and happiness, and it was enough to bring the whole thing together for me. I was beaming with pride for the small part I had played in bringing this about: the people now free to take to the streets without fear of being arrested, attacked, shot at or killed.

Gaddafi was killed in the course of being captured. This didn't surprise me in the least. It wasn't the justice a judicial system would have used, but it was justice in the way a man might kill another man for raping his wife or daughter or murdering his son. Raw, wild, ancient justice. It snapped the whole thing closed with a proper bang, freeing us from having to wait about to see him put on show in a court.

Looking around the new Libya, I thought about all the money he had spent building up the name of his regime, his brand, the green flag – his 'rag of shame' – and all that nonsense, with publicity campaigns and official parties and pompous speeches. And then in a few months – zip, it was all gone. The green flags and green shutters and his slogans were nowhere to be seen. We had eradicated it all, all the symbols at least, in a flash, as if the whole thing had been nothing more than a nightmare.

We were awake again.

Ahmed 'Hamad' Ramadan, the black box of the regime

Inevitably, while in Libya for the months that followed, I became involved in security matters again.

Hamad Ramadan was the man who my late uncle, Mukhtar, had chauffered. Because of his honesty and distaste for their shady dealings, Mukhtar had been slowly moved aside, before taking early retirement and getting out completely.

One day in late October, I got a call to help set up protection for Ramadan at the Matiga hospital. It was feared that Gaddafi might try to have him killed because of all he knew. He had been brought in by a group of Tripoli fighters, who reported that as they were closing in on him, he had tried to commit suicide by shooting himself, but the bullet only grazed the back of his head and so he needed urgent medical attention.

After I had done a round of all the checkpoints on the main roads and entrances, and checked all the perimeter and surrounding landscape for weak spots, I actually got a chance to go in and have a look at him for myself. What was amazing was that I was with Abdu, who was, of course, Mukhtar's son.

I noticed first of all that Ramadan was lying on the new Libyan flag, the monarchy flag. He was old and frail and mumbling a good bit.

I leaned over and said clearly to him, 'You see, you wanted to end your life, but Allah wants you to be punished in this life more before He gets his hands on you in the next. You're a low-life! A murderer! You disgust me!'

Abdu went next and towered over him, this man who had been untouchable up to now, and said, gun in hand, 'Do you remember me? Do you remember?'

Ramadan muttered something.

'I'm Mukhtar Farrara's son.'

'Ah.'

'Yeah. And tell me, was it all worth it? All the shit that you did and the misery you inflicted on Libya? Putting my father into early retirement because of your corrupt ways? Was it worth it?'

I had another go at him, but then one of the commanders came in and told us to stop for fear Ramadan would burst a blood vessel and we'd lose all the intel. I wasn't thinking along those lines, I was so worked up by what I knew of this guy, but of course he was considered one of the black boxes of the Gaddafi regime. I stood back and watched some of our top guys interview him instead.

'Are you OK, Hamad?' the interrogator asked in a brilliant blend of friendliness and a patronising tone. 'Now, Hamad, do you see all these young fellas around? Don't worry about them, they're all like your sons, they're here to protect you so that Gaddafi doesn't get his hands on you. Do you hear? You're safe here, OK?'

'OK, yes.'

'You know the revolution is good for you, Hamad, and everything is going to be all right now.'

'Yes. Allah Akbar, Allah Akbar.'

'Now, we're not going to ask you about the money or the weapon stashes or anything like that for now, Hamad. But we do want to know about the demonstrators. We know that there are up to 50,000 young men who have disappeared from their homes and we just want to know where they are. Don't worry about telling us what you did or didn't do. We're not here to get at you. We just want to find where all those young men are because their time is running out.'

'Oh, I was just an adviser, just an adviser.'

'Come on, Hamad, we know you were the Grand Vizier. We know a lot about you.'

I don't think they got a lot of information out of him on that occasion, maybe because he was very affected by medication, but eventually they managed to get lots of information, including the location of three forty-foot buried containers filled with cash, secured with fingerprint technology.

For me, though, the great thing was to witness the day my cousin was able to stand over the man who had hurt his father and watch that man shake with fear.

I heard that Ramadan was the only man who Gaddafi never raised his voice to; he was the only man to survive all Gaddafi's purges of his closest circles. There were even rumours that they could have been brothers from an illicit relationship – I actually told him how much he looked like Gaddafi.

Preventing civil war

There were ongoing problems with a rogue portion of the Zintani Brigade, and on a couple of occasions local confrontations with them could have got out of hand and spread. Of course, there were well-intentioned and hard-working revolutionaries from all corners of Libya, including from Zintan and Bayda. The bad eggs were the exceptions rather than the rule.

Towards the end of November, I got a phone call about a

group of Zintani who were causing problems in the affluent district of Hay al Andalus, not heeding any laws and disrupting the local community. The Zintani were doing so much looting that there were stories and jokes going around that they had even taken the elephant from the zoo in Tripoli and brought it to Zintan. But more seriously, it was starting to feel like organised crime to me.

I really felt bad for all the great Zintani people I knew whose reputations were being tarnished by the selfish acts of a few trouble-makers. I for one refused to paint them all with the same brush, as I knew there were so many who would object to these criminal actions just as much as I did.

In Hay al Andalus, they had tried to take over a particular villa and the locals had blocked them and wanted to get rid of them once and for all from the neighbourhood. They went to the trouble of issuing the Zintani with a demand, but it was ignored. The Zintani had then brought an AA gun into the town centre and shot up the local council building.

I arrived on the scene and was brought up to the council building where a meeting between the two sides was taking place.

There were about twenty or thirty old men sitting around a huge table having heated arguments about various demands and counter-demands. Some were shouting and I heard one yelling, 'If there has to be war, then let there be war.'

I spotted two Zintani at the far side of the table, sitting there looking very smug, one of them in a flash suit with his hair gelled to glistening. 'That's organised crime right there,' I said to myself.

As I sat down at the table, brigade guys came up to me whispering stuff in my ear about who was who, about what had been said in the room, and about developments on the street. I could see one of the Zintani guys looking over at me and trying to figure out who this non-Libyan-looking fella was.

Eventually things got so heated outside that I had to head out there and try to figure out what to do.

It was too late for talking. The Zintani had gone ahead and taken over the resort, and bunches of locals had gathered and called in their brothers and cousins to help get them out. Among the crowds of men gathering outside, I could see that some were armed and some were drunk, but others were just so fed up with the unruly Zintani that they were ready to take action. The terrible prospect of revolutionaries fighting revolutionaries was there in front of me.

I had a pistol on me, the HK USP .45, a top-of-the-range sidearm that I had picked up at the start of the revolution. But I realised it wasn't the right weapon for what was brewing – in a bringing-a-knife-to-a-gunfight way. I had hoped to avoid it, but decided it was time to take out an automatic again. It was a difficult thing for me to do after the two months that had elapsed since I had left for Ireland, but I felt I had no choice. I jumped in the jeep and sped back to my room. The trouble was, my AK was actually starting to rust and the action on it had become too rough, so I had to clean it up there and then. I took the extra caution too of putting on a bulletproof vest.

Meanwhile, I called my cousin to get a few of our lads together and meet me in Hay al Andalus. The main road was impassable by this time, so I had to go around by a side road to get to the action, about a kilometre short of the resort.

A convoy had formed and they were ready to advance. There were even some of our brigade in amongst the locals. My heart was low as I got out and started trying to figure out what the best course of action would be. What I wanted to do was calm the situation, but I knew just giving orders wouldn't work. These men were not under my control. The thought of lifting my gun to aim at Zintani was terrible. No matter what they had done, these were not Gaddafi soldiers or mercenaries or even civilian loyalists. They were revolutionaries who I had fought with and fought for. I felt it would be murder to kill someone from Zintan, plain and simple.

I could hear a few of the locals making the decision to advance and then starting to move off. A guy came up to me and said, 'Housam, we know you from the France 24 documentary, you can show us what to do.'

This gave me that same old feeling of being responsible for lives, but it also gave me a vague idea of how I might handle this. Thinking on my feet, I said to my guys, 'OK, lads, let's go!'

And as I locked and loaded, they did the same and followed me up to the very front. When we go there, I turned around to address as many of those gathered as I could, making sure to keep my voice positive and encouraging, as if I was going along with this all the way, but actually desperately trying to find a way to divert them.

'Hey,' I said, clutching at straws, 'we need to cover our backs here. You, will you take a platoon back that way and make sure we don't have more Zintani coming in as reinforcements?'

Meanwhile, there were vehicles that I couldn't control getting out ahead, their engines revving, and then I heard them firing off 14.5-mms. And as sure as night follows day, moments later, for the first time in weeks (though it felt much longer) – after all our fight for freedom, all the work done to bring about peace, all the arrests, all the law enforcement, all the seizing of weapons – I heard the *pshoooo, pshoooo, pshoooo* of bullets whizzing by me.

I ran for cover and began shouting out directions to the people around me as I moved, training them on the spot. I got them in off the road and we started running from alcove to alcove up the road, putting myself in the line of fire as little as possible. At one point, a teenager ran up beside me and, obviously recognising me as someone worth impressing, he fired off his machine gun. I grabbed the gun off him in a rage.

'You eejit,' I said, 'our men are up there. *Our* men.'

I can't be sure that he didn't kill someone, and it reinforced my sense of how wrong this whole situation was.

A few of the Zintani had been caught at this stage, and I witnessed how a lack of training can really lead to problems when one guy shouted out to everyone, 'Hey look, lads, I've got one!'

Of course, the mob immediately made for the Zintani, and next thing the guy holding him had to shout at everyone to stay back.

I grabbed this eejit by the collar and said, 'After you calling them over, now you want them to stop?'

I just about managed to get the Zintani into the ambulance before things got completely out of hand. A local lad appeared, limping with some kind of injury to his leg, probably just a twist, not a bullet wound, and he got put into the ambulance. I immediately smelled trouble, picturing the crowds farther back looking into the ambulance as it headed back to the city and seeing one of their own guys inside, injured, and jumping to the wrong conclusions … and becoming eager for retribution. I instructed the driver to go out another way to avoid the crowd.

Thankfully, calls started coming through from various leaders and the message from them started circulating that this would be deemed an act of civil war and that anyone involved in killing would be considered to have murdered. Eventually, things calmed down and it was just drunks and stoned guys calling everyone to attack. 'Don't go back. Go forward!' they were shouting.

'Go home!' I told them.

Justice in democracy?

Back in late October, NATO chief Anders Fogh Rasmussen had come to Libya to mark the formal end of the mission. After 26,000 flights, 10,000 air strikes, 6,000 targets destroyed, 600 tanks or armoured vehicles destroyed and 400 artillery/rocket launchers destroyed, NATO was pulling out of Libya, despite requests from our National Transitional Council for their continued involvement.

I was asked to represent the revolutionaries' views to him and so, in my smartest civilian clothes, glasses and all, I went to meet him at the Rixos Hotel. My attitude was that I wasn't really there to listen to him but to get some key points across, so I made sure I did most of the talking.

To summarise what had been achieved, I pointed out that the prisons were now emptied of the innocent young men and women who had been branded by the regime as subversives but were in fact representative of a great, independent-minded future for Libya. I said I wanted him to know that we were thankful for all the effort that NATO had put into helping achieve this – and I added that I hoped they wouldn't just turn away now and leave us to pick up all the pieces alone. I told him we wanted to establish a democracy, but not necessarily one modelled on Western principles. I said we should be able to keep our Islamic values, and that we now had a unique opportunity to avoid the mistakes other countries had made by creating a new Libyan form of democracy. We had a blank page, I said, and what we needed most from the West was investment.

Such was our optimism at that stage.

❖

After the unity experienced during the revolution itself, it is easy to understand how frustrating it has been for many of us to see Libya struggle with the challenge of setting up a new state system. As a remedy for the trauma caused by years of dictatorship, the country has been tossed a kind of off-the-shelf Democratic Kit for Societies in Transition. The hope was that this would bring peace, safety and normality to the people of Libya – but has it?

First, we were told to establish a multi-party system. This has merely brought to the fore the extreme ideological differences that exist in Libya and given some of them more of a platform than their actual scope in Libyan society would warrant.

Second, we had to establish a free media. This step has led to wealthy and wily businessmen being able to communicate what is effectively propaganda serving their interests and often at the expense of social solidarity.

Third, we had to hold transparent and fair elections. This made those ideological differences even more pronounced and polarised the people even further. It also produced false results because of step two.

Fourth, we had to draft a constitution. This will cast in stone the skewed version of reality that the falsely elected 'representatives' need to establish in order to protect their interests.

The democratic magic spell isn't working for many north African countries post-Arab Spring. Contrary to the idea that it would all develop naturally, the fact is that each step has actually undermined stability and reinforced division. For many, another Arab Winter is coming before we've even had a chance to enjoy a Summer.

What is the solution? For my answer, I turn to all the guys I knew who died fighting in the revolution. I ask them, 'What were you fighting for?' And I know there are nearly as many answers as there were martyrs, but common to them all, I believe, was a wish first and foremost for an end to violence and to give people a chance to get on with their lives without fear of being attacked. In other words, we must be united in peace. How can that be achieved?

Maybe what we need is a creative rather than the dogmatic understanding of democracy. What is democracy? Is it only instruments – elections, free media, and so on – regardless of the society? Or is it about the values of society of equality, tolerance and respect? We need to establish these values in our society through education and example.

Otherwise, 'democracy lite' may be what we get, and it could end up as nothing more than a tool for another form of oppression.

❖

On 5 May 2013, the Libyan General National Congress passed the controversial political isolation law, making it the day Libya was effectively fully liberated. Now anyone who worked in the higher echelons of Gaddafi's regime since its creation in 1969 is barred from working in the new free Libyan government for ten years. For me, this is the making of Libya. Without it, we were slipping back to the corruption that characterised the old regime.

Justice for Adil

The trial of Adil's killer took place in May 2012, while I was working on this book. I took time out to to attend every day of the two-week trial, as did all his friends and family, not surprisingly, considering how much of a hole we all still feel in our lives since his murder.

Although the accused was thoroughly defended by his barrister, all the evidence pointed to his guilt. The CCTV footage showed clearly that the encounter was pure chance, that Adil didn't know this guy at all, and vice versa. We knew most of what had happened already, but we finally found out why – put simply, Adil had been in the wrong place at the wrong time with the wrong people, and because of the colour of his skin, they had mistaken him for someone else. Just because those people hadn't bothered to try to tell one black man from another, Adil was murdered. It was the opposite of justice, the opposite of meaningful, the opposite of good.

We heard details of the murder, and this disturbed me more than anything I'd seen in Libya. Adil had been stabbed fifty-eight times in the head, neck and arms with a machete and a knife. His face had been smashed in an effort to make him unidentifiable. Not even Gaddafi was abused this much by those in the hysterical mob who captured him and forced him into a drain like a rat, the label he had often given us.

In court, through the course of the trial, I found myself keeping a close eye on the accused, watching his reactions and trying to catch some sign that he would suffer as a result of a conviction. I didn't detect any remorse or sadness or doubt in his expressions. One of the newspapers referred to him as 'one of Ireland's most evil criminals' and a 'twisted thug': that's what I saw too. I took a few notes in the courtroom:

When it was explained that there was no blood found on any of the items, the killer raised his hands as if to say … *See, nothing to do with me* … all the time smirking and sniggering …

It infuriated me. I felt compelled, like I had so many times in Libya, to do something about it, to get a word or gesture in on behalf of the victim, to do what Adil would ask me to do if he could. Without him in the court to witness his murderer being put on trial, to point the finger and show the world, I felt legal justice wasn't enough.

During the trial, I had sat at the back of the courtroom, but on the final day, the day of judgment and sentencing, I took up a position as close as I could get to the stand. I spent a lot of time looking at the murderer, scoping him, trying to catch his eye. He complained to the gardaí that I was intimidating him and I was asked to stop.

As the victim impact statements were given by Geraldine and Karen, Adil's partner, he sat there making scoffing sounds and dismissive gestures. I was getting more and more worked up.

What Geraldine said was so true:

> The murder of our beautiful son Adil Essalhi has left us all totally devastated. When Adil was so viciously murdered we could not understand how this could happen to him. He was a loveable son and father, with a very bright future ahead of him. Adil's murder has mentally and psychologically left our family destroyed. Our family will never be the same again. When Adil was killed part of all of us went with him. There is a very big wound left in all of us, which will never heal … But Adil will always be in our hearts and memories forever. He had such a big heart of gold, we will always love him and not a day will go by we won't think of him. He will live in our hearts forever.

Karen spoke about their daughter, who has the same name as my daughter:

Layla, his eldest girl, was sixteen months old when she lost her daddy and like every girl she was a proper little daddy's girl. Adil never had her out of his arms, so it's only obvious that when her daddy wasn't around, there were questions no parent wants to answer or even talk about. Layla always asked about her daddy, 'Where is he? When will he be back?' and 'Why did he leave?'

When the life sentence was handed down, after we all expressed the huge sense of relief, I stood up and caught Adil's murderer's eye. I said quietly in his direction, 'You're finished.'

He looked back at me, saying, 'Wha?'

I shouted out to him, letting my anger break out, and thinking I might even be able to get at him and get in a dig, even if it meant doing a few days in a cell. 'You're finished. You got what you deserve and you'll never smell fresh air again.'

As one of the newspapers put it:

After the verdict, the now twice-convicted killer turned and taunted Mr Essalhi's friends and family. With hate-filled eyes, [he] shouted, 'I guarantee you, I'll be back.'

I shouted back at him and, of course, the judge started banging his gavel and declaring me to be in contempt of court. The guards grabbed me immediately and while they were leading me through into the back, I shouted out in desperation, 'Don't ever let him out! Don't ever let him out!'

❖

They put me into the same holding cell that Adil's murderer had been in before court each day. I sat there in silence looking around

– four walls, a cot-bed, cold hard edges on everything, a bit of meaningless graffiti here and there.

I thought of Libya and all the people like Adil's murderer who I had put away in cells like this the previous summer.

I wished Adil's murderer could be put in one of the blackened cells I'd seen in the foreign security services complex, but I was satisfied at the thought that this would be pretty much the limit of this scumbag's life for the foreseeable future.

Ireland had made this thug, but at least Ireland had also finally put him away for us.

In Arabic, 'Adil' means justice.

Epilogue

Syria

There was no final goodbye for the Lions of the Tripoli Revolutionary Brigade. We went our separate ways bit by bit, coming across one another only once in a while and never for more than a quick chat.

There are people out there now who speak of the Tripoli Revolutionary Brigade as if they knew it well or even represented it in some way, which is not always the truth. Because so many new recruits joined up in the final push towards Tripoli – guys who weren't in Benghazi or in the Nafusa Mountains, guys who didn't put in the weeks of training or fight in the early battles – there are many misguided, ill-informed and even malicious stories circulating about what we were doing. These recruits do not necessarily speak for the values and principles that people like me and those who died fought for. In this way, the original simple idea of that we stood for – justice – could become tarnished, but

I hope this book goes some way towards preventing that from happening.

Proof that justice was all that most of us were ever interested in comes from what happened to us next.

As the Arab Spring took hold in Syria, the Assad regime's brutal response – exactly what Gaddafi would have done in Libya if it hadn't been for NATO and the international intervention – made us all uneasy. Seeing the people there suffering and revolutionaries struggling without international support, we decided it was up to us to help.

A few of us, including Mahdi, went to Syria early in the summer of 2012 and set up a new brigade, the Liwaa al-Umma (Banner of the Nation), to take on this new and even more terrible enemy. The savagery of the war in Syria, the sectarianism on display, and the complications of international agendas at play were so extreme that, as Mahdi said to the *Irish Times* journalist Mary Fitzgerald, it felt like we had just been playing games in Libya.

After a nerve-racking, middle-of-the-night border crossing under olive trees from Turkey, we managed to get into Syria and embarked on a multifaceted mission which involved covert training of local revolutionaries, complicated arms deals, distributing humanitarian aid and witnessing some of the most horrendous effects of unhindered violence imaginable.

But that's another story for another time – a soldier for another summer.

Dublin, 17 February 2013

Acknowledgements

Alhamdulilah (thanks be to God) first and foremost for without Your guidance and blessing I never would have survived to tell this story and may Your grace and mercy shine on the souls of the martyrs who are not with us today.

I would like to express my love and gratitude to Kerry Gallagher and her lovely family Ernie, Cathleen and Cian, Yvonne Townsend, Abdullah Husain, Muneer and Waleed Owen, Ashraf Tumzeen, Moe Buhidma, Nader ElGadi, Mohammed Kattaf and the many people who saw me through this book; to all those who provided support, encouraged me, talked things over, read the many drafts, offered comments and put up with me during the many stressful times.

A special thanks to Ciara Doorley and Breda Purdue for enabling me to publish this book and of course thanks to Ciara Considine, Joanna Smyth, Edel Coffey and all the Hachette Ireland team for assisting in the editing, proofreading, publicity and design. Thanks also to Claire Rourke.

Thanks to my agent Peter O'Connell at TruLit Agency – without you this book would never have found its way to the right publisher. Thank you for your undying patience with my new author's inquisitive nature.

I would like to thank the Essalhi family, Fraj and Geraldine, Amir, Yusef and Nadia. And to Adil's four beautiful children, Tia, Aleem, Aisha and Layla. When you're older and read this book, I want you to know that your father was a great man with a strong heart and so much potential. He was truly the twin I never had.

I would like to thank Matthieu Mabin, who through his amazing camera work and documentary for France 24 captured a piece of history like no other. I wish you the best in the future, my comrade and friend.

I would like to thank Mary Fitzgerald for her great reporting of the truth and keeping the cause and my efforts alive to my fellow Irish people.

I would like to thank Dawud Wharnsby, who allowed me to quote his song. You were an inspiration to me as a young impressionable child and your wise words translated through music inspire me still.

Above all I want to thank my dear mother, father, brother Yusef and sisters Eftaima, Khadija, Zayneb, Karima and Maryam, who supported and encouraged me in spite of all the time it took me away from them. I understand it was a long and difficult journey for you while I was at war and I love you all dearly.

Since the completion of this book I am sorry to say that Wa'el the Greek passed away due to an accident with a firearm in Tripoli after he had travelled to pass on what valuable knowledge he had to the Syrian freedom fighters, may he rest in peace. And to pay my respects to my close childhood friend Hisham Habbash, who lost his life while fighting valiantly on the Syrian battlefields.

To all of the 1,400 men from the Tripoli Brigade who travelled and fought with a bravery unrivalled, I am honoured to have fought by your side and you will forever remain my brothers, no matter how much time or distance comes between us.

Last and not least: I beg forgiveness of all those who have been with me over the course of the years and whose names I have failed to mention.

Housam Najjair

حســـام النجــــار